MORALS AND SOCIETY IN ASIAN PHILOSOPHY

Curzon Studies in Asian Philosophy
Series Editors
Indira Mahalingam and Brian Carr

The **Curzon Studies in Asian Philosophy** address various themes in a manner that does not presuppose the specialist linguistic knowledge which has tended to make these traditions closed to the wider philosophical audience. Among the projected volumes, some reflect recent conferences and others are papers specially written for the series. Some have grown out of recent controversies in the Carfax journal **Asian Philosophy.**

Pali Buddhism
Edited by Frank Hoffman and Deegalle Mahinda

Friendship East and West
Philosophical Perspectives
Edited by Oliver Leaman

The Authority of Experience
Readings on Buddhism and Psychology
Edited by John Pickering

MORALS AND SOCIETY IN ASIAN PHILOSOPHY

edited by
Brian Carr

CURZON

First Published in 1996
by Curzon Press
St John's Studios, Church Road, Richmond
Surrey, TW9 2QA

Typeset in Sabon by LaserScript Ltd, Mitcham
Printed and bound in Great Britain by
TJ Press Limited, Padstow, Cornwall

British Library Cataloguing in Publication Data
A catalogue record of this book is available from the British Library

Library of Congress Cataloguing in Publication Data
A catalog record for this book has been requested

ISBN 0–7007–0345–4

Contents

Preface

The articles included in this collection constitute in effect the proceedings of the First Conference of the recently formed European Society for Asian Philosophy, which was held at the University of Nottingham during August 1993. The articles explore moral and social philosophical issues in the Indian, Chinese, Japanese and Islamic philosophical traditions, both ancient and modern.

The authors of the articles have suitably revised their contributions in the light of the very constructive and lively discussion that was definitive of the First Conference, which in itself gave so much encouragement for the future of the Society. The Second Conference of the Society was held at the University of Exeter in early August 1995 – on the theme *Persons in Asian Philosophy* – and its proceedings will be published in the *Curzon Studies in Asian Philosophy* in due course. A Third Conference is already being planned for August 1997, and is likely to be held at the University of Malta.

Some of these articles have already appeared in the journal *Asian Philosophy*, and are included with the permission of Carfax Publishing Company: those by Robert E Allinson, David E Cooper, Takashi Koizumi and Frank R Podgorski appeared in *Asian Philosophy*, Vol.4, No.2, 1994; those by John Magnus Michelsen and Ian Whicher appeared in *Asian Philosophy*, Vol.5, No.1, 1995.

The newly launched *Curzon Studies in Asian Philosophy* is an ideal format for these proceedings and I am very grateful for the encouragement of the publishers, Malcolm and Martina Campbell. Other collections for the *Curzon Studies in Asian Philosophy* series are in press or under preparation, which are not conference proceedings but special compilations of newly written or previously published papers.

Generous assistance with the First Conference of the Society was provided by David Green of Carfax Publishing Company – from printing and distributing advertising materials to helping with the expenses of our keynote speakers. Assistance was also gratefully received from Curzon Press, from Edinburgh University Press, Macmillan Press, Routledge and others. I would also like to acknowledge the enormous help and support provided by Indira Mahalingam during the formation of the Society and the planning of its conference series.

Brian Carr

Editor's Introduction

Across all philosophical traditions, Western or Asian, a central preoccupation has always been with the fundamental questions of moral and social philosophy, questions which link abstract philosophical enquiry with practical issues of how we should conduct ourselves in our personal and social life and how we can best organise our political institutions. Some traditions have emphasised the personal side, such as Daoism and earlier forms of Buddhism; some have given greater emphasis to the social and political, such as Confucianism and the Islamic tradition. But one thought which emerged clearly from these presentations at the conference and the discussions that followed was that the personal and the social are deeply intertwined. The moral philosophy of the *Bhagavad Gītā* is just one of the most explicit attempts to integrate both dimensions of human action.

Lenn E Goodman (a keynote speaker), in 'Humanism and Islamic Ethics – The Curious Case of Miskawayh', traces the influence on Miskawayh's *On the Refinement of Character* of Aristotelian virtue ethics, and the influence Miskawayh had in turn on al-Ghazālī. Goodman assesses what is lost and what is gained by al-Ghazālī's substitution of pietistic themes for Miskawayh's secularism and humanism.

Two papers explore the work of important figures in Japan. **Takashi Koizumi** (also a keynote speaker), in 'Fukuzawa Yukichi and Religion', follows the changes in that influential thinker's philosophy of religion. Fukuzawa first took a critical standpoint against Christianity from a Utilitarian point of view, came to admit a Unitarian Christianity for a while, but developed his own most original ideas in relation to Buddhism in his later years. **Alistair Swale's** 'The Ethics of Watsuji Tetsurō: A Reappraisal of Western and

Eastern Influences' discusses the contributions of a more recent Japanese philosopher, demonstrating the influence of Hegel in Watsuji's social and ethical thinking.

Continuing the theme of East-West contrasts and influences, **David Loy** in 'Transcendence East and West' raises the question whether south Asia and east Asia can be meaningfully treated together as 'the intuitive East'; he argues on the contrary that the cultural polarity between the Indian-influenced cultures of south Asia and the Chinese-influenced cultures of east Asia is more interesting than that between East and West. **John Magnus Michelsen** in 'The Place of Buddhism in Santayana's Moral Philosophy' discusses the influence of Buddhist though on Santayana's formulation of the notion of 'post-rational morality', and also Santayana's claim that Buddhism suffers from a fundamental contradiction. **David E Cooper** in 'Is Daoism Green?' examines the adoption, by contemporary advocates of 'deep ecology', of the Daoist attacks on convention or artifice: he argues that the implications of Daoism for our environmental attitudes are more complicated than they are usually taken to be.

Three papers directly examine issues in the Indian philosophical tradition. **Ian Whicher's** 'Cessation and Integration in Classical Yoga' challenges the established interpretation of Patañjali's *Yoga-Sūtras* as radically dualistic and ontologically oriented: instead, focusing on the idea of 'cessation', he develops the idea that classical Yoga offers an account of an integrated and embodied state of liberation. **Michael Zammit**, in 'Morals and Society in the Light of Advaita Vedānta – a Reflection', explores the implications of the philosophy of Advaita for our attitudes towards other fellow human beings, and finds a socially important theme embedded in its thesis of the essential identity of the *Ātman*. **Daniel Meyer-Dinkgrafe**, in 'The Function of Theatre in Society: A Reading of the *Nāṭyaśātra*', offers a description and reassessment of the possible role which theatre may play in contemporary society.

Frank R Podgorski, in 'Paths to Perfection: Yoga and Confucian', discusses these two apparently very different philosophies of the development of the self. He argues that they may on the contrary be viewed as complementary and mutually enriching, both affirming the unique richness detected within human experience: Yoga probes inwardly, concentrating on mystical and contemplative insights, whereas Confucianism stresses external possibility of humanity.

Finally, two papers address themes in the philosophical tradition of China. **Xiao Wei's** 'The Characteristics of Confucian Ethics' identifies five themes in Confucianism which together constitute a harmonious, social and practical ethics. But she finds, nevertheless, that these characteristics have a negative and limiting implication for the development of the individual, emphasising as they do a rigid and traditional social structure. Contemporary Chinese philosophy is engaged in reassessing Confucianism in the context of the current social philosophy of China. **Robert E Allinson**, in 'Moral Values and the Daoist Sage in the *Dao De Jing*', attempt to make consistent four apparently contradictory classes of statements in that text concerning moral values: that nothing can be said about the *Dao*; that all values judgements are relative; that the Daoist sage engages in moral behaviour; and that the Daoist sage is amoral or immoral. He distinguishes between the way the Daoist sage appears to the observer outside the *Dao*, and the way he appears to himself.

Contributors

Robert E Allinson, Department of Philosophy, The Chinese University of Hong Kong, Hong Kong

David E Cooper, Department of Philosophy, University of Durham, UK

Lenn E Goodman, Department of Philosophy, Vanderbilt University, Nashville, USA

Takashi Koizumi, Graduate School of Comparative Culture, International Christian University, Tokyo, Japan

David Loy, Faculty of International Studies, Bunkyo University, Chigasaki, Japan

Daniel Meyer-Dinkgrafe, Department of Theatre, Film & Television Studies, University of Wales, Aberystwyth, UK

John Magnus Michelsen, Philosophy Department, University of Victoria, Canada

Frank R Podgorski, Department of Asian Studies, Seton Hall University, South Orange, USA

Alistaire D Swale, East Asian Studies, University of Waikato, New Zealand

Xiao Wei, School of Humanities and Social Sciences, Tsinghua University, Beijing, Peoples Republic of China

Ian Whicher, Dharam Hinduja Institute of Indic Research, Faculty of Divinity, Cambridge University, Cambridge

Michael Zammit, Foundation Studies, University of Malta, Msida, Malta

1

Humanism and Islamic Ethics

The Curious Case of Miskawayh

Lenn E. Goodman

In 945 the Khalifs of Baghdad fell under the control of Buyid dynasts risen from the ranks of their Daylamite soldiery. The century that followed climaxed a period of fragmentation for the no longer young Islamic state. But it was also an era when ambitious princes sought the patina of legitimacy and trappings of stability through patronage of poets, painters, scholars, scientists and philosophers. Commercial and administrative skill, military prowess and discipline were avenues to fortune; and such worldly virtues were widely prized, even as pietism and traditionalism were framing a response. The individualism, occasional secularism, scepticism, even liberalism to be found among the pensioners of the Islamic courts support comparisons of the era to the Italian Renaissance of the 12th century (Kraemer 1986a, b; Mottahedeh, 1980). Confirming the parallel is the systematization of Arabic and Islamic studies during the period. The catalyst in both eras, translated texts of Greek philosophic, scientific, and technical works.

Thinkers trained in Arabic letters and in the Greek sciences laid open by the translation movement of the previous century took Aristotle seriously. But they were also imbued with the values of the court, the chancery, and the military camp. Theirs was the culture of '*adab*, the literature of courtesy and urbanity. Secular values – the distillate of Hellenistic, old Persian, Arab, Byzantine, Jewish, and Syriac traditions, with a leaven of Indian fable and the vivid naturalism of Chinese portraiture and figure painting for critical distance – stood alongside the law and faith of Islam, and, like the philosophic outlook of the Greek teachers, claimed the power of interpreting and judging it. The philosophers of the period, a small group, many of them friends, colleagues, rivals, master and disciple, freely invoked a humanistic ethical discourse and ideal within Islamic culture. Among the most articulate and long lived was Abū 'Alī Aḥmad ibn Muḥammad ibn Miskawayh (ca. 936–1030). His *On the Refinement of Character* has been called 'the most influential work on philosophical ethics' in Islam.[1] But the influence takes a curiously underground route: Miskawayh's ethics were substantially taken over by Abū Ḥāmid al-Ghazālī (1058–1111), the trenchant critic of the Islamic philosophical school whose polemic against neoplatonic Aristotelianism in Islam, *The Incoherence of the Philosophers*, and monumental spiritualising summa *Reviving the Religious Sciences* led to his being called the Proof of Islam in traditional Islamic circles. The *'Iḥyā' 'Ulūm al-Dīn*, as the latter is called in Arabic, draws on many sources and relies tellingly on Miskawayh for its treatment of the virtues. But the perspective is altered subtly but systematically for later ethical thinking in Islam.[2]

Miskawayh was born in Rayy near present day Tehran; he died in his nineties at Isfahan. Reputedly of Zoroastrian background, he was – like his philosophic predecessors al-Fārābī and the Sincere Brethren of Basra[3] – a Shi'ite. He was also a vocal advocate of Persian culture in its struggle with Arab hegemony. While still in his teens he entered the service of the Wazir al-Muḥallabī, a bilingual maecenas, known for his wit and culture, who sought to recapture the glories of the fabled 'Abbasid court in Buyid Baghdad. A poet and prosodist in his own right, in Miskawayh's words, 'he gave new life to forgotten sciences.' Working by day in the chancery, Miskawayh dazzled al-Muḥallabī's salons by night with the learning prized among the literati. After his patron's death in 963, he became librarian and boon companion to the powerful wazir Ibn al-'Amīd, under the Buyid prince Rukn al-Dawla in his native city of Rayy, remaining at his side 'day and night' for seven years. Ibn al-'Amīd was a scholar statesman and a warrior, described by one courtier as 'an Arab in speech (that is, pithy), a philosopher in judgement, and a Persian in manners.' He was also proud, selfish, temperamental and power hungry. Miskawayh praised him for his philosophy, poetry and learning, his skill in art, verse and engineering, tactics, and administration. Himself treasured for his command of the ancient sciences, Miskawayh presided over some ten camel loads (two to five tons) of manuscript folios. On the sacking of his palace by Khorasanian raiders, the wazir learned with relief that his books were intact: 'All my treasures,' he told Miskawayh, 'can be replaced but these.'

Surviving this second patron, Miskawayh stayed on in the service of the wazir's son and successor, who was known as the Doubly Competent, for his mastery of the arts of war and peace. On the deposition of this master, Miskawayh remained in court, serving the greatest of the Buyid monarchs, 'Aḍud al-Dawla, and engaging in embassies in his behalf as the Prince set about rebuilding and enlarging the fortunes of his house. Later he served other monarchs at Baghdad and Rayy and finally retired as court physician to the Khwarizmshah, ruler of Khiva on the Oxus. The story that he answered the disrespect of the young Avicenna (980–1038) by picking up a copy of *The Refinement of Character* and throwing it at him seems out of character for the refined bibliophile but may have been circulated to highlight the one field in which Miskawayh surpassed his formidable successor.

Miskawayh's teacher was the Jacobite Christian Yaḥyā ibn 'Adī (d. 974), a translator and commentator of Plato and Aristotle and a disciple of the great Muslim Neoplatonic Aristotelian al-Fārābī and the Nestorian philosopher Mattā ibn Yūnus. Yaḥyā was a copyist like his father by profession; a collector of manuscripts by avocation. His home was a veritable school of translators and philosophers, Christian and Muslim, including Miskawayh's Boswell al-Tawḥīdī and others of his circle – commentators of Greek works, physicians, theologians, litterateurs, even the son of the famous wazir 'Alī ibn 'Isā. The bibliographer Ibn al-Nadīm, a bookseller by trade, relied on Yaḥyā for booklore and for the erudition stored in his beautifully penned library catalogue. It was from Ibn 'Adī that Miskawayh learned his logic. He later defended the discipline against the charge of an Islamic apologist (or *mutakallim*) that logic was (as its name seemed to imply) just a way of ordering words, retorting that if that much could be inferred from etymology, one could equally conclude that a *mutakallim* was a mere talker.[4]

Miskawayh defended the Greek sciences against all forms of parochialism, but the heart of the cosmopolitanism he imbibed from his teacher is voiced in a passage from Ibn 'Abī's ethics urging that our highest perfection lies in the universal love of humankind as a single race, united by its humanity. Underlying that humanity in turn is our crowning glory, the divinely imparted rational soul, which all men share, and by which indeed all are one. The goal of ethics, Ibn 'Adī wrote, is control of our natural irascibility, allowing our deeper unity to surface in acts of love and compassion (ed. Kurd Ali, pp. 517–18; cf. al-Fārābī, *Kitāb al-Ḥurūf*, ed. Mahdi, pp. 77–80; Walzer, 1963, pp. 33, 222; Kraemer, 1986a, pp. 10, 115). Miskawayh's admiration shows in his choosing the same title for his ethics than Ibn 'Adī had used: *On the Refinement of Character.*

In his compendious annalistic history, *The Experience of Nations and the Outcomes of their Endeavours*, Miskawayh follows the exhaustive annals of al-Ṭabarī down to his own times and then (for the years 951–83) turns strikingly to firsthand experience and eyewitness reports of military, diplomatic and court events. As a court favorite and minister he accompanied Ibn al-'Amīd in the field and was once sent to inventory the goods of a fortress taken from the rival Hamdanid dynasts, which had been betrayed by its venal commander. Ordered to humiliate the loyal slave officer in charge, who had been captured while trying to hold the fort, Miskawayh – neither a paragon and martyr nor a martinet – sent the man back to the conquering prince for his fate to be settled.

Learning was no mere ornament to Miskawayh's courtly role. His masters shared his view that statesmen could learn from the actions of past rulers and from the recovered culture that Miskawayh laid out in a greater and lesser Treasury of the ancient sciences, and in works on ethics, happiness, moral education, logic, the natural sciences, divinity, arithmetic, alchemy and cooking. His intellectual savoir faire is still fresh in al-Tawḥīdī's records of interviews with the learned courtier. His stance towards alchemy shows the tenor of his ethics as well: alchemy is an esoteric science, taught by hints, so that only philosophers may have access to it. Its secrets are deemed dangerous: if they fell into the hands of the ignorant, it is feared, men would abandon cooperation, pursue power only in the form of domination, and pleasures only of the lowest sort. The charge, reflective of a perennial pietist anxiety over *homo faber*, is still made against technology today, and Miskawayh's reply is worthy of a Bacon, a Descartes, or a twentieth century respondent to Heidegger's terror of technological nihilism: real alchemy is simply a branch of mineral science (i.e. chemistry) and need not be confined to an esoteric elite. For those who learn are no longer ignorant. Since mastery of the art depends on philosophic understanding, we can be confident that its practitioners will not misuse it. Here we see a transcendent faith in learning, in the unity of the natural and human sciences, and the transparency of the human will and social organization to the goods that illuminate their course. Our word for what Miskawayh placed his faith in here is humanism, very much in the Socratic tradition that does not isolate act from understanding. Miskawayh's word is *'adab*– manners, culture, the root of *ta'dīb* education, discipline, refinement.

'Adab in its narrowest sense means literature, and literature was a prime vehicle of the refinement Miskawayh counted on. That he wrote on the pure style in poetry as well as on usage and manners is an expression of the nexus of values he most cherished. But *'adab* to Miskawayh was much more than literature and went far beyond mere usage. Combining and universalizing central themes from Plato and Aristotle, Miskawayh saw the humane and humanising manners and mores of a universal human culture as crucial to our fulfillment as individuals and as a species. *'Adab*, he wrote, is the nourishment that gives substance to the mind as food gives substance to the maturing body; it is the content of wisdom – knowledge tested by experience about the good life and its means of attainment. Without it, reason is not reason.[5] Here the sum of human culture, actively assimilated and lived by, provides the material content to Aristotle's phronesis, broadening experience with the aid of history and literature, but also disciplining that experience, through the study of history's lessons and the norms of language, usage and comportment that are made visible in literature. Like his pietist contemporary al-Makkī (d. 996), whose spiritual vademecum was entitled *Food for Hearts*, Miskawayh seeks sustenance for that inner, intentional being that directs our choices. But Miskawayh does not find the substance and the sustenance he seeks in the devotional posture of the heart but in the intellectual focus and clarity of the mind, the rule of reason, nourished not by the *sunna* or example of the Prophet but by *paideia*, the *'adab* of humanity.

In his traditional Islamic foreword, setting out the task of ethics in the context of Islam, Miskawayh follows the Mu'tazilite/Shi'ite voluntaristic reading of the Qur'ān, quoting one of its characteristic oaths: 'By the soul and that which shaped it and breathed into it its wickedness and impiety' – the passage might seem to give comfort to predestinarians; but Miskawayh reads on – 'he who keeps it pure prospers, and he who corrupts it fails!' Miskawayh reads the verses (91:7–10) as mandating a Socratic tendance of the soul: one might forge the same metal into a perfect or a worthless sword (35). The Creator affords the matter of our humanity, but to work up that material through art and culture is our charge.

Society, Miskawayh argues, is our means to this end: each of us is necessary to someone else's perfection, and all of us must cooperate to provide the material base necessary to humanise our existence (14). Once the bare necessities are secured, higher and more intellectual plateaus are sought – each of us advancing in the measure of his capacities and all of us shoring up the weaknesses of the rest (118,

123, cf. 64). The social virtues, then, of friendliness, affability, and cooperativeness, are necessary to human wellbeing, as Aristotle argued; and ascetics are mistaken in seeking perfection outside human society: the life of the anchorite or vagabond stunts our humanity and thwarts our nature. Such men are neither temperate nor just and indeed lack the social theatre in which these virtues are developed (25–26, 139). In the spirit of Ibn ʻAdī, and in perfect agreement with Aristotle, Miskawayh argues that love is the basis of all society – friendship being a more intimate and fellowship a more diffuse form of love (cf. *Nicomachaean Ethics* VIII 9). Humanity itself is named for fellowship (deriving the Arabic *'insān* from *'uns*, and not, as one poet pretended, from *nisyān*, forgetfulness). Even public worship is devised by the religious law to foster human fellowship, neighbourhood by neighbourhood, city by city, and (through the Pilgrimage to Mecca) among the Islamic community throughout the world. It was with this thought in mind – that religion does not isolate but unites humanity – that the wise King Ardashir of Persia (r. 226–241, founder of the Sassanian dynasty) called religion and monarchy twin brothers (125–28).

Piety, in Miskawayh's catalogue of virtues, is defined not in theological terms (as devotion is a few pages further on, as honouring God and His chosen ones, 21–22) but eudaimonistically, as the performance of acts of virtue that enhance and perfect the soul (19). And the virtues in general are defined in the Aristotelian manner, as avenues toward happiness, varying in their implications from person to person and situation to situation. Circumstances must be evaluated with the aid of experience and addressed by way of art (22). The virtues, then, are perfections of character, not, as the command ethics of scripture might suggest to some, matters of mere adherence to stringent behavioural rules.

Popular religion, Miskawayh argues, is a vulgar attempt to trade self-denial in this world for sensory goods in the next – as though a transcendent God would simply serve human appetites and passions (39–40). Like his predecessor Muḥammad ibn Zakariyā' al-Rāzī (d. 925 or 932), a physician philosopher of Epicurean bent (see Goodman, 1971, 1972), Miskawayh follows Galen in arguing that all sensory pleasures presuppose prior lack and pain.[6] He goes on to argue that the ethics of the common mass is (in our terms) conflicted, resting on an inner contradiction: philosophers understand that what is most divine is what furthest transcends the material conditions of pleasure *and* pain. But popular morality simultaneously celebrates the successful hedonist and abhors the conditions of his success. So it responds with awe to the seeming ascetic, whose way of life the common man detests. Without philosophy to reconcile our ascetic and hedonic impulses and direct them toward the higher longings and purer pleasures of the intellectual life, the vulgar oscillate between self-indulgence and shame, never knowing the sources of their embarrassment, let alone the character of its remedy (41, 43, 113, 136).

Like al-Fārābī (tr. R. Walzer, 1985; tr. D. M. Dunlop, 1961) Miskawayh regards religion as a mode of poetry and practice that platonically instills the proper ethos in a people. He does not seek literal truth in scriptural rhetoric, just as he does not find categorical commandments in religious laws. Rather, he sees religious symbolism as a hortatory paradigm, and observance of the laws as a discipline, inuring the character to virtue. He evinces more concern about the quality of a young man's drinking companions than about the fact that young men may violate the religious law by drinking (53). Before coming to philosophy, he confesses, he himself grew up less in the wholesome ethos of the Qur'ān than in the immoralism of the pre-Islamic poets like 'Imru' al-Qays and Nābighah who flaunt the raffish ethos of the desert (see Goodman, 1988). When the romantic ideals of passion and self-assertion are held up to admiration by one's parents and the spirit of such poets is what is most admired by one's prince, it is difficult to free oneself from their grip; only gradually, Miskawayh admits, did he break free of the sensuous and wanton values of the *jāhiliyya* poets, the celebrators of the barbarism of the pre-Islamic age, and wean himself – with the aid of philosophy – from the way of life their songs instilled (45–46).

Manners, Miskawayh argues, make the man. By nature a boy is bad – a liar, cheat and tattletale, spiteful, meddlesome, importunate, jealous, and malicious – a danger to others and even more to himself. But by training, suitable reading, well placed praise and private reproof (lest he become shameless under the blast of condemnation before his fellows), proper diet and discipline, decent demeanour, comportment, dress, companions, and play that is neither exhausting nor debilitating, he can be made a man (51–55). Courtesy (*'adab* again) is not external but organic to morals – as means serve ends in an organism. Even among the lesser animals, the highest are those that come closest to culture: the sexually reproducing species and those that nurture and train their young (and so are amenable to domestication). Man is the highest of the animals because in him the capacity for education is clearest, allowing human intelligence to reclose the arcing circle from Creator to creatures, reuniting with its Source (61–62).

Like Ibn Zur'a (943–1008), a fellow disciple of Ibn 'Adī, who called humanity a horizon[7] Miskawayh makes humanity (*al-insāniyya*) the goal of ethics, to be achieved through the perfection of our identity (*dhāt*) as human beings. That perfection is to be sought through the speculative sciences and practical arts of philosophy. Aristotle collected and organized the relevant arts in much the way that physicians have collected and organised the materia medica God left dispersed for us in the world.[8] Closely following al-Fārābī and a tradition that has been traced back to the Alexandrian Peripatetics (Gutas, 1983, pp. 232–33), Miskawayh catalogues the arts and sciences, showing in detail how theory and practice support one another.

It is commonly imagined that when Aristotle praises the speculative life and the intellectual virtues as what is most distinctively human he is setting his highest good, the contemplative, over and against the eudaimonia attained through exercise of the moral virtues.[9] But the dichotomy is a false one, as will be evident to one who considers that for Aristotle even the appetites and passions of man must have specifically human forms; and so, to be well handled, must be addressed by our distinctively human strengths: we can live as befits our humanity only through the use of reason. So the moral virtues, far from competing with the life of reason, are both presupposed in reason's development and dependent on its use in discovering and defining what is appropriate in concrete circumstances. Since the actual is always ultimately prior to the potential, the properly Aristotelian view is that understanding of the principles necessary to give shape and direction to virtue must be present – not necessarily in the mind of every person who acts virtuously or every adolescent who learns virtue, but clearly in the mind of the statesman or legislator who plots the values that will be implicit in the institutional fabric of a society or ethos of a community. Miskawayh shows his sensitivity to the dovetailing of theory and practice by treating character as the matter to be informed and refined, not merely by discipline but by the arts and sciences, which bring the principles behind virtue to the fore explicitly and train us to use them in the forum of experience. Culture here, literary culture, becomes the educator of character that Plato had sought and al-Fārābī had found, at least for the many, in religion.

Some of the ancients, Miskawayh argues, carried the recognition that happiness depends on transcendence of the physical so far that they denied happiness to be attainable in this life. It is in this sense that Miskawayh reads the notion rejected by Aristotle that no man may be called happy while he lives. It would be disgraceful, Miskaway insists, to hold that a living man who performs good deeds, holds sound beliefs, serves his fellow men and thus in all ways acts as God's deputy is not objectively happy. To be sure intellectual perfection reaches higher than mere moral perfection of our worldly nature; and only intellectual perfection, as Aristotle allowed, endures beyond the grave. But the moral virtues are necessary means to the higher intellectual end; the spiritual goal which is the ultimate aim of philosophy is not attainable by any other means. There are no shortcuts to felicity that bypass the avenues of moral and intellectual self-perfection, as some Sufis of ecstatic and perhaps antinomian inclination were liable to suppose. For the key premise of all mysticism and gnosis, as of all asceticism which pursues a spiritual goal, is that the soul requires purification. And clearly, Miskawayh argues, again citing Aristotle (now on the need for experience), purification is not achieved without living through the stages of our natural human development – undergoing the discipline and acculturation that are, in Miskawayh's view, the object of our existence in this world (74–83). A school is not life, but life is a school.

The fate of Miskawayh's ethics is emblematic of that of Greek philosophy in general in the Islamic milieu. The volume of material absorbed is immense, and orthodoxy does not reject it but builds its house from the inherited materials, much as the early Islamic builders appropriated the structures and stones of Greek basilicas that had been pagan temples, and later used their architectural principles to construct new, distinctively Islamic mosques and palaces. No sentence of Miskawayh's ethics is left unexamined when al-Ghazālī takes over the work. But Miskawayh's distinctive humanism is systematically expunged. Richard Walzer and H. A. R. Gibb showed the heavy dependence of al-Ghazālī's *'Iḥyā'* on Miskawayh, and others have detailed the diffusion of that influence in other writings of al-Ghazālī and of later authors like the pivotal figure Naṣīr al-Dīn al-Ṭūsī (1201–74), the Shi'ite polymath who defected to the conquering Mongol forces in 1247.[10] But in emphasising Miskawayh's formative role and al-Ghazālī's openness to philosophic ethics, Walzer and Gibb rather overstated al-Ghazālī's dependence, slighting his selective preferences for other philosophers' ideas when they better served his purposes, and neglecting to assay the material impact of his displacement of Miskawayh's most distinctive themes in favour of those he drew from traditional Islamic sources and the Sufi pietists like al-Muḥāsibī and al-Makkī – as though an archaeologist were so thrilled to discern the lineaments of a Greek temple in a mosque that he ignored the Muslim worship going on inside.

The most telling effect on Islamic ethics of al-Ghazālī's adoption of Miskawayh's schematism is his contribution to the now almost invisible fusion of virtue ethics with the scriptural ethics of command and prohibition. But, while al-Ghazālī appreciates the powerful methods and edifying conclusions he finds among the fruits of philosophy, he discards the fruit along with the argumentative branch that had sustained it when the conclusions are not to his taste. He is fond of finding traditional texts to support and thereby assimilate (or reappropriate) philosophic ideas. Perhaps the most impressive instance is his book length neoplatonizing gloss of the Qur'anic light and darkness verses.[11] But his deracinating of philosophic theses, excising their argumentative nerve, has a far more systemic impact.

Sensitive to the nisus of Miskawayh's polemic against Sufi austerity, al-Ghazālī suppresses Miskawayh's Aristotelian rejection of the life of solitude as subhuman or superhuman – although he follows Miskawayh closely in the passages that precede and follow. He rejects Miskawayh's social rationale of public worship and suppresses his platonizing proposal that happiness requires the youthful study of mathematics to accustom us to truth and truthfulness. In all, Muhammad Abul Quasem estimates (1974, pp. 119–120) that about one third of Miskawayh's ethics was unacceptable to al-Ghazālī and dropped as quietly as the rest was adopted. We add our characterisation of the clear basis of selection. Whatever was outspokenly humanistic or secular in Miskawayh was dropped by al-Ghazālī, just as he took issue with the Islamic adherents of the philosophic school where he found their metaphysics excessively naturalistic. Walzer and Gibb advert to al-Ghazālī's changes in Miskawayh's ethics but call the elements of *'adab* that are dropped 'merely formal and superficial.'

Al-Ghazālī follows Miskawayh and the Platonic tradition in identifying wisdom, courage and temperance as the virtues of the rational, irascible and appetitive aspects of the personality and in treating justice as the master-virtue that integrates the other three; he follows the later Greek and prior Islamic tradition in listing the remaining virtues under the four cardinal virtues. But Miskawayh identifies the intellectual virtues subsidiary to wisdom rather cognitively as intelligence, retentiveness, reasonableness (conformance of our notions to reality), quickness and strength of apprehension of what follows from the given, clarity of mind (preparedness to recognise and derive abstract concepts), and capacity to learn (ease in grasping theoretical matters). Al-Ghazālī, as the tenor of his work demands, takes a far more spiritual and moral tack. In place of intelligence he lists excellence in deliberation, following al-Fārābī and Aristotle's account, and insisting, as Aristotle had, that practical wisdom is not mere cleverness in finding means to ends but a virtue that deduces what is most conducive in the pursuit of noble aims. He ignores Miskawayh's interest in memory and conceptual clarity and substitutes discernment in matters of controversy (cf. *Nicomachaean Ethics* VI 10) and penetration. In place of reasonableness he puts insight, the ability to hit upon the truth without recourse to proof – a virtue of holymen. To cap his list in the '*Iḥyā*', al-Ghazālī adds an intellectual virtue not found in his earlier ethical work: self-scrutiny, apprehension of the subtle movements and hidden evils of the soul. This is the pietist virtue par excellence (see Goodman, 1983). Without it we would never know our own motives, and even with it they may remain obscure. Where Aristotle relies on reason, the virtue of practical wisdom, to locate the appropriate in concrete circumstances and direct us toward the doable good, al-Ghazālī argues that without recourse to God in prayer and without God's help we mortals would never succeed in finding, let alone appropriating and habituating in our characters, that disposition towards choice in accordance with a mean that Aristotle defined as virtue. Al-Ghazālī is a follower of the Philosophic school when he interprets the *Fātiḥa*, the opening prayer of the Qur'ān, as invoking God's aid in finding the mean, when it beseeches God (1:6) to 'show us the Straight Path.' But he departs radically from the Philosophers when he insists that we are powerless to discover and hew to that path by our own insight and virtue, that all of us, as the Qur'ān is traditionally held to imply, will spend part of eternity in hellfire.[12]

Turning from the intellectual to the moral virtues, we find that under temperance Miskawayh lists modesty, composure (the ability to keep one's soul at rest when the passions are stirring), liberality, integrity, contentment, delicacy or gentility, orderliness, personableness, being accommodating or conciliatory, dignity, and godliness – all virtues of a courtier. He defines contentment as moderation in food and drink, integrity in terms of licit and illicit gain; godliness, as steadiness in fair doings, by which the soul is perfected. Al-Ghazālī lists modesty and liberality under temperance, following Miskawayh, al-Fārābī and the Muslim moralist Ibn Abī Dunyā – but not Aristotle, who treats modesty as an emotional surrogate for virtue appropriate to the young, not a virtue in itself. He also lists forbearance here, the virtue of Job and other prophets, and the fruit of steadfastness, the ability to bear sufferings and losses, which he locates under courage. Following Miskawayh and Avicenna, al-Ghazālī defines forebearance broadly – not confining it to its familiar sense of patience, enlarging it to include resistance to all passions, of pleasure or of pain. He reserves this Qur'ānic virtue for special discussion among our avenues to salvation. Under temperance again he includes another form of self-restraint, foregoing some of our due, using a definition Miskawayh had included under liberality, but adding that such virtues are relevant only for those who are still attached to worldly things. Similarly with thrift and Miskawayh's virtue of orderliness. Even with liberality we can see the same thrust: al-Ghazālī dwells on the dangers of preoccupation with our livelihood, to the detriment of concern with our ultimate destiny. If one must choose between poverty and generosity, he argues, citing al-Muḥāsibī, one must prefer poverty, as the less entangled with worldly things (Sherif, 1975, p. 69).

Al-Ghazālī parallels Miskawayh in defining godliness in terms of good action done for the sake of the perfection in it – but adds: and for the sake of coming nearer to God; thus rendering Miskawayh's eudaimonism theocentric, in keeping with Plato's famous remark (*Theaetetus* 176) that we perfect ourselves as human by becoming as like to God as humanly possible. Miskawayh himself equates actions done for their own sake with actions done to please God. But that is a symmetry, not a reduction. It means that we are pleasing God when our motive is the intrinsic goodness of an act. In al-Ghazālī such symmetries are dangerous. Indeed, they are in a sense, the ultimate danger. God alone is truly generous in the sense of giving without any expectation of a return, but men can approximate such liberality if they are generous for God's sake, or for the sake of their eternal reward. Al-Ghazālī takes care to ensure that canonical eschatology is not dismissed, as the hermeneutics of al-Fārābī tend to do, as a mere symbolism representing something higher. He shows no deontological qualms about setting forth divine favour and the reward of immortality as moral incentives, requiring no apology or deference to the category long recognised by moralists as ultimate: the notion of actions not done for the sake of a reward.

In his properly ethical writings al-Ghazālī follows Miskawayh and

Avicenna in defining contentment as a virtue involving moderation. But in the *'Iḥyā'* he seizes upon the general Aristotelian proviso that virtues must be exercised in the right way, to expand the virtue of contentment into an ascetic principle demanding that we not seek to provide for our needs beyond a single day – a month at most – and give away all that we have beyond that. Even the Aristotelian social virtues of affability, good humour, and cheer are modified in the same sense – made over to conform to the ideals of sobriety and sedateness: one should not laugh unreservedly but emulate the Prophet, who preferred smiling to laughter (Sherif, 1975, p. 185). Jesting, al-Ghazālī urges, again citing the Prophet, leads to falsehood: Muḥammad 'did jest, but he spoke only the truth.' The saintly Ḥasan al-Baṣri, al-Ghazālī reports with admiration, did not laugh for thirty years.

Miskawayh expatiates on liberality – the brightest virtue in a courtier's setting, and the one on which his fortunes most depend. He expands liberality to encompass altruism, magnificence, charitableness, bounty – spending rather more than one really should, a favourite virtue of the Arab poets (see Hamori, 1974, pp. 11, 23) – appreciativeness of great achievement, and the form of self-denial whose ambivalent reception we have noted in al-Ghazālī. Al-Ghazālī, for his part, expands upon the dangers of speech, listing twenty evils of the tongue. He does recognise the Aristotelian mean of cheerfulness and good humour between the glum or morose and clownish buffoonery. But he presents the virtue of exchanging pleasantries at a party and expressing satisfaction with the casual remarks of one's acquaintances as a duty and a chore. Seclusion is to be preferred, and we must look to the model of the Prophet to see how social occasions may be borne with good address. Likewise with tact: we must learn to forego contention and find the mean between pettishness and obsequiousness. But al-Ghazālī complements this advice by reverting to Aristotle for a virtue that neither Miskawayh nor Avicenna included in their catalogues, righteous indignation, here defined as grief at the undeserved good or ill fortunes of those we know or with whom we have something in common. This virtue must be sharply distinguished from envy and spite, which are strictly forbidden but similar in external appearance. The true guide in distinguishing the virtue from the vice is the motive or intention – worldly versus otherworldly goals. A similar canonisation of intention is familiar to philosophers in Spinoza's distinction between piety (al-Ghazālī's godliness) and ambition, which seeks men's approbation, where true piety (also called humanity by Spinoza) seeks their genuine wellbeing.

As Spinoza intimates, this subtle difference of intention demarcating virtues from vices runs all through the catalogue of moral strengths and weaknesses. And the pietist theme of scrutiny of our intentions remains among the most prominent in the ethics of Kant.

Al-Ghazālī follows Miskawayh in defining delicacy or gentility as a kind of inner attachment to what is fair or fine; he follows him again in defining personableness, as Yaḥyā ibn ʻAdī does, in terms of dress, the one aspect of outward appearance beyond demeanour that one can regulate oneself – and with clear effect upon one's mood. Miskawayh says simply that personableness is a love of complementing the soul with fair adornments. One can picture him interviewing would be assistants and explaining the importance of self-presentation, the signs that properly or improperly chosen clothing give about the inner man. But al-Ghazālī puts *greater* emphasis on clothing. The '*Iḥyā*' devotes a full chapter to the Prophet's mode of dress: he wore whatever came to hand, saying that he was just a slave and so dressed as a slave; our ideal clothing is of the coarsest stuff, affording just the necessary coverage and sturdy enough to last no longer than a day and a night – again the theme of trusting God, elevated to ritual proportions. Few but the most saintly will attain the ideal, but lavish clothes are never acceptable. The mean, presentability without luxury or ostentation, becomes a compromise not between excess and deficiency but between a vice and an ideal.

Under courage Miskawayh lists great spiritedness (disdain for the trivial, an Aristotelian ability to bear both honour and humiliation), dauntlessness (confidence in a crisis), fortitude (in bearing and overcoming sufferings, especially those that cause terror), *ḥilm* (that is, Aristotle's mildness or gentleness, now assimilated to the Arabic counterpart of the Roman *clementia*, from which it takes its name – a virtue cultivated by the Khalif Muʻāwiya, who said that if a single thread bound him to his fellow he would not relax his grip on it: 'If he pulled I would yield, but if he yielded, I would pull'), steadiness (especially valuable in fighting to defend one's womenfolk or the religious law), gallantry (eagerness to do great deeds and win glory), and perseverance (sustained command of the soul over the body, applying it like a tool to a task). Al-Ghazālī's response is as much a riposte as an appropriation: he uses the Aristotelian notion that every virtue has its proper sphere to urge that the Realm of Islam is not the proper arena for the courage that is a mean between recklessness and cowardice and quotes God Himself in support: 'Muḥammad is the Apostle of God, and those who are with him are strong against unbelievers but merciful among themselves' (Qur'ān 48:29). Al-Ghazālī also shifts the focus of courage away from warfare, where Aristotle had found its paradigm case, and onto what Muslims call the greater *jihād*, the battle against the passions. He intentionally omits the martial arts from his educational program and treats sports as means of strengthening the body rather than of teaching valour.

Among the subvirtues of courage, al-Ghazālī expands on Miskawayh's list, adding magnificence here, perhaps because courage is needed in making great expenditures. He adopts Aristotle's notion that magnificence is properly shown in honouring the divine and in public works – building mosques, roads, hospitals and bridges – although such activities and the entanglements necessary to support them are not compatible with the self-denying life of the otherworldly ideal. In defining 'dauntless,' al-Ghazālī follows Aristotle's definition of courage as a mean in facing danger and death – a mean, he says, between recklessness and helplessness or desertion. But he redefines gallantry to make goodness and eternal life its object rather than glory. He adds nobility and benevolence to the virtues listed under courage – the former modified from Miskawayh's anatomy of liberality, and the latter defined (as Spinoza will later define humanity) as wanting for all men what one desires for oneself.[13]

Ḥilm is a crucial virtue in al-Ghazālī, as it was in Miskawayh and Ibn 'Adī, because it involves control of anger. It can be simulated, but its true nature acts in cooling the blood, whose heat is necessary to life but harmful in excess. We are attuned, al-Ghazālī argues, to be aroused in defence of ourselves and what is ours; but, if our claims go beyond bare necessity, we must curb our ire and possessiveness over all that is extraneous. Thus self-control is placed in the service of abstemiousness and resignation. Similarly, Miskawayh's virtue of dignity, which in his work means little more than grave demeanour, as it does in the ethics of Yaḥyā, is redefined by al-Ghazālī to become a form of self-respect grounded in a proper valuation of one's worth, and lying at a mean between vanity and abjectness. All the same, al-Ghazālī insists, like most medieval ethicists, that humility, not pride is our proper virtue.

In describing greatness of soul, al-Ghazālī goes back to Aristotle for the recognition that the great man is not overly excited by honours. Recognising the problem for his ideal of renunciation inherent in his acceptance of Aristotle's general principle that externals are needful in the exercise of virtue, al-Ghazālī expands on the dangers of the love of fame and condemns the quest for honours. The point had been an important one in his own life, for the crisis that tested and ultimately confirmed his faith had involved his perception that much of what passed for piety in his time was mere self-seeking.[14] In seeking God in place of worldly regard, some, he explains (the reference is to Sufi practice), pursue apparent humiliation and disgrace. But seclusion, isolation, and migration to lands where one is unknown are the alternatives al-Ghazālī recommends. Here again he alludes to his own life story; for these are in some measure the cures he adopted when his own reputation threatened to overwhelm him: humility and obscurity must displace the quest for worldly greatness, al-Ghazālī argues, responding to a sharp perceived dichotomy between this world's goods and those which he holds more real and more dear. It is always ambiguous, of course, how the efforts of an al-Ghazālī can succeed in extinguishing the sort of worldliness that al-Ghazālī said he found even in the spiritual leaders of his day, and to what extent even the closest self-scrutiny will be deluded, mistaking for spirituality what is in fact mere sublimation of social instincts and acquisitive urges, finding a new vocabulary of selflessness in which to voice the old ambitions, or simply devising a new sphere in which to exercise human emulousness and that self-aggrandisement which projects all evil and inadequacy upon the other and so becomes fanatical and hate-filled. Aristotle thought that the great man does claim the honours due him for his achievements. Cicero confessed that none of his sacrifices and struggles for what he liked to call 'the public thing' would have been made (and they did, to be fair, go further than Aristotle ever went, in that Cicero courted and suffered the martyrdom that Aristotle sidestepped) had it not been for the love of glory and the hope of fame. The spiritual benefits of al-Ghazālī's transvaluation of classical values will remain invisible in the nature of the case, but the material harm of the devaluation of glory is visible in every land that al-Ghazālī's type of otherworldliness has touched.

Al-Ghazālī is attracted to the Aristotelian idea of the mean. He has no difficulty in finding the prooftexts in Qu'rān and *ḥadīth*, the traditions of Muḥammad, that give the notion its Islamic standing. And his comprehension of the Aristotelian doctrine is sophisticated enough that he can use Aristotle's caveats about appropriateness and context to naturalise the Aristotelian theory of virtues in Islam far more effectively than Miskawayh could do by treating that theory as an exotic, an offshoot of the rare and foreign plant Philosophy. In al-Ghazālī's theory of virtues the worries of his theological predecessors about agency – the Ash'arite predestinarian suspicions of bivalent capacities and the occasionalist objections to dispositions resident and fixed in human character – are as quietly forgotten as is the fact that the ethical focus of the Qur'ān and the *ḥadīth* is not on virtues at all but on commands and the example of the Prophet. But to achieve his naturalisation of the Greek concepts and categories, al-Ghazālī had to modify both their form and content: virtue itself was redirected back to positive practice, and the mean in many cases was made a second best to the ascetic extreme, an alternative actively combatted by Aristotle and with graver cause for concern by such medieval successors as Saadiah, al-Fārābī and Maimonides. The mean is retained by al-Ghazālī, but used as he deems appropriate: thus he follows Aristotle in rejecting Plato's claim that justice is no mere compromise and agrees with Miskawayh in describing justice as a mean between doing and suffering wrong – all the while retaining Plato's notion that justice is the sovereign virtue, the result of using wisdom in assigning proper scope to all other goods.

It is evidently because justice engulfs all the other virtues that al-Ghazālī does not, as Miskawayh does, assign it subvirtues at the level of family, household, community, and friends. Al-Ghazālī's is not an assertive, rights claiming theory of justice, either at the level of public interests or at the level of the private, internal demands of the competing interests of the soul. But in his ethical writings proper he does differentiate a properly political justice and a principle of distributive justice overseen by the regulative activities of the conscientious ruler.[15] Like Miskawayh, then, al-Ghazālī does not reject the Aristotelian idea that justice is a social virtue involving give and take – in Islamic terms, proper and improper modes of acquisition. He is as prepared as Miskawayh was to naturalise and in some measure to bracket the more radical claims of Socrates about the preferability of suffering injustice to committing it – despite the Islamic admiration for martyrdom and the spiritual disclaiming of worldly ends. Islam is a polity, not merely a path of otherworldly quest, and that fact must be acknowledged in any Islamic system of ethics, even if the recognition does result in conflicts and tensions.

Al-Ghazālī parts company with Aristotle but follows pietist and mystic tradition in placing love of God ahead of knowledge, making it the fruit of wisdom and turning Aristotle's highest single good into a this-worldly means to an otherworldly aim. He does place speculative wisdom, whose true object is the knowledge of God, above practical wisdom, as Aristotle does. But he even treats practical wisdom as a mean-placing it between the overcleverness of guile (which uses cunning to attain base purposes) and the stubborn witlessness of stolidity (which blocks the lower passions from attaining their proper natural goals). Yet, despite the attractiveness to him of the idea of the mean, which anchors his ethics and theory of action in an Aristotelian social and biological naturalism, al-Ghazālī is under an insistent pressure from a realm whose claims are transcendental and whose goals are given specificity by rejection of the very appetites and impulses that a worldly eudaimonism like that of Miskawayh seeks to channel and modulate but never to deny. This crosspressure of the otherworldly, which defines itself not as the fulfillment of our natural drives but as their antithesis, is a source of ambivalences in al-Ghazālī's ethical scheme and is a commanding motive to him in the suppression of the humanism he finds in Miskawayh, leading him to search in al-Fārābī, Avicenna, Aristotle or Plato, or to dig into the canon of *ḥadīth* or plumb the oracular verses of the Qur'ān for alternative interpretations of the virtues, by which he might formulate an ideal of humanity more closely in tune with his own Islamic ideal.

The resultant ideas of the human virtues do take root in the Islamic context in a way that Miskawayh's do not. Through them, Greek ideas about the mean and the good life, translated into an Islamic idiom that effectively masks their foreign origin and structure, survive to afford the ethical framework for generations of later Muslim thinkers of orthodox stamp. The skeleton is strikingly preserved – Aristotle's profound and profoundly original conceptualisation of the virtues. But, like the mosiacs in the Byzantine basilicas, the faces are deleted or plastered over: where the lithe forms of pagan demigods once danced and later the spiritual lineaments of late antique piety and paideia could once be seen, the space is filled with painted sayings from the Prophet and his Book. The humanism of a Miskawayh, like the intellectualism of al-Fārābī and Avicenna, or the even the prudential and ascetic hedonism of al-Rāzī, do not survive. The prescriptive fountainhead of later Islamic ethics draws upon the pietist and mystical Sufi tradition, the canonical sources, the dialectics of *kalām*. The subsurface engineering may be Greek, but even the classic design motifs visible at the surface are subtly altered, and the waters that flow forth show no signs of how far they have travelled: to the drinker they seem wholly local. The free spirit of Miskawayh, the musky flavor that his odd Persian name suggests, is gone; and rarely in the later history of Islamic ethics will the like of Miskawayh's humanistic views and speculative excursions be seen again.

In al-Ghazālī, as in Aristotle and in Miskawayh, the aim of ethics remains the perfection of the individual. But now the social and cultural dimensions that were critical in defining and refining our humanity are suppressed in favor of the very ideal of isolation that Aristotle rejected and Miskawayh combatted. The perfected individual is no longer one who directs his practical life by habits of reasonableness and whose highest aim is contemplation of nature and its transcendental meaning, but the spiritual seeker, who has, as it were, cut away the middle term and reached directly – as Miskawayh warns one cannot do – for the divine. The discipline now is not simply one of moderation and self-refinement but of ascesis, and the contemplation is gnostic and ecstatic – a quest rather of the heart than of the understanding, leading not to mastery or even self-mastery in this world, nor to a naturalist's inductive synthesis and command, but to detachment from the world and ever closer attachment to the supernal world and preparation for the hereafter.

We are in no position to romanticize Miskawayh as the last hope of a cosmopolitan humanism in Islam. It was not simply narrowness, ignorance or backwardness that grounded the acceptance of al-Ghazālī's ethics and rejection of its more secular and humanistic model. Miskawayh's was a courtier's ethic; and, like his life, it shows the biases of his nature and his role. As in his historiography so in his ethics, Miskawayh is a conspicuous ego. He was criticised in his time for name dropping and trouble making; and his penchants for both, alongside a certain tendency to flatter are still visible in his writing – even though the ability to make trouble can be a virtue in a philosopher, where it is not in a courtier. The flaws of his ethics – its tendency to promote conformity and to breed a cohort of refined but superficial time servers – were as visible to Miskawayh's successors as the personal faults that favoured such biases were to his contemporaries; and it was in part a recognition of such biases that led al-Ghazālī and others to seek authenticity and depth in the canon of the tradition and take refuge in Islam from an ethic that had come to seem to them as empty and superficial as the advice of the courtier Polomius seems to us.

Al-Ghazālī too has faults, again mirrored in his ethics. The exile and partial isolation he made a virtue of were in part a necessity in his own case, and in part a desertion, in his terms, when the patron who had sponsored his polemics against the Ismā'īlī sect fell to assassination, the tactic that gave that sect the name by which it became best known in the West. Al-Ghazālī's meditative ethics is itself escapist in part. It renounces worldly aims on the eudaimonistic grounds that it knows of something better. But it does not attain perfect selflessness for any living subject of its counsels, and it does in effect tend to leave the world's wounds to fester. When Muslim and Arab scholars today look back to Miskawayh's ideals of culture, community and individuality, or juxtapose them with al-Ghazālī recasting of ethics into a Sufi mould, one can feel a sense of loss for the values Miskawayh sought to establish in Islam. Pietism, to be sure, is not as likely a medium as courtesy for the founding of a new humanism – whether secular or theistic. Yet courtliness has had its say and its day in the Islamic lands, and we have the work of Spinoza and of Kant to show us that even mysticism and pietism can anchor a humanistic ethics if a philosopher of clear enough intelligence undertakes the task of construction.

Lenn E Goodman, Department of Philosophy, Vanderbilt University, Nashville, Tennessee 37240, USA.

NOTES

1 Pages from Zurayk's translation (1968) are cited parenthetically below; cf. Arkoun's French translation (1969), Arkoun (1970, 1982) and Ansari (1964). The testimonial is from Richard Walzer and Hamilton Gibb's 1960 article on ethics in the *Encyclopedia of Islam*, s.v. *akhlāq*.
2 See Walzer (1963) 220–35; but cf. M. Abul Quasem (1974, 1975); Sherif (1975).
3 See Ikhwān al-Ṣafā, tr. Goodman (1978).
4 In 932 Mattā debated the grammarian al-Sīrāfī over linguistic relativism versus universality in logic. Yaḥyā pursued the matter in his *Making Clear the Distinction . . .*, ed. Endress (1978) 38–50, 181–93. See Margoliouth (1905), Mahdi (1970); al-Tawḥīdī (Cairo, 1951) 265–66.
5 Cf. Rosenthal (1970) 284–87, 320.
6 Cf. Miskawayh's essay on pleasure in Arkoun (1961/2) pp. 7–19, esp. 10–12.
7 The remark is presented as a paraphrase of Aristotle; see al-Sijistānī, ed. Badawi, 1974, p. 333.
8 See Miskawayh, ed. 1928.
9 Hardie (1988) lays out the problem, pp. 12–28, 336–57.
10 See al-Ṭūsī, tr. Wickens, 1964.
11 See *al-Ghazālī*, tr. Gairdner, 1924.
12 Watt (1963, pp. 67–68); argues that al-Ghazālī must have abandoned virtue ethics after experimenting with it in *The Criterion of Action (Mizān al-'Amal*, lit., 'The Scale of Practice') – a work whose authenticity he questions in whole or part. But cf. Wensinck (1946, ch. 2). It is true that

al-Ghazālī questions the universal adequacy of the model of virtue as choosing a mean between extremes. But so does Aristotle. Al-Ghazālī also questions the adequacy of reason in locating the mean. But he never rejects the idea of the mean. For that idea is Qur'ānic and undergirds his decision to make virtue ethics the backbone of the moral scheme of the *'Iḥyā'*. His insistence on grace should not blind us to his recognition that scriptural deontology is not an end in itself but a means to human felicity in this world and the next. Even at the height of his paeans to Sufi surrender, in the celebrated discussion of *tawakkul* or ultimate trust in God (*'Iḥyā'* XXXV), the core and kernel of piety is not specific behavioural acts but what they reveal and foster in our 'hearts.' Behaviours, whose paradigm is lipservice to the demands of faith, al-Ghazālī insists, are the mere 'hush of the husk.' But this manner of structuring values is virtue ethics, and its source in al-Ghazālī is Miskawayh's Aristotelian reading of the *Qur'ān*.

13 See Sherif (1975) 183 and al-Ghazālī, *Al-Maqṣad al-Asnā* (Cairo, n.d.).

14 See his spiritual autobiography, *Al-Munqidh min al-Ḍalāl*, tr. Watt, 1963.

15 Sherif (1975) p. 72 and *Maqṣad.*

REFERENCES

ABUL QUASEM, MUHAMMAD (1975) *The Ethics of al-Ghazālī: A Composite Ethics in Islam* (Published privately in Petaling Jaya, Selangor, Peninsular Malaysia).

——. (1974) 'Al-Ghazālī's Rejection of Philosophic Ethics,' *Islamic Studies* 13 (1974) 111–127

ANSARI, M. A. H. (1964) *The Ethical Philosophy of Miskawayh* (Aligarh).

ARKOUN, MOHAMMED (1970) *Contribution a l'étude de l'humanisme arabe au IV/Xe siècle: Miskawayh, philosophe et historien* (Paris: Vrin).

——. (1982) *L'humanisme Arabe* (Paris: Vrin).

——. *Encyclopedia of Islam* (New) (Leiden: Brill, 1960, etc.)

Al-Fārābī, *Kitāb al-Ḥurūf*, ed. M. Mahdi (Beirut, 1970)

——. *K. Mabādi 'Arā' 'Ahlu 'l-Madīnatu 'l-Fāḍila* (The Book of the Principles Behind the Beliefs of the People of the Good State), tr. R. Walzer as *Al-Fārābī* on the Perfect State (Oxford: Clarendon Press, 1985).

——. *Fuṣūl al-Madanī*, tr. D. M. Dunlop as *Aphorisms of the Statesman* (Cambridge: Cambridge University Press, 1961).

Al-Ghazālī, *'Iḥyā' 'Ulūm al-Dīn* (Cairo, Lajnat Nashr al-Thaqāfa al-Islāmiyya, 1937/8).

——. *Al-Maqṣad al-Asnā fī Sharḥ Asmā Allāh al-Ḥusnā* (Cairo: Azhar Press, n.d.).

——. *Mishkāt al-Anwār*, tr. W. H. T. Gairdner as *The Niche for Lights* (Lahore: Ashraf, 1952, reprinting the Royal Asiatic Society Monograph 19, 1924).

——. *Mizān al-'Amal* (Cairo, 1910).

——. *Al-Munqidh min al-Ḍalāl*, tr. W. Montgomery Watt in *The Faith and Practice of al-Ghazālī* (London: Allen and Unwin, 1963).

GOODMAN, L. E. (1971) 'The Epicurean Ethic of Muḥammad ibn Zakaiyā' ar-Rāzī,' *Studia Islamica* 34 pp. 5–26.

——. (1972) 'Rāzī's Psychology,' *Philosophical Forum* 4 pp. 26–48.
——. (1983) 'Baḥyā on the Antinomy of Free Will and Predestination,' *Journal of the History of Ideas* 44, pp. 115–130.
——. (1988) 'The Sacred and the Secular: Rival Themes in Arabic Literature,' Halmos Lecture, Tel Aviv: Tel Aviv University, repr. in M. Mir, ed., *Literary Heritage of Classical Islam* (Princeton: Darwin Press, 1993) 287–330.
GUTAS, D. (1983) 'Paul the Persian on the Classification of the Parts of Arisotle's Philosophy,' *Der Islam* 60.
HAMORI, ANDRAS (1974) *On the Art of Medieval Arabic Literature* (Princeton: Princeton University Press).
HARDIE, W.F.R. (1988) *Aristotle's Ethical Theory* (Oxford: Clarendon Press).
Ikhwān al-Safā (ca. 970) *The Case of the Animals vs. Man*, tr. L. E. Goodman (New York, Twayne, 1978).
KRAEMER, JOEL (1986a) *Humanism in the Renaissance of Islam: The Cultural Revival during the Buyid Age* (Leiden, Brill).
——. (1986b) *Philosophy in the Renaissance of Islam* (Leiden, Brill).
MAHDI, MUHSIN (1970) 'Language and Logic in Classical Islam,' in G. E. von Grunebaum, ed., *Logic in Classical Islamic Culture* (Wiesbaden, Harrassowitz).
MARGOLIOUTH, D. S. (1905) 'The Discussion between Abū Bishr Mattā and Abu Sa'īd al-Sīrāfi on the Merits of Logic and Grammar,' *Journal of the Royal Asiatic Society* pp. 129–79.
MISKAWAYH K. *Tahdhīb al-Akhlāq,* tr. Constatine Zurayk (Beirut, American University of Beirut, 1968); tr. M. Arkoun, *Traté d'Ethique* (Institut Francais de Damas, 1969).
——. On pleasure, in Mohammed Arkoun, 'Deux Epitres de Miskawayh,' *Bulletin d'Etudes Orientales* 17 (1961/2).
——. *Kitāb Tartīb al-Sā'ādāt* (Cairo, 1928).
MOTTAHEDEH, ROY (1980) *Loyalty and Leadership in an Early Islamic Society* (Princeton: Princeton University Press).
ROSENTHAL, FRANZ (1970) *Knowledge Triumphant* (Leiden, Brill).
SHERIF, M. A. (1975) *Ghazali's Theory of Virtue* (Albany: SUNY Press).
Al-Sijistānī, *Ṣiwān al-Ḥikma*, ed. A. Badawi (Tehran, 1974).
Al-Tawḥīdī, Abū Hayyān, *Kitāb al-Hawāmil wa 'l-Shawāmil*, eds., A. Amin and A. Saqr (Cairo, 1951) pp. 265–66.
Al-Ṭūṣī, Nasīr al-Dīn, *The Nasirean Ethics* tr. G. M. Wickens (London: Allen and Unwin, 1964).
WALZER, RICHARD (1963) *Greek into Arabic* (Oxford, Cassirer) 220–35.
WATT, WILLIAM MONTGOMERY (1963) *Muslim Intellectual* (Edinburgh, Edinburgh University Press).
WENSINCK, A. J. (1940) *La Pensée de Ghazzali* (Paris, Maisonneuve).
Yaḥyā ibn 'Adī (d. 974) *Making Clear the Distinction between the Two Arts: Philosophical Logic and Arabic Grammar*, ed. G. Endress, *Journal for the History of Arabic Science* 2 (1978) 38–50, 181–93.
——. *Tahdhīb al-Akhlāq*, in M. Kurd Ali, ed., *Rasā'il al-Bulaghā'* (Cairo, 3rd ed., 1946) 517–18.

2

Fukuzawa Yukichi and Religion*

Takashi Koizumi

Fukuzawa Yukichi was the most influential thinker and opinion leader in Japan in the late 19th century. During his long career he published many best-sellers such as *Conditions in the West* (1866–), *An Encouragement of Learning* (1872–), and *An Outline of Civilization* (1875).[1] Fukuzawa also managed a news publishing house, the Jiji Shinpo-sha, beginning in 1882 and authored a series of editorials in his newspaper which had a great impact upon the Japanese intellectual world.

When pressure from foreign diplomats and missionaries finally forced the Meiji government tacitly to admit Christianity in Japan in 1873, Fukuzawa began to write about religion, including Christianity and Buddhism. Indeed, there are more than 80 essays which deal with religious topics included in his *Collected Works* which consist of 21 volumes and a complementary volume published by Iwanami-Shoten in 1958–1963. At first Fukuzawa discussed religion in general from a utilitarian point of view. His attempt at objectivity, however, eroded over the years. Gradually we can see a definite inclination towards Buddhism and the development of a unique philosophy of religion within the context of Buddhism.

In this paper, I wish to clarify the development of Fukuzawa's religious ideas. His ideas were not only of interest to the Japanese intellectuals in the Meiji period; it seems to me that they still have something to say to present-day Japanese intellectuals.

At first glance, Fukuzawa Yukichi seems to be a man who was content to dismiss religion. In a sense, this is correct. In his

* Previously published in *Asian Philosophy*, Vol. 4, No. 2, 1994.

'Autobiography', Fukuzawa relates a boyhood trick he once played on a little shrine dedicated to the god of cereals. He secretly opened the shrine and found there a little stone which was worshipped as a 'holy body'. He threw it away and replaced it with another stone. He was amused that people came to worship the stone he set on the shrine while no misfortune visited him.[2]

His mother, O-Jun, brought up Fukuzawa by herself. His father, Hyakusuke, died when Fukuzawa was one-and-a-half years old.[3] O-Jun was quite a character. Although she nominally supported the True Pure Land sect of Buddhism (Jodo Shinshu), she used to say, 'I feel embarrassed and unable to worship Amida Buddha even though I go to the temple of the True Pure Land Sect'.[4] Fukuzawa was brought up in a non-religious family and, in a way, his way of life may be termed non-religious. Actually he describes his own way of life as 'living and strolling about without religion' in a book he wrote in 1879, *A Popular Theory of National Rights.*[5]

On the other hand, Fukuzawa was not one to treasure one way of thinking. He was conscious of the inconsistency of the ideas in his mind; sometimes he left them untouched, at other times he tried to unify them or select from them what was most appropriate in accordance with the immediate situation. In this sense, we may say that Fukuzawa was a thinker who was able to take on different and apparently inconsistent standpoints both at the same time and at different times, and that he was a follower of the so-called 'situational ethic'.

Now for the question: why was Fukuzawa concerned with religion at all? I have already mentioned one reason given by Fukuzawa: he began to write about religion in general in order to understand how to deal with Christianity, which was first given official recognition in Japan in 1873.

In 1873 the Meiji government was forced to allow the spread of Christianity in Japan.[6] It did, however, attempt to hinder the proclamation of Christianity by means of various policies. Fukuzawa, too, was opposed to Christianity and tried to prevent its spread in Japan. He said that to believe in a foreign religion is the same as if 'a part of one's soul has fallen into the hands of a foreign religion. Such people cannot help but lose their patriotism'.[7]

In a series of speeches entitled 'Essays on religion', given at Mita Speech Hall in 1881, Fukuzawa proclaimed that 'Those who cannot rely on themselves cannot help relying on others'.[8] Therefore, he criticised religious believers, including Buddhists and Christians, because they stood opposed to the principle of independence and self-respect which Fukuzawa regarded as basic to his philosophy of life.

Furthermore, since Fukuzawa maintained a strong antipathy towards Christianity, he regarded Buddhism as a sort of breakwater against the invasion of Christianity, as described in another speech in the series mentioned above:

> Now so-called Christianity comes to Japan and opens churches everywhere. Believers are gradually increasing. We have to say that Christianity invades the Buddhist realm . . . If I were a Buddhist monk, I would not be silent against this invasion. Buddhists might say that they have no helpers against this invasion. But I should say that there are many who will come to their aid. The government and the scholars are strong supporters. I am one of them, of course. However, I do not believe in Buddhism, but I do have reason to help it.[9]

By 'a reason' Fukuzawa means that he sees Buddhism as serving as a bulwark against the invasion of Christianity. Thus, between the period 1873 to 1881, we may say that Fukuzawa was an extrinsic utilitarian in that he supported Buddhism for its usefulness, but was by no means a believer.

In 1884 Fukuzawa changed his standpoint towards religion by withdrawing his opposition to Christianity in his essay entitled 'Our religion is obliged to become Western'.[10] He asserted that since both Buddhism and Christianity could serve the national interest to a great extent, either of them could be adopted. Furthermore, Fukuzawa's eldest son, Ichitaro, met Arthur K. Napp, a Unitarian minister, in the United States and put him in touch with Fukuzawa, as Napp was planning to come to Japan. Fukuzawa was pleased to entertain Napp when he came to Tokyo in 1887. He heartily sympathised with Napp's cause and made a high evaluation of the Unitarian version of Christianity and its utility in Japan. In an essay entitled 'Contributing to the Unitarian magazine', (March 1890) Fukuzawa noted that the Unitarian insistence upon the negation of miracles, the humanness of Jesus and the rational development of morality by human endeavour were all agreeable to him.[11]

On the other hand, on 2 and 3 October of the same year, Fukuzawa published an essay entitled 'How to proclaim religious creed', and concluded that Buddhism was superior to Christianity, especially in comparing their means of evangelisation. He criticised Christianity as having violent methods in the sense that Christian missionaries invited distrust by criticising other religions and destroying Buddhist idols and family altars. In this essay Fukuzawa dealt with how to proclaim religion and insisted that, since religious proclamation aims at catching one's soul, religion should make use of mild and soft methods. He concluded that in this regard, Buddhists were superior to the Christians.[12]

In this essay, Fukuzawa paid special attention to the proclamation method of the True Pure Land sect and sympathised with the advice that a layman ought not to teach Buddhist doctrines in his own way, for if a layman does so, then his behaviour foreshadows the decline of Buddhism. Thus Fukuzawa asserted that a layman has only to listen to and believe what a monk teaches. For Fukuzawa saw and disapproved of the practice of many Christian laymen in which they would engage in enthusiastic discussions of religion and go about preaching their own respective dogma of faith.

Moreover, Fukuzawa expressed his own view concerning the proclamation method of the True Pure Land sect of Buddhism in an essay entitled 'Discussion of the utility and virtue of religion, dealing with the evangelisation of religion from a political viewpoint' (21 July 1885). He pointed out that the proclamation method of the True Pure Land sect was superbly appropriate to a civilised stage in society. He wrote:

> As people develop their knowledge and intelligence, they have come to throw away various superstitions and to proclaim religion in a clear, distinct and rational way. For we find that, historically speaking, the True Pure Land sect followed the Shingon sect and the Tendai sect in due course, and that True Pure Land Buddhism has given reasonable and understandable teachings . . . If a religious preacher tries to appeal to the mind and soul of our people, then he should gradually try to catch their ideas and enter into their feelings by speaking in a gentle manner and by possessing lofty ideals and by not expressing excessively zealous faith to unbelievers.[13]

Thus, Fukuzawa was much impressed by the True Pure Land sect which was not overtly enthusiastic and which kept a reasonable and refined civilised attitude with regard to matters of evangelisation. However, we must add that at that time Fukuzawa was an outsider in his understanding of Buddhism. He did not believe in Buddhism, but recognised the social utility of the True Pure Land sect in Japan.

Ten years after Fukuzawa wrote this essay on the 'Utility and virtue of religion', his attitude towards religion changed again, as can be seen in his famous series of essays entitled 'One hundred stories of old man Fukuzawa', which were begun in 1895.[14] These essays were published serially in the *Jiji Shinpo*, beginning in 1896. In the essays, Fukuzawa still recognised the social utility of Buddhism by viewing it from without, that is, from an objective viewpoint, but he gradually came closer to Buddhism and, as it were, almost entered into its religious framework.

Fukuzawa gradually changed his attitude towards Buddhism through his association with several Buddhists. First of all Fukuzawa had maintained friendly relations with Shichiri Kojun since the last days of the Tokugawa regime. When he visited Nakatsu in Kyushu in 1864, Fukuzawa met Shichiri and was impressed by his remarkable personality. In 1897, Fukuzawa recalled: 'There have been many great scholars in the True Pure Land sect. For example, Shichiri Kojun, a monk of the Mangyoji temple at Hakata in Kyushu, has been called "the present-day Rennyo".'[15] (Rennyo (1415–99) was the greatest restorer of the True Pure Land sect in the Warring States period.[16]) When Fukuzawa was asked to recommend someone to deal with different issues related to Nishi Honganji, he immediately introduced Shichiri Kojun to the authorities. Shichiri, for his part, respected Fukuzawa and had his son enter Keio Gijuku, the school which Fukuzawa had founded in 1868.

In addition, Fukuzawa had friendly relations with Terada Fukuju who was the chief priest of Shinjoji temple at Komagome and often held Buddhist services for the Fukuzawa family. He was sometimes invited to Fukuzawa's home to discuss Buddhism. We find an interesting letter Fukuzawa wrote to Terada:

> Dear Sir,
> I am very pleased to hear that you are in good health. Excuse me for writing so suddenly, but I should like to ask you to come and discuss Buddhist matters with my family members, if you have time to spare. We have discussed Buddhism among ourselves so far, but we need some help from a Buddhist specialist. We would appreciate help from the True Pure Land sect, if possible. We will be happy if you could select and take a mature Buddhist you think best.[17]

Although we cannot identify when the letter was written, it shows that Fukuzawa and the Fukuzawa family members often discussed Buddhism, and that they invited Terada Fukuju and other Buddhists to discuss Buddhist issues, especially as related to the True Pure Land sect.

Shirayama Kenchi was a Buddhist monk of the True Pure Land sect who graduated from Keio Gijuku. He was a chief priest of Seirenji temple at Mita. Fukuzawa wrote a letter to him dated 18 August 1895 which may be paraphrased as follows:

> Dear Sir,
> Since we are supposed to hold the 35th Day Service for the late Teikichi on the coming 20 August, we should like to ask you to visit our house and hold that service. We should like to hear from you a Buddhist sermon also. We will appreciate it very much if you are kind to do so at 5 o'clock on that afternoon.[18]

This letter also shows that, in 1895 at least, Fukuzawa was interested in hearing about Buddhism and in communication with Buddhist priests. (The late Teikichi was a husband of Fukuzawa's eldest daughter named Sato. He died in 1895.)

A Buddhist monk of the Shingon sect named Suge Gakuo graduated from Keio Gijuku University in 1894 and then took up an appointment of Keio University. He wrote a book entitled *Kobo Daishi and Japanese Civilization* in 1895. Since Fukuzawa was impressed by this book, he referred to some passages from it in his 'One hundred stories of old man Fukuzawa' as follows:

> Suge Gakuo, graduate of Keio and monk of the Shingon sect, has quite recently published a book entitled *Kobo Daishi and Japanese Civilization*. Let me quote from his book: 'If we compare the four phrases of the Nirvana Sutra with the Japanese *iroha* phonetic alphabet song, then the following corresponding interpretations can be seen. The first phrase of the Nirvana Sutra, "Ah! Transitory are the things all" (*shogyo mujo*), corresponds to the first phrase of the *iroha* song "Just as anything visible smells and looks good yet it falls and decays quite in an instant" (*I ro wa ni o e do chi ri nu ru wo*). The second phrase of the Sutra, "As they become, so they perish" (*zesho meppo*) corresponds to "So our life cannot be everlasting and permanent" (*wa ga yo ta re zo tsu ne na ra mu*). The third phrase, "Hardly born, are they destroyed" (*shomestu metsui*) corresponds to the third phrase of the *iroha* song "Today crossing over the futile things in the transient world" (*u wi no o ku ya ma kyo ko e te*). Finally, the last phrase of the Nirvana

> Sutra, "To be free from them is bliss" (*jaku metsu iraku*) can be related to "We would never dream a dream in the passing world, rather we would stay in sacredness and purity of immutability" (*a sa ki yu me mi shi ei mo se zu*).'[19]

Fuzukawa was impressed with Suge Gakuo's explanation, for Suge attempted to explain profound Buddhist doctrine by the *iroha* song which most Japanese were familiar with from their childhood. Fukuzawa says that this method is 'the most appropriate proclamation method to interpret the profound Buddhist doctrine by the easiest familiar one'. We can see here that Fukuzawa has gradually become closer to Buddhism itself in his appreciation of the utility of the Buddhist approach to the proclamation of its creed.

As mentioned above, Fukuzawa was inclined to think within the context of Buddhism through his friendly relations with various Buddhist monks. In other words, although he did not believe in Buddhism, he often held conversations with Buddhists he knew, and he came to create his own philosophy of religion within the context of Buddhism. Fukuzawa's unique philosophy of religion found expression in his 'One hundred stories of old man Fukuzawa', which was published in book form in 1896. Here he developed his own philosophy of religion by thinking within the context of the True Pure Land sect:

> We hear that True Pure Land sect teaches that it is better to worship the picture of the principal image of Amida Buddha than its wooden image, and that it is better yet to recite the *nenbutsu* chant in praise of Amida. To try to express the essence of the Buddha by creating a wooden image of Amida coated with gold is merely a means to gain the attention of the vulgar. Since the wooden image does not show the real essence of Amida, we had better abandon the idol and have the image of Buddha in picture form. But since the image of Buddha in picture still has a sort of form and cannot be identified with the real essence of the Buddha, it is better for us to repeat the name of Amida Buddha, that is, *Namu Amida-Butsu*. To tell the truth, Buddha exists in itself without any temple, without any Buddhist monk, and without any Buddhist scriptures. I am very impressed with this means of thinking. I think this is the real spiritual peace, but, to tell the truth, there is no one who agrees with me.[20]

Thus, Fukuzawa made use of the context of the True Pure Land sect and developed his own philosophy of religion which was akin to that of Buddhism in a sense, but was really, as we will see, quite distinct. Fukuzawa urged that people seek real spiritual peace by relying on 'nothingness', in which lies the real virtue of the Buddha. This is what he considered his original spiritual peace.

How did Fukuzawa define this original spiritual peace? We have to discuss his idea of 'Heaven', his theory of identifying human beings with maggots and his two opposing viewpoints of 'mind' in order to explain Fukuzawa's understanding of original spiritual peace.

First, let me discuss Fukuzawa's understanding of 'Heaven'. In the first story of 'One hundred stories of old man Fukuzawa' he wrote:

> People are used to saying that 'Heaven' is God or *Nyorai* meaning *tathagata* or 'thus-come,' but I cannot assert that 'Heaven' is God or *Nyorai*, for I cannot recognize God or *Nyorai* . . . Now we Japanese have been accustomed to saying, 'Heaven did this,' when confronted with a situation in which we do not understand or know what to do. Therefore, I should like to use this word 'Heaven' in order to express the cosmic reality which is so utterly beyond our understanding that we are just in bewilderment . . . By 'Heaven' I mean the mysterious reality of the cosmos which is infinite, eternal, and unfathomable beyond human intellectual power.[21]

Fukuzawa also notes in the sixth story: 'It seems to me that "Heaven" is merely what happens mysteriously and spontaneously without any mover or any first cause'.[22] In short, Fukuzawa thought that 'Heaven' made human beings aware of the fact that they are so ignorant and helpless that 'Heaven' itself is far beyond their understanding. What is more, Fukuzawa was unable to accept a creator of 'Heaven', because he was unable to identify it, and because he thought that if we assume a creator of 'Heaven', then we have to assume another creator of a creator of 'Heaven'. In other words, 'Heaven' is a transcendent, infinite and omnipotent being, but, at the same time, it is that which spontaneously happens; that is, what happens without any cause.

Thus Fukuzawa's 'Heaven' was quite different from the personal God of the Christians. His 'Heaven' is just what happens to be, or, as it were, what spontaneously exists. The Japanese word *shizen*, usually translated as 'nature', perhaps best expresses this notion of 'Heaven' meaning 'spontaneously happening' in Japanese.

According to Fukuzawa, when human beings stand in the presence of 'heaven', they feel themselves to be no more than ignorant, helpless and miserable maggots. Human beings are just creatures who 'happen to be born, eat and sleep on the earth for a short time and then who die in an instant'.[23] Fukuzawa's theory of human beings may be called the theory of 'human beings equal to a maggot'. In other words, Fukuzawa adopted the Buddhist viewpoint of impermanence by recognising the unfathomable cleavage between 'Heaven' and human beings, so that he 'regards this ephemeral world as but a trifle and unimportant; that is, impermanent and considers all human affairs to be a mere jest or joke'.[24]

Fukuzawa named his Buddhist viewpoint of impermanence 'the viewpoint of the original state of mind or the substance of mind' (*kokoro no hontai*).[25] The original state of mind exposes the real impermanence of the ephemeral world. And this impermanence is, to Fukuzawa, the ultimate reality of the present world.

Now an ordinary Buddhist would try to transcend the ephemeral world and reach Nirvana or the Pure Land by all means when he realises the ultimate reality of this ephemeral world by standing upon the viewpoint of this original state of mind. However, Fukuzawa took the standpoint of the original state of mind, but tried to remain in this ephemeral world and tried to live as an independent being with self-respect. He wrote in the 17th story as follows: 'We may say from the viewpoint of the original state of mind that we realize human beings to be but a trifle, an unimportant maggot, while we may say from the viewpoint of the practice of mind or the function of mind, that we live as the noblest and most mysterious being in this world'.[26]

Fukuzawa's viewpoint of assuming two opposite points of mind seems contradictory, but is unique and interesting. To assume two opposite viewpoints, his adoption of both the original state of mind (*kokoro no hontai*) and the practice of mind (*kokoro no hataraki*) is similar to the theory of 'substance and function' (*tai'yo-ron*) of Zhu Xi Neo-Confucianism familiar to most Japanese intellectuals at that time. But Fukuzawa changed the theory of substance (the original state of mind) into the Buddhist view of 'human beings equal to a maggot' and substituted the function of human being to maximise independence and self-respect for the 'function of the mind'. Moreover, Fukuzawa assumed a two-dimensional viewpoint within the this-worldly realm. This constitutes Fukuzawa's original philosophy of religion.

Let us now examine the concrete structure of Fukuzawa's philosophy of religion by assuming that there are horizontally two opposite points from either of which one can move to the other in an instant. Let us assume a right-hand point as that from which one can see the impermanence of the cosmos, that is, the original state of mind. Next, let us assume the left-hand point as the viewpoint from which one can see human beings in terms of their independence and self-respect.

When we take the right-hand point, we realise that the cosmos is what mysteriously and spontaneously happens to be, and that human beings are merely maggots in the presence of the vast and great cosmos in the sense that human beings live and die in an instant. This is similar to the transient life of a maggot in that it lives merely in a jest and passes away in a jest. This is what Fukuzawa considered to be the ultimate reality of the ephemeral world.

On the other hand, there is another viewpoint from which Fukuzawa regarded human beings and the present world. This is the left-hand point to which one can instantly shift. From this left-hand point of view, the situation quite reverses itself. Human beings become instead the most respected beings, that is, independent beings with self-respect. In other words, human beings come to be regarded as the most valuable, inexchangeable beings, and live their lives by respecting themselves as well as others.

When we try to live in this ephemeral world in earnest, we are often confronted with very difficult situations. In these situations, Fukuzawa suggests that we shift from the left-hand to the right-hand viewpoint. In other words, he suggests that we move to the original state of mind; in other words, to the viewpoint of substance of mind. Thus, we can look at ourselves in a quandary as merely living and playing in a transient world like maggots. Let us stop ourselves, asking: 'what makes us so annoyed in our maggot-like life only for 50 years or so? We have nothing important in it; we live in jest'.

Since we live in jest, we need not regard our problem as of life-or-death significance. By standing upon the viewpoint of the original state of mind, we can detach ourselves from our annoyance and look at ourselves coolly. In other words, we can come back to the original state of mind by, as it were, slipping out of our spider's entangled web in this ephemeral world. After we get out of the spider's net, we can embark on a new enterprise again. Then we are going to live another life which is just like playing another joke. Thus, according to Fukuzawa, there is no annoyance at all. We realise that our life is but a jest while we are seriously living a jest-like life. This is what Fukuzawa calls 'The great spiritual peace of life' assuming two opposite and instantly exchangeable viewpoints.[27] And he saw those human beings who were able to adopt this standpoint as people of freedom and of independence.

This idea shows the strength of Fukuzawa's spirit of independence. Fukuzawa says in the 10th story:

> Human minds can work in two apparently opposite modes, but they work in two modes smoothly without contradiction. For the human mind is vast and boundless. Thus we recognize our present life as a jest but at the same time live our life seriously. Since we live seriously, we keep our society in order and at the same time we do not annoy ourselves in our troubles because we recognize our present life as a jest.[28]

Now we may say that Fukuzawa attained this philosophy of religion through cordial ties and discussions with Buddhist believers belonging to the True Pure Land sect, the Shingon sect, and the Rinzai sect of Buddhism.

The last question I wish to ask is: to which sect of Buddhism, the True Pure Land sect on the one hand, or the Shingon and Rinzai sect on the other, did Fukuzawa incline in his philosophy of religion?

In order to answer this question, I should like to consider the view of Shaku Soen, a Buddhist monk and one of Fukuzawa's disciples, whose way of thinking was close to Fukuzawa's. Shaku Soen entered Keio Gijuku in September 1885 and studied directly under Fukuzawa. After graduation, he became the head priest of the Engakuji temple of the Rinzai sect in Kamakura. In March 1903 he wrote an essay entitled 'The significance of religion', which discussed the relationship between the idea of independence and self-respect on the one hand, and Buddhism on the other. He wrote: 'independence and self-respect is what man possesses in nature. Truth in itself is originally independence.'[29] This is similar to what Fukuzawa called the view of the practice of mind or the function of mind.

On the other hand, Shaku Soen continued: 'What does a man feel when he has lost his loving wife or his grandchildren in this transient world, even though he is a scholar or a man of wealth? He cannot help hearing a preaching voice in his soul. This is what I call religion.'[30]

This is the viewpoint of impermanence and is similar to what Fukuzawa called the viewpoint of 'the original state of mind,' or 'substance of mind'. Considering that Shaku Soen's idea of religion is akin to Fukuzawa's philosophy of religion, we may say that

Fukuzawa's idea is close to that of Shaku Soen or Suge Gakuo, who also stressed reliance upon one's own power.

Fukuzawa's philosophy of religion resonates with that of the Rinzai sect or the Shingon sect of Buddhism, for Fukuzawa also stressed the strength of will and spirit of independence and refused reliance upon the power of others (*tariki*), even though he maintained friendly relations with members of the True Pure Land sect who ultimately sought refuge in and reliance upon the power of another, that is, the power of Amida.

Thus we may conclude that although Fukuzawa had friendly relations with the True Pure Land Buddhists, he kept taking the standpoint of this-worldly mindedness because of his strong spirit of independence, for he would not accept reliance upon the assistance of Amida Buddha in order to move to the other-worldly Pure Land.

Takashi Koizumi, Graduate School of Comparative Culture, International Christian University, 3–10–2 Osawa, Mitaka City, Tokyo 181, Japan.

NOTES

1 Over 250,000 copies of Fukuzawa Yukichi's *Conditions in the West* (first series) were said to have been sold. Fukuzawa himself wrote in his Preface to *An Encouragement of Learning* that more than 220,000 copies of the first series of the book were sold. Therefore, we may say that one in 160 Japanese read it in those days. As Fukuzawa wrote in *An Outline of Civilization*, in those days it was hard for common people to read it, so that only several tens of thousands of copies of it were sold. However, such a figure still deserves attention. In any case, his books were so timely that many copies were sold and had a tremendous influence upon intellectuals as well as on common people in the early Meiji period.

2 FUKUZAWA YUKICHI (1959) Autobiography, *Collected Works of Fukuzawa Yukichi* [hereafter *Collected Works*] (Tokyo, Iwanami-Shoten) Vo. 7, pp. 18–19.

3 Ibid., p. 7.

4 Ibid., p. 17.

5 FUKUZAWA YUKICHI (1959) A popular theory of national rights, *Collected Works*, Vol. 4, p. 626, p. 672.

6 The Meiji government announced the prohibition of Christianity in Japan on 15 March 1868, saying:

> Missionary efforts on behalf of Christianity are to be prohibited in Japan, as before. If anyone discovers someone acting in disregard to this decree, he should in due course inform the government office

> concerned with these people. Such informants will be given a reward for this information.

This action was at once reported to foreign countries and raised much protest. It happened that when Iwakura Tomomi, Ambassador Extraordinary and Plenipotentiary of Japan to the United States and European countries, visited Washington in 1872 in order to discuss revision of diplomatic relations with the United States, he received a severe protest from Hamilton Fish (1808–1893), US Secretary of State on 10 February 1872:

> We cannot establish free diplomatic relations with Japan, unless the Japanese government stops the oppression of Christianity in Japan. The insult to our religion is the same as insults to our person. (Japanese Diplomatic Papers, 5 (69), pp. 147–154 (original in English).

On the other hand, Nakamura Keiu contributed to *Shinbun Zasshi* (No. 56) an article entitled 'Imitating a European's letter to the Emperor'. Nakamura insisted that Christianity was the kernel of European spirit, from which the whole of European civilisation was derived. Thus he urged the government to introduce Christianity into Japan before anything else, if the government wished to introduce Western civilisation into Japan.

7 FUKUZAWA YUKICHI (1960) Our religion is obliged to become Western, *Collected Works*, Vol. 9, p. 533.

8 FUKUZAWA YUKICHI (1963) Essays on religion, *Collected Works*, Vol. 20, p. 232.

9 FUKUZAWA YUKICHI (1962) Essays on religion, *Collected Works*, Vol. 19, p. 711.

10 FUKUZAWA Our religion is obliged to become Western, *Collected Works*, Vol. 9, pp. 531–536.

11 FUKUZAWA YUKICHI (1963) Contributing to the Unitarian magazine, *Collected Works*, Vol. 20, pp. 367–369.

12 FUKUZAWA YUKICHI (1960) How to proclaim religious creed, *Collected Works*, Vol. 10, pp. 52–58.

13 FUKUZAWA YUKICHI (1960) Discussion of the utility and virtue of religion, dealing with evangelization of religion from a political viewpoint, *Collected Works*, Vol. 10, pp. 330–332.

14 FUKUZAWA YUKICHI (1959) One hundred stories of old man Fukuzawa, *Collected Works*, Vol. 6, pp. 207–384.

15 FUKUZAWA YUKICHI (1961) Separation of legal succession from lineage, *Collected Works*, Vol. 16, p. 171.

16 This period of constant internal warfare continued from the middle of the 15th century to the middle of the 16th century.

17 FUKUZAWA YUKICHI (1962) A letter to Terada Fukuju, *Collected Works*, Vol. 18, p. 848.

18 FUKUZAWA YUKICHI (1962) A letter to Shirayama Kenchi, *Collected Works*, Vol. 18, p. 684.

19 FUKUZAWA YUKICHI (1959) One hundred stories of old man Fukuzawa: the 70th story, *Collected Works*, Vol. 6, pp. 319–320. I have adopted the

translation of the Nirvana Sutra from V. Srinicasa Sarma's (1983) *A History of Indian Literature*, Vol. 11 (Dehli, Motilal Banarsidass), p. 108. This translation is in turn the English translation of the book entitled, *Geschichte der Indischen Literatur*, written by Maurice Winternits in 1920. Furthermore, I paraphrased the Japanese Iroha Song into English.

20 Ibid., pp. 363–364.
21 Ibid., p. 207.
22 Ibid., p. 219.
23 Ibid., p. 222–223.
24 Ibid., pp. 275–276.
25 Ibid., p. 235.
26 Ibid., p. 235.
27 Ibid., p. 277.
28 Ibid., pp. 226–227.
29 Shaku Soen, The significance of religion, *Keio Gijuku, Gahuko*, 62, September 1885.
30 Ibid.

3

The Ethics of Watsuji Tetsurō

A Reappraisal of Western and Eastern Influences

Alistair Swale

Watsuji Tetsurō, the major Japanese philosopher whose influence spanned from the Pre-War to Post-War periods, received a considerable amount of foreign attention up until the 1960s. This included the attention of such notable scholars as Robert Bellah. Also, La Fleur carried out research covering the Buddhistic aspects of Watsuji's work and Dilworth produced a translation of part of Watsuji's magnum opus, *Ethics*.[1] Yet from the 1970s on, interest in this thinker among non-Japanese waned. It may have been that the Revisionist view of Japan that became predominant since that time led to a disregard for thought considered nationalistic or narcissistic.[2] In Watsuji's case, certain of his works, including *Pilgrimage to the Ancient Temples* and *National Isolation: Japan's Tragedy*,[3] would come into that category. However, whether one wishes to criticise or defend such works, the fact remains that they are perennially popular in their land of origin and so an understanding of them is indispensable.

What I intend to present in this paper is a brief sketch of Watsuji Tetsurō's 'anthropology', including his criticism of three schools of thought within the Western tradition as contained in the work, *Ethics As Anthropology*. It will later be demonstrated that, despite Watsuji's strongly stated objections to certain fundamental aspects of the Western philosophical tradition, his practical ethical philosophy is the product of a significant degree of exchange with Western thinking. In particular, I would like to demonstrate the depth of interrelation between Watsuji and Hegel. It has been customary to emphasise the very obvious intersection with Heideggerian phenomenology, but the fact is that we find something closer to the heart of Watsuji's social and ethical thinking through an examination of the Hegelian influence.

WATSUJI'S ANTHROPOLOGY

Arguably it is the work *Ethics As Anthropology*[4] that best encapsulates the essence of Watsuji's ethical theory. The two volume magnum opus *Ethics* is an amalgam of in fact three distinct strands; his anthropology and anthropological method (denoted in volume one as the preface and chapters one and two); an essentially 'Hegelian' discussion of ethical life (volume one, chapter three) and a discussion that draws mainly on another well-known work, *A Climate* (chapters one and two in volume two). The Hegel-inspired discussion, though significant, is not at the foundation of Watsuji's philosophy. Volume two, which deals with the climatic and historical aspects of human existence, is obviously integral to a comprehensive grasp of Watsuji's thinking but is, nevertheless, arguably inferior to, and perhaps even detracts from the purely 'anthropological' discussion.[5] *Ethics As Anthropology* is a more focused philosophical work with a clearer demonstration of the interplay between Western and Eastern traditions. Thus it provides valuable contextual material enabling insights into the nature and objectives of Watsuji's later work. This is especially so with regard to clarification of the Hegelian input into Watsuji's ethical philosophy on a practical historical and social level.

ETHICS AS ANTHROPOLOGY

In the introduction of *Ethics As Anthropology* the philosophical objective is defined as the clarification of an ethical discourse that ultimately takes a fundamentally different direction to that of the Western tradition. It differs in that the conception of 'man' is radically different from that of the Western 'individual' which has been rendered historically in various forms such as 'individuum', 'anthropos', 'Mensch' or 'man'. He criticises the Western concept of the individual as being limited and excessively abstract. He actually questions whether the individual is an accurate representation of the human condition, whether it is in fact 'real'. Moreover, Watsuji holds that it is only possible to conceive of moral imperatives such as responsibility, sincerity and trust in terms of the collectivity, not the individual.

In the place of 'the individual' Watsuji proposes the concept *Ningen* which, although commonly translated as 'human being', has origins which give it a very different nuance. The character for *Nin* in *Ningen* indeed refers to 'humans', but when combined with *Gen*, which means 'interval', we get an idea of what Watsuji is aiming at. It is human plus that which is trans-individual or inter-individual. A modified version of *Ningen* can be found in Hamaguchi Eshun's term, the 'contextual', which provides a useful contrast to the individual in Western discourse.[6]

This fundamental redefinition of 'human beings' forms the basis of Watsuji's 'anthropology'. He then progresses to a discussion of the human condition in general which he terms *Ningen no Sonzai*. This could be translated severally as 'human existence', 'human place' or, if one were to speculate along Heideggerian lines, the 'beingness of humanity'. The term 'human condition', which is a more natural turn of phrase for the English-speaker, would also suffice, however one would have to bear in mind the specific nuance intended by Watsuji.

Within Watsuji's conception of 'human existence', human relations are referred to as *Aidagara*. These human relations are necessarily not interpersonal relations between individuals but among humans (in the sense of *Ningen*). Moreover, these relations are constituted out of the praxis of human sociality, not out of subjectively mediated states of individual consciousness.[7]

Appertaining to the above definition of *Ningen no Sonzai*, we must also note the historico-geographical aspect embodied in the work, *A Climate*. It is this aspect that distinguishes Watsuji's ethical philosophy from being merely an adaption of Heideggerian philosophy. Indeed, one of the main criticisms that Watsuji had of Heidegger was the lack of adequate attention to the issue of 'spatiality'. Watsuji expanded the human place to incorporate our very environment and this led to his discussion of cultural development in relation to climate.[8]

Watsuji's aim within the scope of *Ethics As Anthropology*, is to introduce a new definition of the human condition, evaluate the attempts of Western philosophy to handle the same problem and finally introduce a methodology which illustrates the conceptual and practical merit of a philosophy grounded in this new conception of human existence.

WATSUJI AND THE WESTERN TRADITION

Watsuji considers that the attempts of a variety of Western thinkers to accurately grasp the human condition have been fundamentally flawed in one regard or another. Essentially, these flaws are rooted in the Western preoccupation with the individual. Nevertheless, Watsuji does recognise that at the foundation of Western philosophy, in particular Aristotelian philosophy, there is a significant degree of intersection with what he himself envisages. He notes that Aristotle's citizen, the *polites*, is defined in terms of the *polis* and not the other way around. Moreover, he notes how the *Ethics* and *Politics* of Aristotle were in fact intended to stand as a whole and not separately. It is the departure from the Aristotelian conception of the human condition and the establishment of a division between the ethical and the political philosophy that is taken by Watsuji to constitute a fundamental error in the development of Western ethical thinking. The history of Western philosophy for him is one of the demise of the early tradition which successive Western thinkers have gradually reclaimed but only begun to approach a full recovery in relatively recent times. The discussion of various Western thinkers in *Ethics As Anthropology* can therefore be characterised as a tracing of this slow course toward the reestablishment of the early 'truth'.

Rather than recount Watsuji's treatment of each philosopher, it would seem beneficial to regroup Watsuji's critique as a response to the following schools of Western thought; the British Empiricist school, featuring the state of nature theories of Hobbes and Locke, the Idealist school featuring Kant, Cohen and also Hegel, and finally the Materialist school featuring Marx and Feuerbach.[9]

To illustrate his point regarding the British Empiricist school, Watsuji criticises the classical 'state of nature' theory within Hobbes as follows:

> The problem with Hobbes' theory can be found by asking the question of how natural morality emerges out of physical nature. Or, conversely, how the atomised individual isolated from nature proceeds to a condition of unity and order.[10]

Watsuji cannot see how all the complex expressions of human existence can be accounted for on the basis of isolated individuals. Drawing on Hegel's critique of Hobbes and Locke, Watsuji also asserts that the social model proposed by Hobbes excludes elements of voluntarism and incidentalness in experiential reality. Hobbes is described as proceeding only on the basis of crude necessities and attempting to explain all other phenomenon simply on that basis. Although this criticism is raised with regard to Hobbes specifically, it implies that all theories that start with the hypothetical individual in a primary natural state share an inability to conceive of society as being more than an agglomerate of atomised individuals.[11]

After making perhaps unjustifiably short work of the British tradition, he moves to Kant who is considered to have made a more thorough attempt at conceiving the fundamental unity of the human condition. In fact Kant also wrote on 'Anthropology' in the latter years of his life and that seems to have inspired Watsuji's own special use of the term to some degree.[12] Nevertheless, in Watsuji's mind, Kant did not succeed in his philosophical objective due to the abstractness of his idealism and his over-preoccupation with the individual. Kant's attempt to bridge the gap between reason and experience is praised but considered bound to fail if the discourse is confined to a discussion of the individual mind. The very tool which Kant employed to fathom the human condition was what in effect precluded an accurate grasp of the human condition.[13]

Hegel, on the other hand, clearly perceived the antithesis of the individual and the whole and sought to resolve it through the three stage dialectic of the Spirit. Watsuji valued Hegel's work highly however, according to Watsuji, Hegel had difficulty in articulating his philosophy in practical terms; he failed to demonstrate how practical custom (which develops into law and legal institutions), is linked to the Absolute Spirit which was essentially 'abstract'. It is concluded, therefore, that Hegel also lost touch with practical existential concerns.[14]

The next stage in Watsuji's anthropological comment on Western ethical philosophy concerns Marx, leading on from a discussion of Hegel and Feuerbach. Marx is praised for having established a practical link between human consciousness and human relations through materialism. His theory has a degree of sophistication in terms of enabling us to grasp the practicality of the human condition and this brings Marx's conception of human relations closer to Watsuji's conception of *Aidagara*. However, Marx is faulted for being morally econocentric and his theory is criticised for being almost bankrupt in terms or providing the basis of a national morality. In other words, it lacks the attempt to create a national morality after the fashion of Hegel's 'ethical nation' in *The System of Ethical Life*.[15]

Overall, Watsuji sees a tendency in Western thought to be torn between two extremes; one atomistic and the other holistic, neither of which succeeds in articulating the human totality. Watsuji is adamant that neither the individual nor an abstract universal are adequate for correctly conceptualising the human condition.

The alternative that Watsuji espouses is an interpretative exploration of human existence. However, there are special criteria for the manner of exploration that he considers legitimate in the interpretative analysis of phenomena. Watsuji maintains that we can only countenance phenomena in relation to an absolute totality. Individuals, in the Western sense, are not recognised for the very reason that they are isolated, dissociated expressions of human existence.[16] This problematic aspect of the individual is dissolved through the reconceptualisation of human beings and human relations (*Aidagara*) within human existence. Through *Aidagara*, humans partake of the totality of human existence. This totality is not something beyond *Ningen* or *Aidagara* but, in fact, the practical matrix of those elements.

In the above sense Watsjui's totality constitutes an open field wherein the scholar can seek to reapprehend the deep ethical structures of life. These ethical structures are taken to be already part of the fabric of human existence but they must be 'realised' through the purposeful use of language for them to become practical. Watsuji's human existence is deliberately left somewhat open-ended and in that sense there is a strong affinity in his method to Heidegger's formulation of the question of Being. Nevertheless, Watsuji forsakes Heidegger's phenomenology in favour of a Diltheyesque interpretation of the various 'expressions' of human existence encountered in everyday life.[17]

By framing the academic enquiry in the above manner and by putting constraints on the field of legitimate phenomena, Watsuji seems to have avoided the Western pitfall of attempting to fathom the external world through individual perception and in terms of individuals alone. In addition, through the resolution of all phenomena into an Absolute which is subjective, he would claim to have escaped from the problems of the subject/object dichotomy as well.

Theoretically at least, one may feel that Watsuji has succeeded in solving many of the problems that he points out in Western philosophy. Yet there are problematic implications regarding the reframing of ethical inquiry in this manner. Not least of these is the implication of a reconstitution of human beings which excludes the 'individual'.[18] But, putting this issue to one side, it would seem that priority should be attached to clarification of what kind of 'Absolute' Watsuji is working with, as this has a large bearing on what criticisms might legitimately apply.

WATSUJI AND THE ABSOLUTE; EASTERN AND WESTERN INFLUENCES

The influence of the two great Asian traditions, Buddhism and Confucianism, are obvious in Watsuji's work. The Buddhist tradition is overtly incorporated in the adoption of the Buddhist concepts of '*Senru*', a Buddhist notion of an absolute totality and '*Loka*', a Sanskrit word denoting 'place' in the world. Also, Watsuji's discussion of 'negativity' displays an ostensible debt of inspiration from Nishida Kitarō's 'nothingness'. In addition, with regard to Confucian influence, Watsuji posits Confucian-style 'cardinal relations' within these broader Buddhist concepts just mentioned.[19]

La Fleur, in his aforementioned research, emphasised a profoundly Buddhist influence. This would seem to be justified in that Watsuji posits human relations within a totality referred to with a Buddhist term, *Senru*. Bur as Kōsaka states, Watsuji's orientation is actually essentially secular, unlike Nishida's.[20] We get an important clue to the nature of Watsuji's attitude to the great Asian traditions in his discussion of cardinal relations at the start of *Ethics As Anthropology*. He insists that he is not attempting to reify Neo-Confucian philosophy and approaches making a disclaimer regarding any association with it. This could be construed as an attempt to palliate an eclectic tendency but, on the contrary, it is in fact an attempt to frame something beyond the constraints of the grand traditions.

A close examination of the main body of Watsuji's texts reveals that Watsuji's Absolute has a clearly secular aspect to it and it is apparent that Hegelian philosophy plays a significant role in this regard. The nature and extent of that influence is discussed in the following section.

HEGEL IN *ETHICS AS ANTHROPOLOGY*

Watsuji noted how Hegel took the elements of Kant's work and reworked them in a radical way with a view to capturing the totality beyond the individual. He also notes that despite the Protestant background that Kant and Hegel held in common there was in Hegel's time a strong influence which emerged to compete with Protestantism in the form of Romanticism; especially in relation to the revival of interest in Classical Greek works. Hegel redefined Schelling's subject as 'spirit' and combined it within an Aristotelian totality whereby he hoped to promulgate the practical subject. Watsuji remarks that although Hegel's philosophy of the spirit does not overtly include 'ethics' one can consider this philosophy as the broadening of ethics to include a broader aspect of human existence through 'spirit'. Consequently, Hegel's philosophy of spirit represents an advance from mere moral consciousness. Nevertheless he notes that whereas Hegel's earlier works represent a consistent devotion to Spirit this was later 'compromised' in favour of 'Religion' and 'Absolute Knowledge'. Even so, he still admires Hegel's on-going attempt to promulgate a practical morality which encompassed human relations, culture and ethics under the aegis of one 'Spirit'.[21]

Watsuji traces the development of Hegel's spiritual philosophy from *The System of Ethical Life*, a work which was never used in lectures and was written at around the same time as the work *On the Scientific Treatment of Natural Law*. This early philosophy formed the basis of Hegel's *Phenomenology of Spirit* and represents for Watsuji the beginning of a 'correct' Absolute Ethics.

Although the title, *The System of Ethical Life*, suggests a fairly exclusive concern for ethical philosophy, it is regarded by Watsuji as better understood as 'social philosophy' after the style of Aristotle and consequently coming closer to Watsuji's own definition of 'ethics'. He says that, despite the use of some of Schellings 'hard' terminology and 'vagueness', it is clear that Hegel was trying to capture the wholeness of humanity, (viz *Ningen*). The goal of *The System of Ethical Life* was the Ethic of the Absolute Idea, which was the arrival at the wholeness and unity of life where all 'difference' ceases to exist through a dialectical process of resolution fully played out.

The focal point of 'difference' is the dualism of 'part' and 'whole' and this forms a dominant theme throughout the commentary. Hegel conceived reality in terms of an organic whole which goes through a dialectic process of resolution. For Hegel, and also for Watsuji, the particular has no meaning, in fact cannot be considered 'real' in the true sense of the word outside of the Whole. Individuality is postulated not as a self-contained individual, but rather an individual containing all the contradictions of the whole and the particular.

The process of resolution toward the Absolute in the sphere of ethical life proceeds through various levels. It starts on the level of 'Nature' where the whole is hidden and man is left struggling to tap into it. The individual also lives as part of a 'Volk' or 'People' which, although an abstraction, has a 'mysterious link' to the individual, with the totality itself 'floating' above and beyond. This vision had enormous appeal to Watsuji, along with the depiction of the concept of 'Intuition' in Hegel's thought where the individual searches for the Absolute, albeit initially 'outside' of himself in the objectified 'whole'. It is precisely this problematic aspect of 'objectification' that Watsuji tackles in the section on methodology in *Ethics As Anthropology* and seeks to solve interpretatively. Nevertheless, the above is still a discussion in a 'Natural' and not 'Absolute' context, only an intermediary level of Natural Ethics or Intuition.[22] The focus of Watsuji's interest lies in the latter stages of Hegel's argument.

The next stage in Hegel's 'System' is 'Ethical Life As A System At Rest'. In the system at rest particularity ceases and ethics as a universality becomes a concrete reality. This concrete universal can be conceived in three ways;

i) Absolute ethical life which is 'absolute intuition immediately'.
ii) Relative ethical life, where legal right and 'honesty' are fashioned.
iii) Ethical life of 'trust', where identity and difference reach their 'indifference point'.[23]

This framework establishes the parameters for the process of moving towards clarification of the Absolute form of ethical life. It conforms to Watsuji's own perception of what ethical life should ultimately entail in that it provides for the resolution of the particular and the totality into a whole that shares one identity and draws its moral impetus from 'trust' as opposed to 'objectified' legal conventions. Yet rather than being something that is simply 'close' to Watsuji's conception, it is pertinent to note how this framework comes to structure Watsuji's later discourse. The theme of one society, based on legal right and 'honesty' embodying the morality of a self-interested Bourgeoisie (viz the West) in contradistinction to another (anonymous) society which embodies the ideal expression of ethical life and draws its moral impetus from 'trust', is reproduced in almost exactly the same sense as Hegel in other contexts. We may also note how the motif of a 'system in motion' *vis-à-vis* a 'system at rest' emerges in the section on methodology where Watsuji states that the objective of ethics is to capture the human being in its *dynamic* aspect.[24]

Some of these themes are further developed when Watsuji moves on in his commentary to discuss *On the Scientific Treatment of Nature Law.* In this work we find the three stages of the 'Universal Government' reproduced indirectly through a discussion of:

i) Hobbes and Locke, (c.f. 'particularism').
ii) Kant and Fichte's Formalism, (c.f. 'ideal abstract universality').
iii) Hegel's own discussion, (c.f. 'concrete universalism').

Overall there are two main complaints of Hegel regarding i) and ii) and Watsuji concurs with them. The first is the failure to reconcile 'Indifference' and 'Difference' (or perhaps part and whole, one might say). The second is the divorcing of ideal universal freedom and the nature of particular practical freedoms.[25] For Hegel freedom had to be expressed with the absolute or in an absolute synthesis of the parts. These themes are also built into later parts of Watsuji's own discourse. The first sections of the discussion on methodology in particular indicate that Watsjui's academic mission could well be framed to address the same issues (although he was not necessarily preoccupied with 'freedom').

One further area of Hegel's work that Watsuji continues to indicate considerable proclivity towards but ultimately adapts into a different position is the discussion of law in relation to 'custom'. Watsuji considered the problem of the natural specificity of a particular culture or Volk very important. Hegel depicts the cultural context of the Volk as being in a state of flux, where sometimes Law can get out of synchronisation with its cultural context. If this process is ignored then chaos ensues, but if we can accurately perceive these movements the hope of realising the Absolute moment remains. Cosmopolitanism is a 'nonmoment'; rather our duty is to pursue a 'more beautiful' moment, to seek a direct view of the self in the Whole, the Absolute Spirit. This is profoundly similar to Watsuji's undertaking in *A Climate* and also parallels the views expressed in the first section of *Ethics As Anthropology.*[26]

Nevertheless, Hegel's practical conception would still seem to be different to that of Watsuji's in certain ways. For example, if we refer to Hegel's discussion of the Spartans in *The System of Ethical Life* we may note that Watsuji is not inclined to admire the positive aspect of 'recognition' that is entailed in such an expression of political culture.[27] Also, when Hegel uses ancient Rome as an example of private interest leading to the ruin of all, he interprets it in a broader sense to criticise the West rather than strictly in the sense that Hegel meant by it. Overall, as Hegel's later philosophy develops, Watsuji indicates increasing estrangement.

The ultimate point of divergence is that Watsuji does not accept the conception of the final stage of the Absolute Spirit as defined by Hegel, which he considers highly problematic. His commentary on *The Phenomenology of Spirit* makes this clear. During this discussion Watsuji does not proceed to the topic of 'religion' as one might expect but rather to the failure to achieve a nation of the Absolute Ethic. He remarks that whereas the *The System of Ethical Life* had the family as its major turning point, the *Phenomenology* has the 'ethical nation' as merely a point of transition. Watsuji indicates dissatisfaction that the 'ethical nation' has lost preeminence to religion.

As if to seal the division between himself and Hegel Watsuji picks up on the tension in Hegel's work between Philosophy and Law. The problem lies in the fact that the former is reflective and the latter starts from a concept of intention and is abstract. These two are eventually combined into a schema of Ethical Life which, i) starts with the family, ii) leads to Bourgeois society, which introduces the hope of iii) the country as the Ethical Spirit. But Watsuji considers that iii), as part of the basis of i) and ii) are not feasible in terms of philosophy or philosophical advance. Watsuji requires clarification of how law and other institutions are constituted through self-consciousness. In other words, how the tension between looking at consciousness and analysing the structure of humanity (*Ningen*) can be removed.[28] To posit the Spirit as the 'thinking Spirit' is not sufficient. The weakness of Hegel's philosophy is that he tried to grasp moments of existence only in terms of the development of ideas and the advance of concepts to the point that 'thought' became the basis for discussing human existence and its foundation. Watsuji says that if the Spirit is a real idea, then the 'unity of self' cannot help but be on the level of thought as well. This Idealism undermines Hegel's philosophy in Watsuji's eyes and it is that same weakness that was soon to be brought out by his very own disciples and ultimately used as the basis for establishing a completely opposing philosophy to Idealism, namely the Materialism of Feuerbach and Marx.

Overall, Watsuji pronounces that Hegel's work is indeed an 'analysis of the structure of human existence', although not the definitive one. Watsuji admires Hegel's treatment of the particular and the totality as it grasps the relation between individual and society through expanding on the subject to a point of semi-objectification via intuition. It is Ethics, not as subjective consciousness but individual action in a social sense and, more importantly, Hegel is analysing concrete moments of human existence. Yet for reasons outlined above, Hegel's intention is not carried through.

Regarding the elements of Hegelian philosophy that are particularly influential on Watsuji's philosophy we should note how Hegel's distinction between 'private' Bourgeois 'morals' and the Absolute Ethic, (c.f. 'Moralität' and 'Sittlichkeit'), fundamentally structures Watsuji's criticism of Western society and ethics as presented in the first section of *Ethics As Anthropology*. With more specific regard to the concept of the Absolute, we note that when Watsuji picks up on the theme of Volk and Polis the aspect of denial of the individual in favour of the Absolute is construed as a kind of negation similar to his own in the construction of the Absolute(*Kū*). Indeed he praises Hegel for incorporating some notion of *Kū* in his philosophy of humanity.[29] Nevertheless, with its dialectic of double negation Watsuji's Absolute is probably more reminiscent of the Hegelian Absolute than the other way around. Though owing some debt of inspiration to the philosophy of Nishida Kitarō, it is, in an important sense, an adaptation of the Hegelian model.

ETHICS AND THE HEGELIAN INFLUENCE

Ethics As Anthropology shows us that Watsuji is primarily interested in the thrust of Hegel's earlier work. This is particularly so with regard to Hegel's investigation of practical expressions of ethical life which Watsuji continued to value highly and employ as a framework for later work himself. That Watsuji continued to regard Hegel highly right up until the time of the writing of *Ethics* is evidenced by the construction of chapter three in the first volume. Below is a translation of the table of contents for chapter three alongside an abbreviated table of contents for Part Three of *The Elements of the Philosophy of Right*, Hegel's final major opus:[30]

Ethics

Ch. III Ethical Organisation

1) **Private existence as defective communality**
2) **The Family**
   i. The community of two persons –sexual love, husband and wife
   ii. The community of three persons –blood relations and off-spring
   iii. Fraternal community –siblings
   iv. The structure of the family and the ethical implications
3) **Kinship**
4) **Territorial community** –from the community of neighbours to the community of the homeland

Philosophy of Right

Part III Ethical Life

Section One: The Family
Love
Moments of the family
A. Marriage
B. The Family's Resources
C. The Upbringing of Children and the Dissolution of the Family

Section Two: Civil Society
A Society of persons
The Development of Particularity
Moments of Civil Society
A. The System of Needs
B. The Administration of Justice
C. The Police and the Corporation

Section Three: The State
The State as Ethical Idea and Objective Freedom

5) **Economic organisation**
   – and the problem of self-interested society
6) **Cultural community**
   – from the community of companions to the [community of] folk.
7) **The state**

Moments of the state
A. Constitutional Law
   I. The Internal Constitution
   II. External Sovereignty
B. International Law
C. World History

While not mirroring each other section by section, it is readily apparent that the development of the discussion of the former generally parallels that of the latter. In particular, we may note the very obvious correlation between the sections that deal with the family, the sections appearing under the broad themes of community/economic organisation and civil society respectively, along with the extremely obvious parallel in the progression to a discussion of the state and world history.

One significant difference between *Ethics As Anthropology* and *Ethics*, however, is the fact that Watsuji does not discuss Hegel directly but only generally quotes him to indicate points of difference. Indeed the longest section that refers to Hegel only lasts for approximately four pages and is devoted to explaining Watsuji's ultimate rejection of the Hegelian model of civil society. Hegel saw Bourgeois social relations and morality as entailing a positive advance within the process of development toward the highest form of ethical life. However, Watsuji saw it as being an unavoidable but essentially *pathological* expression. In particular, Watsuji highlights Hegel's treatment of 'the corporation' as signifying a degree of endorsement for the defective organisation and morality of Bourgeois society. These are rejected as being ultimately the expression of modern capitalist society, more specifically *Western* society. Indeed, it is considered part of the particular destiny of the Japanese nation to resist and eventually overcome this pathological form of ethical life through the establishment of a higher form of ethical life. As a consequence, the state in *Ethics* is highly particularised and reflects Watsuji's ideal of the 'ethical nation' pertaining to the earlier Hegelian works as covered in *Ethics As Anthropology*.[31]

The purpose of the following chapters in *Ethics* which deal with the geo-historical currents of world history come into clearer relief when considered in the light of the above. They signify an attempt to outline first of all the cultural and moral specificity of the Japanese people and indicate how the Japanese nation, within the broad flow of world history, has come to be in a position to fulfil the ultimate aim of clarifying a form of ethical life that reaches 'Indifference', i.e. which entails no contradictions in the terms of Individuals versus the State, part versus the whole or Subject versus Object. This is essentially the fulfillment of the philosophical objective as laid out in *Ethics As Anthropology.*[32]

CONCLUSION

The above examination of the Hegelian input into *Ethics As Anthropology* and *Ethics* clarifies the practical social and historical aspects of Watsuji's ethical philosophy and indicates a greater unity of construction that would otherwise be lost if one were to limit one's purview simply to the Eastern traditions of thought. This does raise the question of how the Eastern and Western elements of his philosophy are integrated. I have argued that Watsuji was not trying to reify Confucianism or the Buddhist tradition through his philosophy. Yet the fact remains that at the very root of his ethical philosophy there are essentially 'Eastern' concepts of the human being and the Absolute. The most plausible explanation for the way in which these elements hang together is to suggest that Watsuji's ethical philosophy was in an important regard a particularised version of the Hegelian enterprise where the direction of the early philosophy was expanded to attribute to the nation, along with the historical and cultural specificity it embodied, a far greater significance. Concepts such as '*Senru*', '*Loka*' and 'the five cardinal relations' are raised precisely because they are part and parcel of the ethical *particularity* of the Japanese people. Yet they are not incorporated in their original sense because Watsuji is ultimately trying to solve a philosophical problem which is essentially new and requires a completely new methodology. This methodology ultimately necessitates therefore a rejection of Hegelian Idealism and Watsuji can be interpreted as speaking of 'ethical life' more or less in terms of his own discourse.

The Hegelian influence in Watsuji's work was never kept secret. The lecture notes published after his death indicate that Watsuji lectured on Hegel as a matter of course. Watsuji clearly pursues an agenda that transcends both East and West and that is what enables him to build elements of both traditions into his philosophy without a sense of contradiction.[33]

The overall implication for evaluating Watsuji's ethical philosophy, in particular his conception of the Absolute, is that while the structure and the process of attaining it bear great resemblance to the ethical philosophy of Hegel, the root is something that transcends Hegel. It is a particularised absolute drawing on the traditions, or perhaps more to the point the 'practical experience' across time and through space, of the Japanese. Yet Watsuji's methodology does not permit this to become a mere reification, a mere traditionalism. It is an attempt at an integrated exploration of human existence taking account of parameters that belong neither to 'Hegel' nor to 'Buddhism' or to 'Confucianism'. Watsuji was in an important sense a philosophical pioneer in the cause of clarification of ethical life with specific regard to his own point in time and place.

The response we might make if we are to perhaps evaluate the success of this undertaking, is to comment in terms of the framework of *The System of Ethical Life*. We might say that Watsuji walked a very fine line between transcending the mere 'morality' (*moralität*) of Bourgeois society through the apprehension of a higher form of ethical life and mistakenly reifying the elements of 'Natural' ethical life within his own society and culture as expressions of the 'Absolute'.

Alistair Swale, East Asian Studies, University of Waikato, Hamilton, New Zealand

NOTES

1 R. Bellah, Japan's Cultural Identity in *Journal of Asian Studies*, No. 24, pp. 570–581. W. R. La Fleur, Buddhist Emptiness In The Ethics And Aesthetics Of Watsuji Tetsuro, *Religious Studies* No. 14.
D. A. Dilworth, The Significance Of Ethics As The Study Of Man (Trans. of 'Ningen no Gaku to Shite no Rinrigaku no Igi' in *Rinrigaku*) Monumenta Nipponica, XXXVI.

2 The term 'Narcissistic' is employed in R. Bellah, idem.

3 Both works as yet untranslated. See Watsuji Tetsurō, *Kojijunrei* (Pilgrimage to the Ancient Temples) *&* *Sakoku* (National Seclusion, Japan's Tragedy), *Watsuji Tetsurō Zenshu (WTZ), Vols 2 & 15*, Iwanami Shoten, 1977. English title of *Sakoju* as per G. Piovesana, *Recent Japanese Philosophical Thought 1862–1962: A Survey*, Sophia University Press, 1968, p. 135.

4 Watsuji Tetsurō, *Ningen no Gaku to Shite no Rinrigaku,* WTZ, op. cit., Vol. 9, pp. 9–10. Title as per Piovesana, ibid., see pp. 131–145 for a brief survey of Watsuji's thought.

5 Regarding the academic merits of *A Climate* it has to be conceded that the fundamental structure of the work is over-simplistic and the method of supporting his thesis is overly reliant on subjective impressions.

6 Watsuji, op. cit., pp. 13–21, especially pp. 20–21. See Hamaguchi Eshun, *Nihonjinrashisa no Saihakken*, Kodansha, 1988, pp. 62–67.
7 Watsuji, *Ningen no Gaku . . .*, op. cit., p. 25 & 127.
8 Watsuji Tetsuro, *A Climate*, trans. of *Fūdo* by G. Bownas, Ministry Of Education, 1961. See also M. Sakabe, *Watsuji Tetsurō, NijūSeiki Shisōka Bunkō* (17), Iwanami Shoten, 1986, pp. 102–118 for a discussion of *Fudō* as providing insights into how Watsuji's anthropology is applied to the phenomenal world.
9 Watsuji's discussion of Cohen and Feuerbach have been excluded for clarity and also because they are not strictly speaking the main focus of Watsuji's interest.
10 Watsuji, *Ningen no Gaku . . .*, op. cit., p. 89.
11 Watsuji, ibid., p. 154–156.
12 See I. Kant, *Anthropology From a Pragmatic Point of View.* Trans. by Mary Gregor, Martinus Nijhoff, 1974. See also Kaneko Takezo, commentary following *Ningen no Gaku . . .*, ibid., pp. 496–7.
13 Watsuji, *Ningen no Gaku . . .*, op. cit., pp. 58–60.
14 Watsuji, ibid., p. 102.
15 G. W. F. Hegel, *The System of Ethical Life*, ed. and trans. by H. S. Harris and T. M. Knox, State University of New York Press, 1979. See Watsuji, ibid., p.126 for criticism of Marx's econocentrism and pp. 127–129 for the discussion of Marx in relation to Hegel.
16 Watsuji, ibid., pp. 102.
17 Martin Heidegger, *Being And Time*, trans. by J McQuarrie and E. Robinson, SCM Press, 1962, p. 24. Watsuji's methodology owes much to Heidegger (see Watsuji, *Ningen no Gaku . . .*, ibid., p. 131 for Watsuji's acknowledgement of this). But there is a very deliberate break from Heidegger's lead when Watsuji espouses the Interpretivist approach of Dilthey (see Watsuji, ibid., pp. 168–185 for his discussion of shortcomings in Heidegger's Phenomenology).
18 If we exclude the individual from within the compass of legitimate ethical inquiry we lose, for example, the notion of individual accountability for actions. A communalist perspective taken to its extreme means that conduct can be rationalised in terms of a cultural or social imperative. For a discussion of how the above could apply to historical circumstances, see Maruyama Masao, 'The Theory and Psychology of Ultranationalism' in *Thought and Behaviour in Modern Japanese Politics*, ed. by Ivan Morris, Oxford University Press, 1963, pp. 1–24.
19 The book is in fact dedicated to Nishida and he figures as an important leader outside of the Western tradition (see Watsuji, ibid., p. 129). For the discussion of Buddhist concepts see Watsuji, ibid., pp. 21–25.
20 M. Kōsaka, *Watsuji Tetsurō to Nishida Kitaro*, Shinchōsha, 1964, pp. 110–111.
21 See Watsuji, *Ningen no Gaku . . .*, op. cit., pp. 74–75 (to page 109 for the entire commentary of Hegel). We can see something of how important Watsuji considered Hegel to be by observing the relevant amount of space dedicated to each philosopher; Aristotle (13 pp.), Kant (10 pp.), Cohen (14 pp.), Hegel (35 pp.), Feuerbach (10 pp.) and Marx (11 pp.).
22 See Watsuji, ibid., pp. 130–168 for the section on methodology in *Ethics*

As Anthropology, especially pp. 154–168 regarding the relative merits of Heidegger and Dilthey. An aspect of this section of *The System of Ethical Life* which seems relevant to Japanese society, but is not in fact raised, is the 'Volk' (tribe or people) which takes on a universal aspect of morality where the individual is completely subsumed. Religion becomes the religion of the tribe or the 'tibal God' (often the tribal king as well). Given the pronouncements made by Hegel regarding the 'Orient' and the implications regarding the role of the Emperor in Japan at the time, it is rather baffling that Watsuji chose not to say anything more explicitly about it (see Watsuji Tetsuro, *Ningen no Gaku . . .*, ibid., pp. 85–88). It should be noted of course that Hegel was going into a discussion of the 'Negative' aspect of 'Nature' where Difference wreaks 'havoc', (Harris, op. cit., p. 44, 45). Certainly Watsuji felt that his own society was beyond that level and he also perhaps felt sure that his country would not be given to such a propensity in the future.

23 See Harris, op. cit., p. 56 for English terminology regarding the system at rest.

24 Watsuji, *Rinrigaku*, Vol. I, pp. 28 & 285 re 'trust'. See *Ningen no Gaku . . .*, op. cit., pp. 176–177 re the dynamic aspect of human existence.

25 Watsuji, *Ningen no Gaku . . .*, ibid., p. 101–102.

26 Watsuji, ibid., pp. 97–99 and pp. 184–185 regarding what Watsuji terms 'the excavation of tradition'.

27 See Watsuji, ibid., pp. 128–129 and Harris, op. cit., pp. 58–60.

28 This is a tension between practical and philosophical concerns that is also discussed by Harris, ibid., p. 63–64.

29 Regarding Watsuji's Absolute construed as *Kū*, see Watsuji, *Ningen no Gaku . . .*, op. cit., pp. 35–37. Regarding *Kū* in Hegel's philosophy of humanity, see Watsuji, ibid., pp. 108–109 and *Rinrigaku*, op. cit., Vol.I, p. 245.

30 Hegel, G.W.F., *The Elements of the Philosophy of Right*, G. W. Allen (ed.), Cambridge University Press, 1991. See Table of Contents for English renditions; the subsections under each theme have been abridged.

31 Watsuji, *Rinrigaku*, op. cit., Vol I, pp. 594–595; Watsuji describes the state as a 'self-consciously comprehensive *ethical* [my italics] organisation' using the same terminology for ethical as that employed in the commentary on Hegel's *System of Ethical Life*. Note especially the reference to the (historically and culturally) 'exclusive' nature of the state even though it is in essence 'public' and therefore in a sense universal.

32 Watsuji, *Ningen no Gaku . . .*, op. cit., pp. 184–185.

33 Katsube Mitake, *Watsuji Rinrigaku Nōto*, Tōsho Sensho 38, 1979, pp. 171–196.

4
Transcendence East and West

David Loy

> Oh, East is East, and West is West, and never the twain shall meet, Till Earth and Sky stand presently at God's great Judgment Seat . . .
>
> Rudyard Kipling, 'The Ballad of East and West'

The twain have long since met, but there is a deeper problem with Kipling's blithe verse: the assumption that East *is* East, that we can make useful generalizations about *the* East. What follows is a critique of the notion that South Asia and East Asia can be meaningfully lumped together into, e.g., 'the intuitive East' or 'the mystic Orient'. My argument is that the cultural polarity between the Indian-influenced cultures of south Asia and the Chinese-influenced cultures of East Asia is more interesting than that between 'East' and 'West'. This paper is an experiment that pushes this opposite generalization to see how far we can ride it and how illuminating it can be.

Needless to say, the amount of relevant data here is indigestible, so part one confines itself to noticing what I think are the most significant contrasts. (Much of this information is taken from Hajime Nakamura's encyclopedic *Ways of Thinking of Eastern Peoples*.) Part two outlines the pattern in those differences, which reduces to differing attitudes towards *transcendence*: the distinction between sacred and secular is one of the most fundamental determinates of Indian ways of thinking, whereas China and Japan are more this-worldly in assigning primary value to – and thereby *sacralising* – socio-political structures. Part two also considers the various types of transcendence, and why an overt transcendental dimension arose in certain places but not in others.

Part three reflects on where 'the West' fits into this schema. If (in the compensatory stereotype to be developed below) East Asia and South Asia are already cultural opposites, where does the West fit into that polarity? Curiously, India and Japan each seem to have more in common with the West than with each other. That is because Western civilisation, like Indian, is rooted in a strong sacred/secular bifurcation, yet the historical eclipse of the sacred has transformed Western societies into more secular nations now similar in some ways to China and Japan, which lack India's transcendental reference-point. But this perspective is misleading because in the most important sense a transcendental *dimension* is unavoidable: when we do not apprehend or project a transcendental realm, we end up sacralising some aspect of the secular, since we feel a need to ground ourselves in one or another ultimate concern. In East Asia, the transcendental dimension has remained embedded in the *sacred authority* of social and political hierarchies, whereas in the West the transcendental has been gradually internalised into the supposedly autonomous and self-directed *individual*. These differences underlie many of the political and economic tensions between East Asia and the West today.

I

1. Traditional **Indian** culture displays a strong preference for universals over particulars. For example, Indian thought has a preponderance of (and the Sanskrit language has a preference for) abstract notions, which are treated as if they were concrete realities. Emphasis being on the unity of things, the ever-changing manifestations of the phenomenal world tend to be devalued as illusory. Accordingly, there is a lack of historical and geographical consciousness: not the specific but the general is important.

In contrast, traditional **Chinese** culture prefers particulars over universals. The Chinese language has a more concrete flavor with a large number of metaphors. Chinese literature includes detailed geography, historiography and biography, because specific places, historical events and the people that made them are all important.

In a pattern that will be repeated, **Japanese** culture may be viewed as extrapolating these Chinese traits, for it also emphasises sensible and concrete events. Nakamura terms this Japanese tendency *phenomenalism*. In contrast to Indian inclination toward an Absolute transcendent to the phenomenal world, and Chinese understanding of the Dao as a more dynamic ground of changing phenomena, for Japanese the phenomenal world *is* the absolute (Nakamura 219, 315).

2. In **India** the highest value was placed on the religious goal of one's individual self merging into the Universal Self. There was little discussion of the problems with social structures, such concerns being subverted by the belief that each self is ultimately nondual with other selves. This world was devalued into a means to prepare for another: '*The ancient Indians led their life on this side of heaven with the expectation of a life after death*' (Nakamura 161; his italics). Emphasis was on passive, forbearing and introspective behaviour and the subjective comprehension of one's personality (in contrast with modern Western emphasis on scientific, i.e. objective, comprehension of the personality), along with a tendency to abstain from action.

China was more worldly in placing the highest value on the family. One is not concerned to transcend this world but identifies with one's family and works for its welfare. Ancestors are worshipped in order to gain prosperity in this life. The religious goal of Daoism and Chan Buddhism is not to experience another realm but to become aware of the true nature of this one; the miraculous function of Chan is 'fetching water and chopping wood.'

The phenomenalism of **Japanese** culture meant that the sacred is not separate from this world but suffused in all things, even trees and grass. No profound reflections on the soul or death are found in Shinto, the only indigenous religion: death understood as impurity. Zen Buddhism emphasises the spiritual significance of everyday life: tea-drinking, flower-arranging, killing others, and, when necessary, oneself. Not-killing is the first precept in Indian religions (wars were fought mainly by mercenaries), yet Zen first became popular because it taught the samurai how to kill and how to die – that is, how to play their role in what Nakamura calls the social nexus. He notes that there are very few instances in Japanese history of individuals sacrificing themselves for universal principles such as religion and truth, yet innumerable samurai (and other vassals) sacrificed themselves for their lord: not because he was any better than any other lord, but simply because he was their lord. Indian renunciants abstained from work and begged for their food; Chinese Buddhists were more practical (Baizhang declared that 'a day without working is a day without eating'); Japanese Buddhism came to repudiate most traditional spiritual disciplines in favour of those that promote productive activities. This exemplifies a general trait that Robert Bellah considers the most important characteristic of Japanese society:

its goal-oriented behaviour (Bellah 188), which reflects a this-worldly orientation.

3. **Indian** pessimism about the possibilities of this world of *saṁsāra* implied a submissive attitude toward one's fate; *karma* was understood to mean that one is regulated by an invisible power beyond immediate control. In contrast, 'everyday mind' is enlightenment in **Chinese** Chan. Mahayana Buddhism, which claimed that *saṁsāra* is not other than *nirvana*, did not survive in India yet became the one Indian school of thought to thrive north of the Himalaya. Chinese thinkers understood human nature to be basically good, as part of the larger natural law. Since nature is not opposed to man, we do not need to conquer it but to harmonise with it; natural disasters are a sign that the ruler has lost his mandate to govern. For both the social system and the physical environment, harmony is the key concept. In the religious sphere, this implied syncretism among the three major Chinese religions, widely believed to be essentially the same. This syncretic tendency may also be seen in the way that different Buddhist doctrines were formally organised into a hierarchical system (e.g., in the T'ien-t'ai school), rather than such systems resulting from the logical development of their relationships. This attitude towards religious teachings was part of a general conservative emphasis on the authority of antiquity overruling abstract principles such as logical consistency. Confucius said that he merely imitated and revived past customs. Later no independent school of thought was allowed to exist in opposition to Confucianism; intellectual life became confined to commentary on the traditional classics.

The **Japanese** too have never viewed the natural world as cursed. Love of nature developed into a subtle appreciation of minute, delicate, transitory things (e.g., cherry blossoms). Their phenomenalism accepted human dispositions, desires and sentiments as natural too and therefore not to be struggled against. Later alcohol, meat-eating and marriage were allowed for priests – not to weaken the influence of Buddhism, as has been argued, but to ratify abuses which had become common. Even more than in China, emphasis on the harmony of the social nexus meant there was hardly any interest in potentially divisive argument and critique. Nakamura notes (402) even a lack of will to drive home an idea, and the sociologist Chie Nakane also notices that there is little social sanction in Japan for entertaining ideas and opinions that are different from the head of one's family or community. Virtue is simple and unproblematic: the highest value is placed on honesty, understood as straightforward truthfulness and loyalty to one's superior, rather than commitment to some abstract moral code. In discourse logical rules are neglected; the primary importance placed on one's limited social nexus means there is little inclination to make each person's understanding rational or universal. In these ways Chinese and Japanese culture devalue the *authority* of abstract thought.

4. In traditional **India** political leaders rarely interfered with religious institutions. On the contrary, kings tended to defer to sages and spiritual organizations, for the highest authority was the universal law or *dharma*, understood as the foundation of the world on which all things are grounded, a universal Truth transcending the transitory affairs of humans. The desire for a direct relationship with the Absolute led to emphasising one's own efforts. The Buddha appointed no successor, whereas one's spiritual lineage became extremely important in Chinese and Japanese Buddhism. Indians had little racial or national consciousness, and their many legends and myths contain very few national heroes. It was a virtue to offer one's property and life for the happiness of others, yet self-sacrifice on behalf of a particular race or nation was not taught. In short, India did not absolutise or 'transcendentalise' the State.

In **China** and **Japan** there was much greater esteem for the hierarchy that structured the social nexus, and corresponding emphasis on formalism in behaviour which usually accompanies such esteem. In both countries the primary value placed on rank and social position subordinated religious values: *religious institutions became dominated and controlled by secular authorities*, who neutralised the threat that such sacred authority (*dharma*) offered to their power and appropriated that authority for their own political ends. Sakyamuni had had to choose between becoming a world-monarch or a world-saviour (a Buddha); the two were not conflated in India, nor was there ever much doubt about which was the nobler accomplishment. Starting with the Tang dynasty, the Chinese emperor gradually became deified, coming to be viewed as a Buddha himself. Under his rule property rights existed but not freedom by law. The conception of human rights that developed in the West – that one can have the protection of law against one's own government – had some Indian equivalent in the respect for the *dharma* but both notions were (and generally still are) alien to Chinese and Japanese political institutions, which did not tolerate other authority.

Japan perfected this tendency to identify religious and secular authority. Only in Japan did the mythology that accounts for creation of the world also found the imperial family. In China dynasties were overthrown, yet in Japan the same family has reigned since the beginning of history. Chinese Confucianism allowed for revolution, should the emperor lose the mandate of heaven. Japan has no place for this because its imperial authority is not derived from any abstract principle such as divine right but *abides in his person* – which means he cannot lose it. The importance of this for Japanese society may be appreciated from the stress Nakamura places on 'the tendency to emphasize, and unconditioned belief in, a limited social nexus', which takes form in the 'absolute devotion to a specific individual symbolic of the social nexus': that is, emperor worship (Nakamura 407ff.)

Religion in Japan was not considered important in itself; as Nakamura says, its value was its utility in serving as the foundation of the state. He also points out the problem with this: 'the inclination to regard as absolute a limited specific human nexus naturally brings about a tendency to disregard any allegedly universal law of humanity that every man ought to observe at any place at any time' (Nakamura 579, 393). Since the social nexus is primary, hierarchical relationships and rules of propriety take precedence over the individual. Emphasis is on complete dedication to one's social collective. This makes good and evil a matter of social morality: what profits the group or harms its welfare. Although the family was the predominant social unit, as in China, the whole Japanese nation was regarded as the extended family of the father-emperor. In order to win a place in Japanese society, Buddhism too had to promote such civic virtues as loyalty to the emperor and devotion to one's parents, concepts alien to Indian Buddhism. The original Mahayana goal was the happiness of all sentient beings; in Japan this became the prosperity of the imperial family.

The cost of this absolute devotion to a particular individual who symbolized the human nexus, as opposed to the Indian way of symbolizing the cosmos in an impersonal way, was more than a loss of personal freedom: it was a lack of individuality. Unlike the contracted and delimited responsibilities in European feudalism, a Japanese vassal devoted his whole existence to his lord. It is a simple way to solve the problems of ultimate value and social relationships – by conflating them – but at a considerabie price. Bellah's *Tokugawa Religion* concludes:

> Religion reinforced commitment to the central value system by making that value system meaningful in an ultimate sense. The

> family and the nation were not merely secular collectivities but were also religious entities. Parents and political superiors had something of the sacred about them, were merely the lower echelons of the divine. Fulfillment of one's obligations to these superordinates had an ultimate meaning (194).

Herman Ooms' more recent study *Tokugawa Ideology* agrees and adds that, in accordance with this, '[m]ilitary regimentation came to inform the model of the social order.' And today? 'That obsession with order has continued undiminished' (297).

The basic problem is that such an order allows for no 'categorical imperative' which transcends the limitations of one's particular human nexus. It is because all things were judged according to that nexus that ecclesiastical authorities in Japan were always subservient to secular authorities. As Max Weber put it, the state was not a patron of religion, as in India, but a religious police. Religious institutions in Japan have never had much authority, nor have men of religion been respected as much as in India or the West. Nakamura emphasises the weakness of the Japanese religious consciousness and concludes that 'religion, in the true sense of the word, never deeply took root on Japanese soil' (530). But if there is no escaping religion, in the most important sense of the word – if to deny the authority of the sacred is to end up sacralising secular authority – we can see that the religion of the Japanese people is . . . Japanese society.

II

Nakamura summarises his study as follows: in India ultimate value is placed on religion, in China on the family, and in Japan on the state. However, this may be further simplified. In China the extended family functioned as a small state, while in Japan the state was one big family. Both are *this-worldly* in assigning primary value to those societal structures. The Indian emphasis on religion means that India is not this worldly because this world is understood (and devalued) by juxtaposing it with another possibility: there is constant reference to a transcendental realm. From the East Asian perspective, one can see that the distinction between this phenomenal world of *saṁsāra* and a 'higher' sacred reality is a fundamental determinate of Indian ways of thinking. From an Indian perspective one could say that it is the absence of such a transcendental/secular distinction that has determined many of the characteristics of Chinese and Japanese culture.

This does not mean that the Japanese and Chinese traditions lack a transcendental or sacred *dimension.* Elsewhere I have argued that such a sacred aspect is unavoidable: our need to ground or secure ourselves compels us to make an ultimate commitment somewhere, so that even when we consciously deny any spiritual reality, our worldly pursuits take on a religious-like urgency (Loy, 'Nonduality' and 'Trying'). In East Asia we can detect that religious dimension in the sacred authority appropriated by secular rulers. The Chinese emperor became deified, and the authority of the Japanese emperor was even greater because irrevocable. *Without an authoritative trascendental realm understood as separate from the secular, the sacred dimension manifests itself in East Asia as the social structure: the consequence is that human beings are more tightly embedded within society.* The social collective is taken to be more important than the individuals that compose it – or more real than the persons that can be abstracted from it.

In East Asia hierarchical (and, by more democratic standards, oppressive) social relations came to be accepted much like the weather because they too were perceived as natural: that is, as not needing to be explained, much less open to significant reform. Describing the situation in Japan before the Meiji Restoration, Wolferen notes that 'the political arrangements of the Tokugawa period were presented as perfect in that they confirmed to the order found in the manifold natural phenomena of heaven and earth' (337).

This attitude seems peculiar and unnecessary to us because we can view it from 'outside,' in this instance less from an Indian perspective than from a Western one, which did not accept hierarchical political and economic structures as natural and whose modern history has been punctuated by radical attempts at social improvement. The disastrous consequences of so many of those efforts means we should hesitate before denigrating the East Asian model of social relations. Loyalty to people becomes attractive when we remember all the killing that has been done on behalf of abstractions such as God or the future socialist utopia; yet when that devotion plugs into a hierarchical social structure itself unaccountable to any 'higher' dimension, we should not be surprised that a sacred ideology sometimes becomes indistinguishable from militant nationalism.

These reflections suggest that transcendence also includes the authority of ethical universalism (usually understood to be derived from such a 'higher world'). Today the otherworldly aspect of the sacred has been largely eclipsed in Western society, while the function of such universal values has expanded to fill much of the breach, ranging from legal inscriptions such as the U.S. Bill of Rights to our informal sense of fair play. In that sense the transcendental is still very much with us, and indeed it has been necessary to protect the newly evolved individual from his state and to regulate his competition with other individuals. It is not by chance that this form of transcendence has also been lacking in East Asia.

Yet even this understanding of transcendence is not yet broad enough. The full implications of the term are suggested by its etymology: Lt. *trans* + *scendere*, to climb *over* or rise *above*. Most generally, transcendence is that which takes us *out of* the given world by providing a theoretical perspective on it. The etymologies of these words reveal how much our vocabulary for 'higher' thought processes involves 'rising above' the given, *which allows the possibility of leverage over, of changing that given*. This too is consistent with the contrasts we have noticed between Indian preference for an abstract, theoretical (metaphysical) perspective on life, versus Chinese concreteness and Japanese phenomenalism. Historically, the fulcrum that Archimedes needed to move the Earth has been provided by the transcendental, whether we understand it as the realisation of another reality or as a product of the human imagination. To borrow Renan's comment about the supernatural, the transcendental is the way in which the ideal has made its appearance in human affairs.

III

With this trivalent understanding of transcendence – as higher realm, as ethical universal, and as critical perspective on the given – we are ready to address what is perhaps the most interesting question: why did an explicitly transcendental dimension arise in certain places, such as India, and not in others, such as China and Japan?

> 'Transcendence,' whether it takes the form of divine revelation or of theoretical cosmology, implies a search for authority outside the institutionalized offices and structures of the seeker's society. Even its most concrete form, the law code, implies a transfer of authority from the holders of office to the written rule. Transcendental impulses therefore constitute, by definition, an implicit challenge to traditional authority and indicate some dissatisfaction with it . . .
>
> [N]ew transcendental visions are . . . likely to be presented by

> persons in a precariously independent, interstitial – or at least exposed and somewhat solitary – position in society; they are therefore particularly likely to occur in societies sufficiently differentiated to have specialized social roles with distinct bases of authority, but not complex enough to have integrated these roles into functionally differentiated structures. (Humphreys 92, 112)

Humphreys argues for this by referring to axial-age (first millennium B.C.) Greece. She finds the necessary precondition for a transcendental perspective on society in the privileged and relatively independent position of its intellectuals, such as the sophists, whose special linguistic skills provided 'the ability to recreate social relationships and manipulate them in thought' (111). However, her conclusion may be applied more widely. She could also have cited the role of the 'interstitial' Hebrew prophets – especially Amos, Isaiah and Jeremiah – who developed the ethical monotheism of Judaism established by the Mosaic covenant. Inspired by Yahweh, they understood themselves as intermediaries to the children of Israel, charged to fulminate against the impious people and particularly their rulers. Max Weber drew attention to how their precarious position was supported by their ability to alternate between prophesizing in towns and withdrawing into the hills.

The case of India supports Humphreys' conclusion even better. According to Louis Dumont, a two-stage process created fertile conditions for the development of a transcendental perspective. The first occurred in the Vedas, whose 'extreme development of specialized macro-religious action and representation' exalted the role of priests into a pre-eminence never thereafter lost. By the time of the Brāhmaṇas (probably 800 – 500 B.C.), 'the priest was supreme, though the king was his master.' Soon afterwards there appeared 'a full-fledged and peculiar social role outside society proper: the renouncer, as an individual-outside-the-world, inventor or adept of a "discipline of salvation" and of its social concomitant, best called the Indian sect' (Dumont 162–3).

Dumont wonders why political rulers assented to the loss of their pre-eminence. Everything falls into place, he says, once we start with the king as 'priest-cum-ruler': then the Indian development becomes understandable as 'a differentiation within this institution, whereby the king lost his (official) religious function in favor of the priest. In other words, kingship had been "secularized", as we say, at an early date' (Dumont 165). The fragile distinction between secular authority and sacred authority acquired a firm institutional foundation. Our problem in perceiving this is that we usually take that distinction for granted, whereas it now begins to look more like the exception than the rule.

The meaning of this distinction becomes more apparent and more important when we consider what occurred in some other civilizations such as Mesopotamia and Egypt – or rather what did not occur, since there was no such differentiation. In Mesopotamia, the scribes who composed the educated elite never challenged the authority of the priest-cum-king. The most important religious practices were not public and in fact there seems to have been little religious role for the common people. Instead, the main religious rituals were performed by religious specialists, including the king:

> It is from the heart [i.e., the king] of the community, but almost unbeknownst to it, that the divine benediction radiated. None of them could break with the practices: the king because he was the only guarantor of an order that depended on them; the people because they believed they benefited from them, without participating directly; the priests because their entire education pushed them into preserving what they had acquired . . . (Garelli 153)

In twelfth-century Egypt the Pharaoh Akhenaten attempted to establish the sole worship of Aten the sun-disc, but soon after his death there was a return to the traditional polytheistic cultus. 'One major reason for this was the divine status of the Pharaoh himself. It was through the Pharaoh that the divine order benefited society. A break in the continuity of kingly ritual could have had disastrous social consequences' (Smart 289).

The parallels are remarkable: in Mesopotamia and Egypt, as in China and Japan, the sacral dimension was not suffused throughout society, for it functioned through rulers who were as much religious as political authorities. Unlike India, Greece and Judea, there was no clear distinction between secular and sacred authority, and therefore no alternative transcendental perspective to challenge the inherent conservatism of such societies.

In China the situation was more complex than this model suggests, although it nonetheless fits into this pattern. The *Shijing* (Book of Poetry) and *Shujing* (Book of Documents), the first extensive literary texts, envision an all-encompassing social, political and cultural order in which people relate to each other according to a highly-structured system of familial and political roles.

> All of these roles and role relationships are governed by elaborate normative rules of behavior (*li*). The human order is not closed off from the cosmic order. Within the cosmos, the various gods of mountains, rivers, winds, stars, and localities, and the ancestral spirits also play their roles. Within the larger political order of the cosmos, the rulers of men must, in fact, relate themselves by proper ritual behavior (*li*) to the governing spirits of the universe as well as to each other. At the apex of the human order is the universal kingship, which is the central focus of communication, as it were, between the king, who is ultimately responsible for the maintenance of the normative human order, and the supreme God or Heaven (*shang ti, t'ien*), who maintains harmony and order in the world of the spirits presiding over the forces of nature as well as over the world of ancestral spirits. (Schwartz 58–9).

Again, there is functional equivalence between the lack of sacred/secular dualism and the role of religio-political authority as nodal point of communication between the human and the cosmic order. As with Mesopotamia and Egypt, there is a sacral dimension in society, but it manifests through the apex of the social pyramid and therefore serves to sacralise that hierarchy. This is in striking contrast to transcendence in Humphreys' sense: a challenge to traditional authority which allows for the possibility of everyone having his or her own personal relationship with that transcendental order.

Obvious counter-examples spring to mind for China, most notably Confucius himself and Daoist sages such as Zhuang Zi. Yet both support my thesis. Confucius, although a precariously independent and 'interstitial' intellectual, did not challenge the transcendental function of the political order: he emphasised respect for it, he wanted to be employed by it, and his legacy became used as an apologetic for it. He allowed for the possibility of revolution, but only if the king failed in his divine duty to preserve the human order by maintaining communication with the divine order. Daoist sages such as Zhuang Zi had their own personal experience of the Dao, yet the critique of society which followed from that was employed not to reform social relations but to withdraw from them. For the Daoists of his time, the alternative was not political reform but being co-opted and corrupted by the powers-that-be. Thus neither Confucians nor Daoists offered any serious challenge to the secular-cum-sacred authority of the political rulers. By the time Buddhism arrived, it was too late to challenge the pattern that had been established. This was even more true in Japan, where Buddhism was first imported as an aristocratic religion to support the prosperity of the imperial family.

Mesopotamia, Egypt, China and Japan versus India, Judea and Greece: all of them validate Humphreys' criterion of transcendence as involving a search for authority outside institutionalised offices and structures. Such an authority never became established in the first four civilizations; it did in India, Judea and Greece, thanks to 'interstitial' world-renouncers, prophets and intellectuals, respectively. In the first four cases, an effective transcendental/secular bifurcation did not occur, but we have seen that that does not mean they lacked a sacral dimension. Rather, it means that political power and religious authority never became distinguished, which accounts for the conservatism of their hierarchical social structures.

III

Where does 'West' fit into this scheme? If Asia already contains its own polarity between South and East Asian traditions, the West can no longer simply be defined as the 'other' of the East. Can it be defined using our trivalent understanding of transcendence?

Historically as well as geographically, Europe is closer to India. The Aryans who settled in India were closely related to those who peopled Europe, and Greek, Latin and the major European languages evolved from the same Indo-European root as the Sanskrit family of languages. In antiquity and the Middle Ages, Indian culture diffused into Europe through West Asia and the Mediterranean. Today, of course, the nation-states of the West are secular societies much preoccupied with the opportunities provided by this life and this world, yet this does not quite bring us to the situation in China and Japan. As Nietzsche predicted, the gradual attenuation of the 'higher world' has left the West with the painful task of revaluing a devalued objectified world, ushering in an age of nihilism which seems far from over. We suspect there is something unique about our situation today that fails to fit into the pattern analysed above. The above contrast between India and China/Japan concluded that the alternative to a transcendental vs. secular distinction is tighter embeddedness in a sacralised social hierarchy. Yet this was not true in England in 1649, France in 1789, Russia in 1917. As God abdicated from Western society, the desire to reform economic and political structures (whose authority was no longer buttressed by His authority) did not diminish but became more urgent. The results have been mixed: understanding society as a human construction which should be reconstructed has led to various types of democracy and individual rights as well as to horrible experiments in social engineering that have caused incalculable suffering.

Then what has happened to the transcendental dimension in the modern West? If the sacred cannot die, where has it gone?

When we remember that the transcendental is, most broadly, that which provides a perspective on the world and leverage for changing it, the answer becomes evident: the transcendental dimension was *internalised* to become the supposedly autonomous, self-directed *individual* who began to develop at the time of the Renaissance. Later Luther assisted this development by sanctioning a more private relationship with God. Instead of having faith in a corporate church, now everyone must work it out for oneself. The importance of this can hardly be overemphasised. *Personally having a direct line to Transcendence provides the leverage to challenge all this-worldly authority, both in religious as well as in secular institutions.* Convinced he was following God's will, Luther refused to shut up: 'Here I stand; I can do no other.' This ratified a principle that we today take for granted: one's personal understanding and moral principles can provide an appropriate perspective to confront social structures. Luther was more than a prophet: after him everyone had to become his or her own prophet. Eventually God could disappear as a causal principle because by then His role had been largely assumed by the self-sufficient self-consciousness that Descartes described. Each became the prophet of his own viewpoint.

Contrary to our usual understanding, then, transcendence has not disappeared from the West; it just went inside and became the Cartesian self. The result was an increasingly anxious individual who relied on his own judgement, who measured the world according to his own standards, and who could use his own internal resources to challenge the present situation, the social environment as well as the physical one. As an increasingly ultimate commitment, the possibilities and dangers of such a Cartesian subject were unprecedented. The question today is whether our interdependent world can survive such a self much longer.

IV

We end up with three different cultural paradigms for the relationship between sacred and secular, transcendental and worldly. Summing up the problems with each of these paradigms also reveals something discomforting about our needs: they seem to be contradictory. In response to the quest for an ideal transcendental realm, we must live in this world and strive to improve it without ever expecting to perfect it. In response to the alienation that results from individualism and objectification of the world, we need to become one with the world, with less sense of separation from it. Yet in reaction to the problem with embeddedness in a 'natural' social order, which sacralises and thereby fixates political and economic structures, there is also need for the transcendence that grants us perspective on, and creative leverage over, those structures.

A new cultural paradigm does not seem to be the sort of thing that can be consciously constructed, but we may conclude by noticing that Huayan, a school of Chinese Buddhism, proffers a worldview that suggests how all three of these needs might be met. The Hua-yen doctrine perceives transcendence in the mutual interpenetration of all phenomena, and therefore derives universalist values from our identification with that whole. It locates the sacred dimension in this world, not by privileging particular social structures of even *homo sapiens*, but by sacralising the totality. The crisis of the biosphere testifies to our need for this type of universalist perspective: not for a 'higher world' that is other than and therefore opposed to this world, but for the kind of overview that is able to evaluate and respond to the needs of the whole because it is not limited by the demands of a specific nexus (such as one's own social class or nation). Since trees and whales and the ozone layer cannot vote or protest, we must realise that their needs are our needs. Maybe that is what is unique about *homo sapiens*: we are the species which can transcend itself and make that leap to identify with everything. Perhaps the challenge for us today is whether we will actually be able to do so. If, rather than being one particular bit of it, each of us is nondual with the entire universe, as Mahayana Buddhism claims, our needs for nonduality and for transcendence may be satisfied at the same time.[1]

David Loy, Faculty of International Studies, Bunkyo University, Chigasaki 253, Japan

NOTE

1 A longer version of this paper was originally published, under the title 'Transcendence East and West: A New Stereotype', in the U.S. philosophy journal *Man and World* 26 (1993), 403–427.

REFERENCES

BELLAH, ROBERT N. (1957) *Tokugawa Religion: The Cultural Roots of Modern Japan* (New York: The Free Press).

DUMONT, LOUIS (1975) On the Comparative Understanding of Non-Modern Civilizations, *Daedalus*, 104, pp. 153–172.

GARELLI, PAUL (1975) The Changing Facets of Conservative Mesopotamian Thought, *Daedalus*, 104, pp. 47–56.

HUMPHREYS, S.C. (1975) 'Transcendence' and Intellectual Roles: The Ancient Greek Case, *Daedalus*, 104, pp. 91–118.

LOY, DAVID (1990) The Nonduality of Life and Death: A Buddhist View of Repression, *Philosophy East and West*, 40, pp. 151–174.

—— (1992) Trying to Become Real: A Buddhist Critique of Some Secular Heresies, *International Philosophical Quarterly*, 32, pp. 403–425.

—— (1993) Transcendence East and West: A New Stereotype, *Man and World*, 26, pp. 403–427.

NAKAMURA, HAJIME (1964) *Ways of Thinking of Eastern Peoples*, ed. and trans. Philip P. Wiener (Honolulu: University of Hawaii Press).

NAKANE, CHIE (1973) *Japanese Society* (Harmondsworth: Pelican).

OOMS, HERMAN (1986) *Tokugawa Ideology: Early Constructs*, 1570–1680 (Princeton, NJ: Princeton University Press).

SCHWARTZ, BENJAMIN I. (1975) Transcendence in Ancient China, *Daedalus*, 104, pp. 57–68.

SMART, NINIAN (1969) *The Religious Experience of Mankind* (London: Collins).

WOLFEREN, KAREL VAN (1989) *The Enigma of Japanese Power: People and Politics in a Stateless Nation* (London: Macmillan).

5

The Place of Buddhism in Santayana's Moral Philosophy*

John Magnus Michelsen

Like so many other philosophers whose origins were in Europe of the 19th century, the Spanish-American philosopher George Santayana (1863–1952) had strong affinities with the systems of thought of ancient India, and Buddhism in particular. Although Santayana's knowledge of Indian philosophy was not extensive, it was – I believe – deep. The most interesting aspect of the relationship between Santayana's philosophy and that of India may well be the fact that Santayana developed almost exclusively within the Western tradition a philosophy which is very much akin to Buddhism. It is therefore appropriate to talk of *affinity* rather than of *influence*. This affinity finds its expression in Santayana's thoroughgoing scepticism, in his conception of the spiritual life, and in his moral philosophy. Although these three facets of his thought are interdependent, it is primarily upon an aspect of his moral philosophy that I will focus in this paper. What I will show is that reference to Buddhism becomes an essential feature in his formulation of the notion of *post-rational morality*, which is that 'phase' of morality which involves an effort to subordinate all precepts to one that points to some single eventual good. Post-rational morality is synonymous with the *spiritual life*, an essential feature of which is *detachment*; and that is why the Buddhists can be said to be the 'true masters' of the subject.

In order to understand this notion of post-rational morality, it has to be placed in the larger context. Santayana distinguishes three phases of morality: pre-rational morality, rational ethics, and post-rational morality. Although there is the suggestion that these are

* Previously published in *Asian Philosophy* Vol. 5, No. 1, 1995.

successive stages in the development of a culture, and that the so-called post-rational phase is borne of despair and belongs to the ages of decadence, this is not really his considered view. The three phases are *aspects* of moral life which may be realised in the same moment, even though one phase or another may be most clearly manifested in a particular individual or culture in a particular historical period.

That aspect of morality which is said to be *pre*-rational has to do with the *foundation* of morality, and the fact that this is said by Santayana to be 'morality proper' betrays the fundamental relativism and naturalism of his position. According to this view, morality is founded on instinct and expressive of passion; it exists on the level of radical elementary preferences, accommodating a multiplicity of goods which are ultimately unstable in themselves and incompatible with one another. To deem anything *good* is to express certain affinities between that thing and the person forming that judgement; and the judgement is unassailable provided that the affinity is real, which means that the judgement is based on adequate self-knowledge and knowledge of the thing in question. This qualification shows that Santayana's relativism is not of the naive and sophomoric kind according to which the mere *opinion* that something is good is unassailable. Santayana's relativism is not one of *opinion* but of *nature*; it is therefore inseparable from his naturalism. This naturalistic conception of the good is sometimes elaborated in terms of the notion of *intent*, which has to do with the active operation and the forward-directed character of action. In order for a thing or a situation to be deemed to be *really* good, it must somehow respond to that intent, which sets up its own standard and forms the basis for moral judgement. Although intent does not rest upon any moral principle, being itself the basis of moral principles, it does rest upon the physical habit and necessity of things; it rests upon "the propulsive essence of animals and of the universal flux, which renders forms possible but unstable and either helpful or hurtful to one another".[1]

This appeal to nature rather than opinion does not form the basis for any sort of absolutism. Desires, ambitions, and ideals come into conflict not only between individuals, nations and religious traditions, but also within each individual. It is possible that agents in conflict may be so far apart in nature and ideals that if they meet they can meet "only to poison or to crush one another". As far as conflicts between humans are concerned, however, it is possible that the humanity in them is "definable ideally . . . by a partially identical function and intent". If so, it is possible to rise above their mutual opposition by studying their own nature, and they may come to realise that they "were hardly doing justice to themselves when they did such great injustice to others".[2]

And it is here that *rational ethics* comes into play, for the principles of *harmony*, *synthesis*, and *integration* are here central. Rational ethics is a theoretical attempt to bring order into the chaos of the instincts and impulses which form the basis of morality and are by Santayana labelled 'pre-rational morality'. Pre-rational or 'intuitive' morality, as he also calls it, is adequate as long as it simply enforces "these obvious and universal laws which are indispensable to any society"; but it is not adequate to resolve conflicts between rival authorities: for that it is necessary to appeal to "the only real authority, to experience, reason, and human nature in the living man".[3]

It is worth noting at this stage that, whereas Santayana speaks of pre-rational and post-rational *moralities*, he speaks of rational *ethics*. Why is this? Is there no such thing as rational *morality*? In a very real sense no, for a rational morality would imply not only perfect self-knowledge but also perfect knowledge of the world and others, and – in fact – a perfect sympathy with the goods of others. This kind of morality has never existed and it is in fact beyond our reach. In lieu of a rational *morality* we therefore have rational *ethics*, which for Santayana is the mere *idea* of a rational morality. In the absence of perfect self-knowledge and perfect sympathy, which would entail perfect humanity and perfect justice, we may observe "the general principles of these ideal things [and] sketch the ground-plan of a true common-wealth".[4] The true masters of this science are for Santayana – and not surprisingly – the ancient Greeks, and above all Socrates, Plato and Aristotle. But to say this is not to claim that ancient Greek society embodied a perfectly rational *morality*, which veneration of the Greeks might lead one to attribute to them if one did not make this distinction between morality and ethics.

Central to the concerns of rational ethics is the phenomenon of *volition*. The will is the expression of an animal's living interest and preference and manifests therefore a radical bias. It is the role of reason to render will consistent and far-reaching. Rational ethics, unlike the pre-rational, seeks to be *complete*; and, unlike intuitive morality, rational ethics rests upon the impulse to *reflect*. Reflection upon the individual and society, upon *self* and *other*, reveals that:

> Sympathy and justice are simply an expression of the soul's interests, arising when we consider other men's lives so intently

> that something in us initiates and re-enacts their experience, so that we move partly in unison with their movement, recognise the reality and initial legitimacy of their interests, and consequently regard their aims in our action, in so far as our own status and purposes have become identical with theirs.[5]

This rational reflection, which demands consistency and completeness, also demands that existence be viewed *as a whole*; and it shows that, although the instincts and preferences upon which morality rests are individual, egoism is not a particularly rational position to adopt; for there is something quite problematic about the notion of the individual self: "the same principle that creates the ideal of a self creates the ideal of a family or an institution".[6] The reason for this is that what a biographer may define as an individual's life is ultimately not a significant unity: "All the substances and efficient processes that figure within it come from elsewhere and continue beyond; while all the rational objects and interests to which it refers have a transpersonal status".[7] (Although Santayana does not at this point make reference to it, affinities with the Buddhist doctrine of *Anatta* are quite apparent.) Another way to express the inadequacies of an ethics of egoism and metaphysics of the self is to show that there is a significant difference between *pleasure* and *happiness*: if the former can be said to be the satisfaction of instinct or the aim of impulse, the latter is the aim of reason: "The direct aim of reason is harmony; yet harmony, when made to rule in life, gives reason a noble satisfaction which we call happiness." The reason why happiness belongs in the realm of the rational is that it is impossible without *discipline*, and this is something the intuitive moralist rejects.

> It is discipline that renders man rational and capable of happiness by suppressing without hatred what needs to be suppressed to attain a beautiful naturalness. Discipline discredits the random pleasures of illusion, hope, and triumph, and substitutes those which are self-reproductive, perennial and serene, because they express an equilibrium maintained with reality.[8]

These effects of discipline are not unrelated to the element of sympathy touched upon above. Sympathy has a natural base in such things as parental and sexual instincts, but in order to find one's happiness in the exercise of this sympathy, one has to "lay one's foundations deeper in nature and to expand the range of one's being".[9]

If it is the role of rational ethics to bring order and harmony to the multifarious and conflicting individual instincts and passions, to promote happiness through the deepening and expansion of one's being and to demonstrate the untenability of the egoism/altruism and the self/other dichotomies by adopting a holistic point of view through reflection upon experience – what need is there for anything other than pre-rational morality transformed by rational ethics? Why bring in or establish a third phase, post-rational morality? I believe Santayana's answer lies ultimately in the fact that rational ethics is, as mentioned above, a system of thought: it is the mere *idea* of rational morality. Human history shows that such rational structures of thought do not translate into rational modes of behaviour, and to Santayana, given his general philosophical position, this is not surprising. There does exist a need for post-rational morality, which is essentially a religious dimension of human existence: it is synonymous with the spiritual life.

The relationship and perfect continuity between the three phases of morality are brought out in the following passage:

> Now you cannot have a harmony of nothings, and rational ethics would be impossible if pre-rational morality were annulled. And as the impulse to establish harmony, and the love of order, are themselves natural and pre-rational passions, so an ulterior shift to post-rational morality introduces a new natural and pre-rational passion, the demand for harmony not merely within the human psyche or within the human world, but between this world and the psyche on the one hand and the universe, the truth, or God on the other.[10]

One might express this by saying that, although rational ethics adopts a holistic point of view, post-rational morality does so in an ultimate sense, by placing both the individual and the natural world in the context of the transcendent reality postulated by religious systems. But more important, in my view, is the distinction between rational ethics as *a system of thought* and post-rational morality as *a way of life* – the spiritual life.

Post-rational morality is borne of despair – despair over the failure of reason. These systems of morality are "experiments in redemption".[11] Santayana considers a number of such experiments which have occurred throughout human history: Epicureanism, Cynicism, Stoicism, Islam, Platonism, Christianity and Buddhism. Since my concern here is primarily with the role that Buddhism plays, I will not discuss the other 'experiments in redemption', except to say enough about Christianity to bring out the contrast with Buddhism. It is after all striking that a philosopher who was so much a product of Catholic Christian culture should come to recognise an Eastern religion as a superior expression of the spiritual life.

There is for Santayana a certain double aspect to Christianity. On the one hand, the soul of the gospel is really post-rational, which is to say that it recognises that all earthly things are vanity, and that its effort at redemption takes the form of renunciation of the world, an emptying of the will as regards all human desires, thereby realising a deeper peace through contemplation and mystical detachment. On the other hand, Christianity's Jewish heritage made this renunciation of the world temporary and partial only, for it never gave up the pre-rational craving for a delectable promised land; and although it conceives of a life of the soul in the beyond, hope of a new order in *this* world has never been abandoned. Since the emptying of the will of desire and the renunciation of the world were half-hearted only, there has been within Christianity a tendency towards a destructive extreme in its asceticism and its cult of suffering. Buddhism, being 'a purely negative system', would not allow such extremism: "For a discipline that is looked upon as merely temporary can contradict nature more boldly than one intended to take nature's place".[12] And Santayana elaborates:

> The hope of unimaginable benefits to ensue could drive religion to greater frenzies than it could have fallen into if its object had been merely to silence the will. Christianity persecuted, tortured, and burned . . . It kindled wars, and nursed furious hatreds and ambitions . . . All this would have been impossible if, like Buddhism, it had looked only to peace and the liberation of souls. Man [in Christianity], far from being freed from his natural passions, was plunged into artificial ones quite as violent and much more disappointing. Buddhism had tried to quiet a sick world with anesthetics; Christianity sought to purge it with fire.[13]

Buddhism then is for Santayana 'a purely negative system', by which he means – I believe – that it is a system which through its spiritual discipline somehow seeks 'to take nature's place'. And this in turn means that its 'experiment in redemption' takes the form of a practice of detachment which seeks to silence the will, liberate the soul and bring about peace. Seeking to 'replace' nature, it does not 'contradict' it, which is to say that it does not promote violence, hatred and strife among people, or between body and soul. That Buddhism is an eirenic religion which seeks to liberate the individual through a practice of detachment is of course not news to anyone familiar with it. Rather than give a detailed account of this religious philosophy, what is important for us is to understand how Santayana conceives of this form of the spiritual life and – most importantly – what function this highest form of post-rational morality performs in moral life.

I have said above that Santayana characterises Buddhism as a purely *negative* system, and he adds to this that it is wholly *pessimistic*. He does not refer explicitly to the Four Noble Truths, but we recognise the characterisation as an expression of that wisdom, and realise that he does not speak pejoratively. Since every Buddhistic virtue is said to be viewed as 'merely removing guilt and alleviating suffering', Santayana also says that Buddhism is purely *remedial*; and it is this which has enabled it to keep morality pure – "free from that admixture of worldly and partisan precepts with which less pessimistic systems are encumbered".[14] Elaborating upon the superiority of this system of morality, he continues:

> If there is something in a purely remedial system of morality which seems one-sided and extreme, we must call to mind the far less excusable one-sidedness of those moralities of prejudice to which we are accustomed in the Occident – the ethics of irrational acquisitiveness, irrational faith, and irrational honour. Buddhistic morality, so reasonable and beautifully persuasive, rising so willingly to the ideal of sanctity, merits in comparison the profoundest respect. It is lifted as far above the crudities of intuitionism as the whisperings of an angel are above a schoolboy's code.[15]

While it is clear that the superiority of Buddhism lies in its pessimistic and remedial nature, I believe that this in turn is inseparable from its epistemological and ontological conception of the world, for it is this which fosters the practice of detachment from the world which for Santayana is the essence of the spiritual life. This could ultimately not be elaborated upon without going into the complex and central topic of the practice of meditation; a few words about Santayana's conception of the spiritual life, and of how this relates to morality, will, however, have to suffice.

Central to Santayana's philosophy is the distinction between *existence* and *essence*. The realm of existence is the natural world, the dynamic world of flux, the world of temporal entities which are subject to generation and corruption. The realm of essence, by contrast, is the realm of eternal and immutable entities; essences are the forms or aspects that existent objects may manifest for a time, but many essences are not ever manifested in existence; the realm of essence is infinite. This basic distinction is therefore at heart the distinction between the temporal and the eternal; put in Platonic terms it is the distinction between *Becoming* and *Being*, and in terms of Buddhist philosophy it is the distinction between *Saṁsāra* and *Nirvāṇa*. It is important to realise that, for Santayana, essences – being eternal – are *non-temporal*, which is different from saying that they are *everlasting*. If there were any everlasting entities, such as the gods and souls postulated by various religions, they would be temporal, albeit of infinite temporal extent, and not eternal. Santayana is one with the Buddhists in believing neither in the existence of gods nor in the reality of enduring selves.

The following passage makes it clear that Santayana sees a close connection between his own fundamental ontology and that of Buddhism;

> So Nirvana may be called annihilation in that it annihilates personality, desire and temporal existence; yet the 'Buddha teaches that all beings are from eternity abiding in Nirvana' so that far from being nothing Nirvana embraces the whole realm of essence – pure Being in its infinite implications – from which, of course, existence is excluded; because since existence is necessarily in flux and is centred in some arbitrary moment, it itself exists only by exclusion and with one foot in the grave.[16]

Now the spiritual life, for Santayana, is life in the eternal; which is to say that, although it is a life which is a possibility for a natural being in the natural world, it is a life which transcends the natural world to the greatest possible extent and attends in the fullest possible way to the realm of essence, to the eternal aspect that temporal things wear. The key to realising this life in the eternal is *detachment*, and Santayana makes it very clear that by this he does not mean *indifference*. To be detached from a thing is, spiritually speaking, to regard it with joy; it is to detach it "from the world that besets and threatens it", and to attach it to the spirit "to which it is an eternal possession".

> But this thing eternally possessed by the spirit is not the thing as the world knows and prizes it; it is not the person, or nation or

> religion as it asserts and flaunts itself, in a mortal anxiety to be dominant; it is only that thing in its eternal essence, out of which the stress and the doubt of existence has wholly passed.[17]

This passage points to the fact that the realm of *existence* can be distinguished from the realm of *essence* in less metaphysical terms by saying that the former is the world of care, anxiety, desire, fear and passion; whereas the latter is the world freed from these stresses and doubts. In a sense it is of course misleading to speak of two *worlds*, for it is the same world which is experienced in different ways: *Saṁsāra* and *Nirvāṇa* are in a sense the same world and to attain the capacity to sense the ultimate in the immediate is to be freed from anxiety; it is to realise the Pyrrhonian ideal of *ataraxia*, or tranquillity.

The spiritual life entails a complete transformation of the person: in being liberated from oneself one comes to feel for the first time that one *is* oneself; in being liberated from the world one becomes capable of a universal love of nature. Santayana elaborates:

> Your detachment will not be spiritual unless it is universal; it will then bring you liberation at once from the world and from yourself. This will neither destroy your natural gifts and duties nor add to them; but it will enable you to exercise them without illusion and in far-seeing harmony with their real function and end. Detachment leaves you content to be where you are, and what you are . . . yet in your physical particularity detachment makes you ideally impartial; and in enlightening your mind it is likely to render your action also more successful and generous.[18]

In this last remark about the connection between enlightenment and action we have a clue to the connection between the spiritual life and morality; for just as the spiritual life transforms the individual, so does it also transform morality, and it effects what reason can not. A post-rational morality has value to the extent that it retains some natural impulse and restores natural morality. It will be recalled that natural, or pre-rational, morality is the multiplicity of variable and conflicting natural desires, instincts and impulses; and that rational ethics is an intellectual attempt to bring order and harmony into natural morality, an attempt at which it can be at best only partially successful. Post-rational morality is the subordination of all precepts to some single eventual good. In the case of Christianity, this is presumably the salvation and eternal life of the soul in the afterlife; and this rests upon faith in the divine and redeeming nature of Christ. In the case of

Buddhism it is the Bodhisattva ideal of enlightenment, which involves the overcoming of greed, hatred and the delusion of an ego isolated from other happenings and existences; and this realisation of the Buddha nature within ourselves rests not upon the kind of faith that is central to Christianity, but rather upon the spiritual discipline of meditation. I hope it has been clear from my brief account that Santayana's conception of the spiritual life is close to that ideal.

Although post-rational morality is said to subordinate all precepts to some single eventual good, it should not be thought that it is Santayana's view that morality is *based* on the sort of religious system which constitutes post-rational morality; morality has an entirely natural *genesis*, but it has a wholly ideal or spiritual *telos*. What remains is to explain how this spiritual life 'restores' natural morality and why it is that Buddhism is the superior form of post-rational morality. Speaking generally, Santayana says that:

> Systems of post-rational morality are not original works: they are versions of natural morality translated into different metaphysical languages, each of which adds its peculiar flavour, its own genius and poetry, to the plain sense of the common original.[19]

As an example, he gives the law of Karma, which is the natural experience of retribution and the fact of character 'ideally extended and made precise'. In the law of Karma a particular observation about life is raised to such a level of eminence that we come to imagine it as underlying and explaining all empirical observations. This 'imaginary extension of the law of moral continuity and natural retribution' becomes a dogma which – although it institutes a deeper spiritual law – contains certain dangers; for it rests on what Santayana calls 'the fantastic metaphysics' of the transmigration of souls, and – by making my future entirely dependent on my former conduct – the law tends to deny the fact that the efforts of others can have a real influence over my salvation through works of love, pity, science or prayer. In other words, systems of post-rational morality tend in the direction of faith in the supernatural, which may issue in destructive superstition, from which even the Buddhistic law of Karma may not be immune. (Whether Santayana has an adequate understanding of this law may well be a matter for debate.)

Although some metaphysical dogma or moral fable may be an inescapable aspect of any post-rational morality, the value of any such system depends on the extent to which it restores natural morality. It works best when the symbolism is not deceptive, when the 'supernatural machinery' becomes a poetic echo of experience which does not offend intelligence. "True sages and true civilisations can accordingly flourish under a dispensation nominally supernatural; for that supernaturalism may have become a sincere form in which imagination clothes a rational and human wisdom"[20].

Although the sophisticated Buddhist would no doubt say that dogma and faith in supernatural machinery are completely obviated in Buddhism, I believe Santayana would be inclined to say that in Buddhism they are reduced to their minimum; in any case, this freedom from dogma is no doubt related to the negative, pessimistic and purely remedial character of its orientation discussed above. It is because of its freedom from superstitious dogma that Buddhism is able to work to redeem us from the illusion which is the fountain of our troubles: "Ignorance is to be enlightened, passion calmed, mistaken destiny revoked; only what the innermost being desiderates, only what can really quiet the longings embodied in any particular will, is to occupy the redeemed mind."[21] Buddhism was able, he said, to "pierce to the genuine principles of happiness and misery"[22], and "to combine universal sympathy with perfect spirituality"[23].

And this perfect spirituality, with the attendant consequences for the moral life, is ultimately made possible through the spiritual discipline of meditation – something to which Santayana does not give nearly enough explicit attention. It is through this practice, and not through dogmas and doctrines, that the individual realises that detachment which is liberation both from the world and from the self. The moral power of Buddhism does not lie in the discipline of the Eightfold Path if this is conceived of as but one ethical code among others; its power lies in its capacity to transform natural morality as such through the transformation of the individual as the result of spiritual practice. This is why Buddhism, more than any other religious system or post-rational morality, is of universal relevance and universal appeal, and this is why "It is lifted as far above the crudities of intuitionism as the whisperings of an angel are above a schoolboy's code"[24].

John Magnus Michelsen, Department of Philosophy, University of Victoria, Victoria BC, Canada V8W 3P4.

NOTES

1 Santayana, George (1962) *Reason in Science* (London, Collier) p. 154.
2 *Reason in Science*, pp. 158–159.
3 *Reason in Science*, pp. 163, 164.
4 *Reason in Science*, p. 171.
5 *Reason in Science*, p. 175.
6 *Reason in Science*, p. 177.
7 *Reason in Science*, p. 188.
8 *Reason in Science*, p. 179.
9 *Reason in Science*, p. 182.
10 Santayana, George (1940) Apologia pro mente sua, in: P. A. Schilpp (Ed.) *The Philosophy of George Santayana* (hereafter PGS) (New York, Tudor Publishing) p. 563.
11 *Reason in Science*, p. 189.
12 *Reason in Science*, p. 201.
13 Ibid.
14 *Reason in Science*, p. 205.
15 *Reason in Science*, p. 206.
16 Santayana, George (1957) *Platonism and the Spiritual Life* (hereafter *Platonism*) (New York, Harper Torchbooks, p. 30).
17 *Platonism*, p. 271.
18 PGS, p. 571.
19 *Reason in Science*, p. 204.
20 *Reason in Science*, p. 209.
21 Santayana, George (1962) *Reason in Religion* (London, Collier Books) p. 155.
22 *Reason in Religion*, p. 156.
23 *Reason in Religion*, p. 155.
24 *Reason in Science*, p. 206.

6

Is Daoism 'Green'?*

David E. Cooper

I

'The green movement should learn from ancient civilizations', urges a recent Chinese author, 'so as to reconstruct the world of values for . . . modern man'.[1] Many people in that movement, those of a 'deep' hue of green, have been following this advice. Unlike their 'shallow' colleagues, they deny the capacity of mainstream Western approaches, such as utilitarianism or natural rights theory, to foster those values which, as they see it, 'modern man' requires if he is to stop pillaging his environment. Some have turned for inspiration to aboriginal cultures in which, one is told, the natural environment is held sacred. Others look for a source in the philosophies of the ancient Asian civilisations. A head-count of this second group would, I suspect, show that it is daoist thought which is deemed to hold most promise for 'reconstructing' an environmental ethic. So, for example, one pair of authors construe Zhuang Zi's parable of the cook who follows the *dao* when carving meat as teaching a lesson that 'green movements all over the world are striving to achieve' – that of 'operating according to the law of nature without inappropriate human intervention'.[2] For Fritjof Capra, in his best-seller *The Tao of Physics*, the very survival of our civilisation depends on heeding the daoist message of 'a oneness of the universe' and 'harmony with the natural environment'.[3]

Someone may wonder how any moral lesson is to be gleaned from ancient masters who could treat considerations of benevolence and

* Previously published in *Asian Philosophy, Vol. 4, No. 2, 1994.*

righteousness as symptoms of decay (*Dao De Jing*, 38), or find conventional 'goodness and fairness . . . as odious . . . as vice and depravity' (*Zhuang Zi*, 8d).[4] The reply would be: it is precisely the failure of the Western tradition to acknowledge values beyond those 'artificial' ones (in Hume's sense) which facilitate social cooperation that debars it from accommodating an adequate environmental ethic. Whether these more primordial, pre-conventional values should be labelled 'moral' is a semantic question which should not divert us from identifying and promoting them.

I hope to do three things in this paper. First, I try to identify those aspects of daoist thought which *prima facie* are sympathetic to 'green' concerns. Second, however, I argue that it is much more difficult than it first appears to discern a 'green' message in those aspects. Finally, I suggest that, on a certain construal of daoist thought, there is nevertheless a rather deeper aspect which is, so to speak, environmentally friendly.

There are four alleged themes in daoist thought which 'deep' environmentalists have variously adduced in support of the attitudes towards nature which they favour – respect for nature, a sense of harmony with it, and so on. These themes might be labeled 'holism', 'anti-pragmatism', 'primitivism', and 'femininity'. Put them together, and you have the idea that Daoism incorporates a vision of the unity of everything in the universe, including ourselves; an hostility towards the pragmatic, means-end mentality held responsible for so much environmental devastation; an ideal of a primitive, back-to-nature form of life; and a rejection of a dominating, intrusive, 'masculine' stance towards nature in favour of a yielding, passive, 'feminine' one. Since 'deep' environmentalists share just these antipathies and sympathies, Daoism is therefore well-suited to provide them with a philosophical currency. Or so it is claimed.

Given the readiness with which some environmentalists invoke daoist authority, it is perhaps worth reminding ourselves that the contribution of the classical masters to 'green' issues will be at best indirect. Zhou, Qin and Han China was no bed of roses, but it did not confront today's ecological issues. Hence it would be anachronistic, for example, to suppose that Lao Zi's plea for population control and restrictions on travel expressed a concern for 'sustainable development' or energy conservation (80).

II

Let us now examine the four themes and their alleged contribution to an adequate 'eco-philosophy', beginning with the theme of 'holism'. When ecologists speak of holistic systems, they are referring, in Capra's words, to systems in 'dynamic balance', where the existence of each element depends upon its place in the system, as does the integrity of the system upon each element. Some of them, like proponents of the 'Gaia hypothesis', urge us to see the whole natural order as one giant system of this kind.[5] We then interfere in this order at the risk of destroying its balance. In Daoism, too, there is much talk of oneness or unity, as when the *Dao De Jing* states that 'it is the One that makes [things] what they are' (39). But this is not the holism of the ecologists. References to 'the One' seem to fall into two main, and related, groups. There are those, first, which emphasise the undifferentiated, unarticulated character of the nameless' *dao* which was 'the beginning of heaven and earth'. Second, there are those references, especially frequent in the *Zhuang Zi*, which register the conviction that all the distinctions we make are the artificial products of convention and language. Thus, 'contrasts' like that between pleasure and pain are 'so many sounds . . . fleeting modalities of the universal being . . . there is nothing real except that universal norm' (2b).

It might be said that, different as such 'metaphysical' holism is from the ecologists' version, it must nevertheless encourage a sense of harmony with the natural order that in turn promotes attitudes of respect and care for nature. Surely, however, it is hard to see why such an abstract doctrine *must* inspire any particular sense or emotion. The 'futurist' leader, Marinetti, thought that it was through technology that one could best experience such harmony with the natural order, as when 'the man at the steering-wheel' feels joined to 'the centre of the earth' by gravitational force. 'Greens', with their 'nostalgia for Homeric cheeses and legendary spinning-wheels', debar themselves from that 'union' with nature that is most fully obtained by seizing hold of it and moulding it.[6] It is not obvious that this is a less appropriate emotional response to an abstract holism than is a 'greener', hands-off one.

The second theme is what I have called 'anti-pragmatism'. It is by now a cliché that many environmental ills can be put at the door of the *Zweckrationalität* of modernity, of our modern inability to value actions 'for their own sake', distinct from what they contribute by way of supposed, usually material benefits. Several commentators have then appealed, by way of an antidote to this mentality, to the daoist masters' praise of 'uselessness'. ('Shouldn't one rejoice at being good-for-nothing?', asked Zhuang Zi rhetorically (1f)). What is being praised here, one author tells us, is the 'aesthetic attitude toward life', that attitude which, following Kant, is 'disinterested' and rejoices in the intrinsic qualities of things, unconcerned with their practical pay-off.[7]

There are two problems here. The first concerns the interpretation of the 'uselessness' passages. When Zhuang Zi rejoices in his good-for-nothingness, he compares himself to an ailanthus tree whose fibrous, knotty wood preserves it from 'the axe and the delinquent'. And when Lao Zi warns us against pursuing goals, the point seems to be, as often as not, that we are then more likely to attain them. Like the *dao* itself, it is because the sage 'never attempts to become great that [he] succeeds in becoming great' (34). By not contending for things, he obtains them, since no one bothers to contend against him (22). Whether or not Lao Zi's is a 'brilliantly wicked philosophy of self-protection',[8] there is surely a Machiavellian streak in Daoism which calls into question its alleged hostility towards a pragmatic outlook on life. But suppose we waive that consideration and agree that Daoism preaches a 'disinterested', 'aesthetic' stance. There is then the problem of seeing why this should, in any way, be an environmentally friendly one. It was in thoroughly aesthetic terms that many of the best-known enthusiasts for technology in the 19th and 20th centuries couched their enthusiasm. For Marx, nature is there as the plastic medium for the self-expressive activities through which human beings realise their productive 'essence'. For Spengler, the new 'Faustian man' is the technologist, the epitome of creative energy. For Le Corbusier, the true 'spirit of the modern age' should reside in the synthesis of the aesthetic with the technical. Perhaps we should behave in a 'disinterested', 'aesthetic' manner, and perhaps Daoism urges us to. But in the absence of further argument, we need to know why it is the 'greens' rather than their enemies who authentically represent this aestheticised ethic.

The third theme is that of 'primitivism'. Only the most romantic propose that human beings should return to a genuinely primitive form of social and economic life. But many people do urge that we should try to live *more* primitively – in small autonomous communities, perhaps, with a much reduced reliance upon technology. Some do so in the name of sustainable development, but others argue that a more primitive existence than ours has become is intrinsically valuable, for it offers a direct intimacy with nature, unmediated by the paraphernalia of technology. How much of a precedent for this ideal does Daoism represent? There is no denying the admiration apparent in daoist art for 'the wild man', the solitary mountain-dweller, so that, as Lin Yutang put it, someone with a 'hidden desire to go about with . . . bare feet goes to Taoism' rather than to Confucianism.[9] Nor should one ignore the *Zhuang Zi*'s mention of the 'resurgence of vitality' which 'communion with nature' can afford (19a). (Though one is, I believe, entitled to ignore the dithyrambs to 'naturalism' in Chapter 9, one of the more obviously unsatisfactory accretions to the original text). But these provide an insufficient basis for any 'green' ideal of primitivism. Maybe 'the wild man's' existence is admired less for its positive aspects than out of disgust for the way city life had developed. And one should note that at one point in the *Zhuang Zi*, 'retiring from the world . . . to solitary places' is described as a mark of 'craziness' (15a–b). As for the bracing, revitalising effects of a spell in the country, that can be conceded by almost everyone, including the tired businessman whose ideal, once he has taken this tonic, is as far from primitivism as could be imagined.

It is arguable that, in the *Dao De Jing*, there is to be found an ideal which deserves to be called 'primitivism' – a doctrine which a recent commentator calls 'primitive innatism'. But there is nothing, as it stands, 'green' about this doctrine. Rather, it reflects Lao Zi's conviction that we should 'vacate . . . social, linguistic conditioning' and 'abandon all language guides to behaviour', so that we are then free to heed our untutored, innate impulses, to 'follow our natural bent, unembellished by culture and language'.[10] This is not in itself a message of economic and social primitivism, proclaimed in the name of intimacy with the natural order. The simple agrarian life in small communities is at most an implication of the message, for it seems to have been Lao Zi's belief that people who did manage to 'vacate' or 'abandon' language to the recommended extent would be incapable of operating a more complex and sophisticated mode of existence. It is important to recognise, furthermore, that Lao Zi's 'primitive innatism' was not endorsed by Zhuang Zi. Our artificial linguistic perspectives doubtless distort, but mankind is too far along the road of linguistic acculturation to turn back and start all over again, guided only by its innate instincts. When he writes that 'in our days, to raise water, the ancient people's bucket has been abandoned for the counterbalanced ladle, and no one feels a need to return to the bucket' (14d), the point is both literal and metaphorical. Literally, it is a criticism of those Luddites whose nostalgia for the past makes them resist 'technological innovation'. Metaphorically, it is an attack on the doctrine by which Luddism might well be inspired – 'primitive innatism'.

The name of the final theme, 'femininity', goes proxy for a battery of terms – 'submissiveness', 'affable passivity', 'non-contention', 'non-imposition', 'letting things be', 'going with the grain' – which denote, in the classic texts, the kind of attitude or style of behaviour we are urged to cultivate in emulation, it is said, of the *dao* itself. Such an attitude and style are at least part of what is indicated by the expression *wu wei*. Those who invoke daoist authority in support of the green movement construe this call to 'femininity' as containing or implying an attack on the attitudes towards the environment which have come to prevail in modern times. Those attitudes are 'masculine', viewing nature as a 'macho' might view a woman, as something to dominate, penetrate, violate, and use for one's pleasure. Environmentalists are further encouraged by those anecdotes, like the one told by *Zhuang Zi* of the nobleman who fatally feeds a sea-bird a casserole and wine (18e), which apparently warn of the perils of trying to regiment or pervert the course of nature.

I am unconvinced that the 'femininity' passages or these anecdotes can really serve the 'green' purpose. First, it should be recalled that Lao Zi praises 'femininity' for the same reason he praises water – 'for attacking that which is hard and strong nothing can surpass it' (78). The environmental message, perhaps, is not that we should refrain from trying to 'overcome' nature and mould it to our purposes, but that we should do all this in the subtle, flexible way that a seductive woman follows in capturing her man. As for Zhuang Zi's tale, perhaps its moral is simply that we should not intervene in nature in a ham-fisted manner. Had the nobleman enjoyed the services of a biochemist able to alter the sea-bird's digestive system, it is not obvious that Zhuang Zi would have objected to its unnatural diet. Second, there is an obvious difficulty in conscripting an ideal of 'feminine' quietude and passivity on the side of 'the green movement' once the prevailing ideology has become – as 'greens' are keen to stress it has – one of environmental exploitation. For why should that ideal not support passive acquiescence in this prevailing ideology? Not going against the grain, it could be argued, means *inter alia* not kicking against the political and economic *status quo*, despite nostalgic yearnings for a happier past. Only 'in favourable times', says Zhuang Zi, would the sage attempt to 'reform the world by returning to its lost simplicity' (16b). In unfavourable times, he keeps himself to himself, 'indifferent' and 'detached' – not at all the type to demonstrate against seal culls or nuclear plants.

III

I have argued that none of the four alleged daoist themes can provide firm support for a 'deep' environmental ethic. Daoists and 'deep' environmentalists may both be 'holists', but in different senses, and the daoist version is too philosophically remote to yield any obvious practical lessons. Daoism is not so clearly 'anti-pragmatist' as some imagine, and if it does preach a kind of aestheticism, this need have no environmentally friendly implications. Daoist 'primitivism' is of a different species from that enjoined by many 'greens', and is anyway rejected by Zhuang Zi. Daoist 'femininity' may be a good deal more Machiavellian than some suppose: and even if it is not, its message may be one of political quietude rather than 'green' activism.

Despite this, there is in daoism a line of thought to inspire what might be called an inner resistance to the spirit of technological dominion. I shall try to bring this out by relating remarks in the *Zhuang Zi* to the position of the one notable 20th century philosopher to have both concerned himself with technology and expressed a debt to daoism – Martin Heidegger.

Let us first recall Zhuang Zi's sage who eschewed reformation of the world by returning it to its 'lost simplicity'. For Heidegger, too, it is pointless to 'rebel helplessly' against the technological age and 'curse it as the work of the devil' (307).[11] But nor, he insists, should a person 'push on blindly with technology'. Instead, 'here and now and in little things', the person should foster within himself a sense of the danger of technological culture, preparing himself for a different way of life should that culture ever collapse. A person can be in, yet not of, the technological world. Likewise, the sage keeps himself 'detached' from his age, 'indifferent' to its fortunes, keeping himself to himself and kindling 'the notion of primitive perfection' which, should 'favourable times' ever return, would contribute to 'reforming the world' (16b).

For both thinkers, crucially, the attitude a person should foster is one of 'letting things be', a slogan which clearly suggests something more than simply letting things take their course. It is tempting to construe it as follows: ordinarily we do not let things reveal themselves to our thought as they are in themselves, since they are veiled by the artifices of language and conventional schemes of interpretation. To 'let things be' is then to allow things to show themselves as they intrinsically are. But this cannot be right, since neither for Heidegger nor (as we saw) Zhuang Zi is it possible to think about things in the absence of language.

The slogan, I suggest, is a triple injunction. It enjoins us, first, to recognise that no one perspective on how things are is privileged and entitled to exclude others. In particular, the technological 'way of revealing' things, as instruments for our use, should not drive out other ways. Things must be allowed to show themselves in a variety of lights. Second, because any system of knowledge or science is itself conventional, propositional knowledge should not be elevated above the unsystematic 'know how' which we obtain, not through examining things, but through practical engagement with them. And if we are to know things in this manner, as Zhuang Zi's swimmer knows water, we must remain open to their qualities, without imposing preconceptions upon them. Finally, although we cannot represent things except through language, words need not be vehicles for representation. They can – or once could – be responses, uncluttered by artifice and convention, to intimations of the *dao*, the way of Being. Before language became, as Heidegger puts it, 'a mere container for [mankind's] sundry preoccupations', there was 'simple saying', the bringing of 'the unspoken word of Being to language' (239).[12] The thought is anticipated in the *Zhuang Zi*. 'Preliminary to all discourses, there pre-exists an innate harmony in all beings'. Language which responds to this 'harmony' is 'natural' and 'spontaneous', hence 'fitting' and able to set up sympathetic 'vibrations' in other people (27a). It is the language of those whom Heidegger called 'poets'.

But how might 'letting things be', so construed, foster an appropriate attitude towards nature and technology? To begin with, the injunction to remain open to many perspectives is especially directed against technologism, for what makes this so dangerous, according to Heidegger, is precisely its capacity to 'drive out every other possibility of revealing', to the degree that we forget there are other possibilities (309). Increasingly, that is, things lose any meaning beyond the one they enjoy as components within the technological enterprise – as tools, say, or resources. Perhaps it was this danger which one master in the *Zhuang Zi* sensed when he reprimanded the Yellow Emperor for the latter's desire to control the harvest and the seasons: 'to entrust [nature] to you, would be to the loss of all beings

. . . the sun and the moon would soon be extinguished' (11c). Things would cease to be what, from other perspectives, they are if 'lording it over nature' were to prevail.

Second, the demotion of representational knowledge militates against the technological enterprise if, as both our philosophers believe, esteem for such knowledge is deeply implicated in that enterprise. 'The love of knowledge, inventions, and innovation', says Zhuang Zi, 'is responsible for all the ills of the world'. (10d). And for Heidegger, the pursuit of 'objective' knowledge requires that same distancing of enquirers from the objects of their enquiries as inspires the view of nature as a resource for our utilisation (pp. 302ff). Practical 'know-how', of the kind manifested by Zhuang Zi's swimmer or bell-maker, or by Heidegger's peasants and craftsmen, calls on the other hand for a respect for one's materials or milieu, a quiet readiness to be guided by them and to 'fuse' with them. ('Water has become my medium', says the swimmer, 'and it supports me because I am one with it' (19I)).

To the extent, finally, that the injunction to cultivate a 'natural' and 'spontaneous' use of words is also a call to remember pre-conventional 'old ways' of talking, it enjoins an inner 'detachment' from the artificality – nowhere more apparent than in the technological enterprise – of modern times. Not only that, but the complexity of an artificially ordered life has turned us into 'chatterers', as Heidegger puts it. We need to 'chatter' so much because there is so much business to conduct, with the result that language itself is now only seen as what it has largely, in practice, become – a utilitarian device for the conduct of business (a repertoire of communicative speech-acts, say). 'To use words but rarely is to be natural', said Lao Zi (23). Hence, to foster a 'natural' use of words requires us to stand aside from, if not against, a mode of existence where the premium is upon 'chattering', to the exclusion of the 'simple saying' which characterised an age less geared to the complex management of nature than even Lao Zi's, let alone our own.

David E. Cooper, Department of Philosophy, University of Durham, 50 Old Elvet, Durham DH1 3HN, U.K.

NOTES

1 Fok Tou-Hui, quoted in Simon Sui-cheong Chau & Fung Kam Song, (1990) Ancient wisdom and sustainable development from a Chinese

perspective, in: J. R. & J. G. ENGEL (Eds) *Ethics of Environment and Development* (London: Belhaven), p. 230.

2 CHAU & SONG, op. cit., note 1, p. 230.

3 CAPRA, FRITJOF (1983) *The Tao of Physics* (London: Fonana) pp. 339–340.

4 *Dao De Jing*, trans. D. C. LAU (1985) (Harmondsworth: Penguin). References in the text are to chapter numbers; *Zhuang Zi*, trans. D. BRYCE (from L. Wieger's French translation), in: L. WIEGER (1984) *Wisdom of the Daoist Masters* (Lampeter: Llanerch). References in the text are to chapter numbers and section letters.

5 For a sophisticated treatment of ecological holism, see FREYA MATHEWS (1991) *The Ecological Self* (London: Routledge).

6 Quoted in LIONEL TRILLING (1972) *Sincerity and Authenticity* (Oxford: Oxford University Press) pp. 129–130.

7 JOSEPH WU (1985) Taoism, in: D. H. BISHOP (Ed.) *Chinese Thought: An Introduction* (Delhi: Motilal Banarsidass) p. 54.

8 LIN YUTANG (1936) *My Country and its People* (London: Heinemann) p. 112.

9 Ibid., pp. 109–10.

10 CHAD, HANSEN (1991) Classical Chinese ethics, in: P. SINGER (Ed.) *A Companion to Ethics* (Oxford: Blackwell) p. 77.

11 The question concerning technology, in: *Martin Heidegger: Basic Writings* (1978) trans. D. F. KRELL (London: Routledge & Kegan Paul). References in the text are to the page numbers of this book.

12 Letter on Humanism, *Basic Writings*, op. cit., note 11.

7

Cessation and Integration in Classical Yoga*

Ian Whicher

What is Yoga philosophy and how can it enrich our understanding of human nature? What is the relationship between self-understanding, morality and spiritual emancipation in Yoga thought? As a response to these questions, my paper will explore, within the Hindu tradition, Patañjali's (c third century CE) authoritative system (*darśana*) of Classical Yoga – a philosophical perspective which has, I submit, far too often been looked upon as excessively spiritual to the point of being a world-denying philosophy, indifferent to moral endeavour, neglecting the world of nature and culture, and overlooking human reality, vitality and creativity.

Contrary to the arguments presented by many scholars, which associate Yoga exclusively with extreme asceticism, mortification, denial and the renunciation and extrication of material existence (*prakṛti*) in favour of disembodied liberation – an elevanted and isolated spiritual state (*puruṣa*) – I will argue that Patañjali's Yoga can be seen as a responsible engagement, in various ways, of spirit (*purusạ* = Self, pure consciousness) and matter (*prakṛti* = mind, body, nature) resulting in a highly developed and transformed human nature, an integrated and embodied state of liberated selfhood (*jīvanmukti*). In support of the above thesis, textual evidence has been drawn from the two main authoritative sources of Classical Yoga: *the Yoga-Sūtras* (*YS*) of Patañjali and the *Vyāsa-Bhāṣya* (*VB*) of Vyāsa (c 500–600 CE).[1]

* Previously published in *Asian Philosophy*, Vol. 5, No. 1, 1995.

CESSATION (*NIRODHA*): TRANSFORMATION OR NEGATION OF THE MIND?

In Patañjali's central definition of Yoga, Yoga is defined "as the cessation of [the misidentification with] the modifications (*vṛtti*) of the mind (*citta*)".[1] '*Nirodha*' ('cessation') is one of the most difficult terms employed in the *YS* and its meaning plays a crucial role for a proper comprehension of Patañjali's system of Yoga. The 'attainment' of liberation is based on the progressive purification of mind (*sattvaśuddhi*) and the increasing light of knowledge (*jñāna*) that takes place in the process of *nirodha*. Since, as I shall now argue, the misunderstanding of this process has been fundamental to the misapprehension of the meaning of Patañjali's Yoga, there is a need to clarify it.

The word '*nirodha*' is derived from *ni*: ('down, into') and *rudh*: 'to obstruct, arrest, stop, restrain, prevent'.[3] In some well-known translations of *YS* 1.2, *nirodha* has been rendered as 'suppression',[4] 'inhibition',[5] 'restriction',[6] 'cessation',[7] and 'restraint'.[8] These meanings, I submit, are highly problematic, erroneous or misleading if understood, as many scholars understand them, with a view which emphasises *nirodha* as an ontological negation or dissolution of the mind and its functioning. I suggest that any attempt to interpret Patañjali's Yoga as a practice which seeks to annihilate or suppress the mind and its modifications for the purpose of gaining liberation grossly distorts the intended meaning of Yoga as defined in Patañjali. In regard to the process of *nirodha*, the wide range of methods in the *YS* indicates an emphasis on the ongoing application of yogic techniques, not a deadening of the mental faculties wherein the operations of consciousness, including our perceptual and ethical natures, are switched off. By defining *nirodha* as 'cessation', I mean to imply the 'undoing' of the conjunction (*saṃyoga*) between *puruṣa*, the 'Seer' (*draṣṭṛ*) and *prakṛti*, the 'seeable' (*dṛśya*), the conjunction with Vyāsa explains as a mental superimposition (*adhyāropa*),[9] resulting in the confusion of identity between *puruṣa* and the mental processes. Our intrinsic nature as *puruṣa* becomes *as if* misidentified with the mental processes (*vṛtti*) thereby creating, in the words of Vyāsa, "a mental self born of delusion".[10] *Nirodha*, I suggest, refers to the cessation of the worldly, empirical effects of the *vṛttis* on the *yogin's* consciousness, not the complete cessation of *vṛttis* themselves. *Nirodha* means to cease the congenital, epistemological power of the *vṛttis* over the *yogin*, i.e. *nirodha* is the epistemological cessation of *vṛttis* in the form of the congenital ignorance (*avidyā*) of our true spiritual identity and ultimate destiny.[11]

One will naturally ask how practitioners who attempt to obey any teachings resulting in death to their minds would have the capacity to comprehend or carry out any further instructions. Perhaps, more importantly, how could one function practically as a human being without the faculties of thinking, memory, discrimination and reason, and an individual I-sense with which one can distinguish oneself from other people and the world? Surely such a person would have to be mad or unconscious. If all the great Yoga masters of the past had obliterated or so thoroughly suppressed their minds in order to become liberated, how did they speak, teach, reason, remember, empathize, or even use the word 'I'? The mind and the body are the only vehicles in which to attain liberation. It is the mind, as Yoga readily admits, that must be utilised to study and listen to the guru; it is the mind that is needed to follow a spiritual path to liberation; and it is equally the mind that is required by the aspirant in order to function as a human being in day-to-day life.

By advising or explaining that the mind and its various faculties are to be negated, suppressed or abolished, many scholars, teachers and writers on Yoga have, I maintain, missed the point of practising Yoga. For it is not the *mind*, but rather the exclusive identification with material existence as one's true Self which is the source of all human difficulties and dissatisfaction (*duḥkha*); it is a specific state of consciousness or cognitive error evidenced *in* the mind and not the mind *itself*, which is at issue. Misidentification refers to the process wherein our self-identity conforms (*sārūpya*) to the changing nature of *vṛtti*.[12] *Avidyā* – the root affliction (*kleśa*) in Yoga which gives rise to four other afflictions: I-am-ness/egoity (*asmitā*), attachment (*rāga*), aversion (*dveṣa*) and the desire for continuity or fear of death (*abhiniveśa*)[13] – is a positive misconstruction of reality which mistakes *puruṣa* for prakṛtic existence. It is the condition of misidentification – the saṃsāric condition of self and world – and not the mind in total which must be eradicated in Yoga. Any advice to destroy the mind is, it seems to me, detrimental to a human being and to the practice of Yoga. How could progress on the path of Yoga be made with such an approach? What would the ethical ramifications be? The belief that mental annihilation leads to spiritual liberation has become a popular and unfortunate teaching of modern interpretations of Yoga. Despite the fact that it is neither truly yogic, practical, logic, nor appealing and, furthermore, may be destructive for aspirants, recent teachings and works on Yoga have often prescribed the negation or suppression of the mind, ego and thoughts as the primary means to self-emancipation.[14] This stance, I submit, is a gross misrepresentation of Yoga; a confused, misleading and, at best, naïve attempt at conveying the depth and profundity of the practice termed by Patañjali as *nirodha*.

It is my contention that *nirodha* denotes an epistemological emphasis and refers to the transformation of self-understanding, not the ontological cessation of *prakṛti* (i.e. the mind and *vṛttis*). *Nirodha* thus is not, as some have explained, an inward movement that annihilates or suppresses *vṛttis* or thoughts, nor is it the non-existence or absence of *vṛtti*; rather, *nirodha* involves a progressive expansion of perception which eventually reveals our true identity as *puruṣa*. Elsewhere,[15] I have argued that *cittavṛtti* describes the very basis of all the empirical selves: under the influence of *avidyā* the unenlightened person's mental processes (*vṛtti*) generate and are ineluctably driven by deeply rooted impressions (*saṃskāras*) and personality traits (*vāsanās*) sustaining an afflicted I-sense (*asmitā*).[16] Seen in the above context, *cittavṛtti* can be understood as a generic term standing for a misconceived knowledge (*viparyaya-jñāna*)[17] or error, which is structured in the network of our psychological make-up and veils our identity as *puruṣa*. The epistemic distortion or erroneous knowledge (*mithyā-jñāna*)[18] functioning as the *vṛtti* of *viparyaya* acts as the basis for all misidentification with *vṛttis* in the unenlightened mode (*vyutthāna*) of being.[19] In short, our afflicted identity rooted in spiritual ignorance functions through *viparyaya*. Oddly enough, this fundamental insight, which can be attributed to Vyāsa,[20] has not clearly noted by scholars. I have attempted to clarify Vyāsa's position and furthermore suggest that this insight into the nature of *viparyaya* has profound implications for our understanding of Patañjali's whole system.

Accordingly, *cittavṛtti* does not stand for all cognitions or emotive processes in the mind but is the very seed (*bīja*) mechanism of *puruṣa*'s misidentification with *prakṛti* and from which all other *vṛttis* or thoughts arise and are appropriated in the unenlightened state of mind. Spiritual, ignorance gives rise to a malfunctioning of *vṛtti* which in Yoga can be corrected, thereby allowing for the 'right' functioning of *vṛtti*.[21] *Cittavṛtti* is an analogical understanding of consciousness in that the consciousness which has become the mind is analogous to *puruṣa*'s consciousness.[22] It is the *cittavṛtti* as our confused and mistaken identity of *puruṣa*, not our *vṛttis*, thoughts and experiences *in total* which must be brought to a state of definitive cessation.

ALONENESS (*KAIVALYA*) AND INTEGRATION

I would now like to contend that in Yoga the state of liberation or 'aloneness' (*kaivalya*) in no way destroys or negates the personality of the *yogin*. Rather, *kaivalya* can be seen as a state in which all the obstacles preventing an immanent and purified relationship or engagement of person and spirit (*puruṣa*) have been removed. The mind, which previously functioned under the sway of ignorance colouring and blocking our perception of authentic identity, has now become purified and no longer operates as a locus of misidentification and dissatisfaction (*duḥkha*). *Sattva*, the finest quality (*guṇa*) of the mind, has the capacity to be perfectly lucid/transparent, like a dust-free mirror in which the light of *puruṣa* is clearly reflected and the discriminative discernment (*vivekakhyāti*)[23] between *puruṣa* and the mind can take place.[24] The crucial point to be made here is that *prakṛti* ceases to perform an obstructing role in *kaivalya*. The mind has been transformed, liberated from the egocentric world of attachment, its former afflicted nature abolished; and *puruṣa*, left alone, is never again confused with all the relational acts, intentions and volitions of empirical existence. There being no power of misidentification remaining (i.e. in *nirbīja-samādhi*),[25] the mind can no longer operate within the context of the afflictions, impressions, *karmas* and consequent cycles of *saṃsāra* implying a mistaken identity of selfhood subject to birth and death.

The *YS* has often been regarded as promoting the severance of *puruṣa* from *prakṛti*; concepts such as liberation, cessation, detachment, etc., have been interpreted in an explicitly negative light. Max Müller, citing Bhoja Rāja's commentary (11th century CE), refers to Yoga as 'separation' (*viyoga*).[26] More recently, numerous other scholars, including Eliade, Koelman, Feuerstein and Larson, have endorsed this interpretation, i.e. the absolute separateness of *puruṣa* and *prakṛti*.[27] In asserting the absolute separation of *puruṣa* and *prakṛti*, scholars and non-scholars alike have tended to disregard the possibility for other fresh hermeneutical options and this has surely proved detrimental to Patañjali's Yoga by continuing a tradition based on a misreading of the *Yoga-Sūtras* and Vyāsa's commentary. Accordingly, the absolute separation of *puruṣa* and *prakṛti* can only be interpreted as a disembodied state implying death to the physical body. Yet, interestingly, *YS* 2.9 states that even the wise possess the 'desire for continuity' for life. What *is* involved in Yoga is the death of the egoic identity which generates notions of one being a subject trapped in a particular body-mind.

Yoga is a practical way of life implying physical training, exertion of will power and acts of decision because Yoga deals with the complete human situation and provides real freedom, not just a theory of liberation. To this end, Patañjali outlined an 'eight-limbed' path (*aṣṭāṅga-yoga*) dealing with the physical, moral, psychological and spiritual dimensions of the *yogin*, an integral path which emphasises organic continuity, balance and integration[28] in contrast to the discontinuity, imbalance and disintegration inherent in *saṃyoga*. The idea of cosmic balance and of the mutual support and upholding of the various parts of nature and society is not foreign to Yoga thought. Vyāsa deals with the theory of 'nine causes' or types of causation according to tradition.[29] The ninth type of cause is termed *dhṛti*, meaning 'support', 'sustenance'. Based on Vyāsa's explanation of *dhṛti* we can see how mutuality and sustenance are understood as essential conditions for the maintenance of the natural and social world. There is an organic interdependence of all living entities wherein all (i.e. the elements, animals, humans and divine bodies) work together for the 'good' of the whole and for each other. At this point I would like to emphasise a much overlooked aspect of Yoga thought. Far from being exclusively a subjectively-orientated and introverted path of withdrawal from life, classical Yoga acknowledges the intrinsic value of 'support' and 'sustenance' and the interdependence of all living entities, thus upholding organic continuity, balance and integration within the natural and social world. Having attained to that insight (*prajñā*) which is 'truth-bearing' (*ṛtaṃ-bharā*),[30] the *yogin* perceives the natural order of cosmic life, 'unites' with and embodies that order. To be ensconced in ignorance implies a disunion with the natural order of life.

In contradistinction to the above interpretation of Yoga as 'separation', I am suggesting that far from being incompatible principles, *puruṣa* and *prakṛti* can engage or participate in harmony, having attained a balance or equilibrium together. The enstatic consciousness of *puruṣa* can co-exist with the mind and indeed all of *prakṛti*.[31] The *yogin* fully reconciles the eternally unchanging Seer with the eternally changing realm of relative states of consciousness only by allowing the mind in the practice of *samādhi* to dwell in its pure sattvic nature in the 'image of *puruṣa*', and then to be engaged once again in the field of relative existence. The process of *nirodha* culminates in *asaṃprajñāta-samādhi*,[32] the supra-cognitive awareness where the Seer abides in its own form.[33] According to Vyāsa, the repeated practice of the temporary 'experiences' of enstasy gradually matures the *yogin's* consciousness into *kaivalya*, permanent liberation. The stability of the consciousness in *kaivalya* should not be misconstrued as being sheer inactivity, pacifism or lethargy; rather, stability in *samādhi* allows for a harmony in activity, where the *guṇas* do not conflict with each other and are attuned to *puruṣa*. One is no longer in conflict with oneself and the world. We need not read Patañjali as saying that the culmination of all yogic endeavour, *kaivalya*, is a static finality or inactive, isolated, solipsistic state of being. In fact, *YS* 4.34 tells us that *kaivalya* has as its foundation the very heart of the unlimited dynamism or power of consciousness (*citiśakti*) that is *puruṣa*.[34] In terms of our primary analogue of empirical life (*cittavṛtti*), *puruṣa* is not seen to be active. In terms of *puruṣa*'s inexhaustibility, *puruṣa* is supremely active. To conclude that *puruṣa* is incapable of any activity whatsoever simply amounts to a tautological statement. In the liberated condition, it can be said that *prakṛti* is so integrated in the *yogin's* consciousness that it has become 'one' with the *yogin*. *Kaivalya* incorporates a perfectly integrated psychological consciousness and the independence of pure consciousness, yet pure consciousness to which the realm of the *guṇas* is completely attuned and integrated. Through the consummate phase of supra-cognitive *samādhi*, in *dharma-megha* ('cloud of *dharma*'), a permanent identity shift – from the perspective of the human personality to *puruṣa* – takes place. No longer dependent on knowledge (*vṛtti*) and fully detached from the world of misidentification, the *yogin* yet retains the power of discernment, omniscience[35] and activity.[36] The autotransparent knower, knowledge and action coexist in a state of mutual attunement.

The culmination of the Yoga system is found when, following from *dharma-megha samādhi*,[37] the mind and action are freed from misidentification and affliction[38] and one is no longer deluded regarding one's true identity. At this phase of practice one is disconnected from all patterns of egoically-motivated action. The *karma* of such an adept is said to be neither 'pure', nor 'impure', nor 'mixed'.[39] Though transcending the normative conventions and obligations of karmic behaviour, the *yogin* acts morally not as an extrinsic response and out of obedience to an external moral code of conduct, but as an intrinsic response and as a matter of natural, purified inclination. The stainless luminosity of *puruṣa* is revealed as one's fundamental nature; the *yogin* does not act samsarically and is wholly detached from the egoic fruits of action. The yogin does not, for example, indulge in the fruits of ritual action, in the merit (*puṇya*) and demerit (*apuṇya*) generated by good and bad observance of traditional ritualistic religion. By the practice of a detached ethic, the yogin must transcend this ritualistic, self-centred mentality. This does not imply that the *yogin* loses all orientation for action. Detachment, in its highest form (*para-vairāgya*),[40] is defined by Vyasa as a 'clarity of knowledge' (*jñāna-prasāda*).[41] Only attachment (and compulsive desire), not action itself, sets in motion the law of moral causation (*karma*) by which a person is implicated in *saṃsāra*. The *yogin* is said to be neither attached to virtue nor non-virtue, is no longer oriented within the egological patterns of thought as in *saṃyoga*. This does not mean, as some scholars have misleadingly concluded, that the spiritual adept is free to commit immoral acts,[42] or that the *yogin* is motivated by selfish concerns.[43] Acts must not only be performed in the spirit of unselfishness (i.e. sacrifice), or non-attachment, they must also be morally sound and justifiable. If action depended solely on one's frame of mind, it would be the best excuse for immoral behaviour. Moreover, the *yogin's* spiritual journey – far from being, as Feuerstein describes it,[44] an "a-moral process" – is a highly moral process! The *yogin's* commitment to the sattvification of consciousness, including the cultivation of moral virtues such as compassion (*karuṇā*)[45] and non-harming (*ahiṃsā*)[46] is not an 'a-moral' enterprise, nor is it an expression of indifference, aloofness or an uncaring attitude to others. Moral disciplines are engaged as a natural outgrowth of intelligent self-understanding and commitment to self-transcendence which takes consciousness out of (ec-stasis) its identification with the rigid structure of the monadic ego, thereby reversing the inveterate tendency of this ego to inflate itself at the expense of its responsibility in relation to others.

Having defined the 'goal' of Yoga as 'aloneness' (*kaivalya*), the question must now be asked: what kind of 'aloneness' was Patañjali talking about? 'Aloneness', I submit, is not the isolation of the Seer (*puruṣa*) separate from the seeable (*prakṛti*), as is unfortunately far too often maintained as the goal of Yoga, but refers to the aloneness of the power of 'seeing'[47] in its innate purity and clarity without any epistemological distortion or moral defilement. The cultivation of *nirodha* uproots the compulsive tendency to reify the world and oneself (i.e. that pervading sense of separate ego irrevocably divided from the encompassing world) with an awareness which reveals the transcendent, yet immanent, Seer. *Puruṣa* is said to be 'alone' not because there is an opposition or a separation, but simply because there is no misconception of *puruṣa*'s identity. Yoga is not, as one scholar would have us think, a Cartesian-like dichotomy (of thinker and thing).[48] Nor can Yoga be described as a metaphysical union of an individual self with the objective world of nature or more subtle realms of *prakṛti*. More appropriately, Yoga can be seen to unfold states of epistemic oneness (*samādhi*) – the non-separation of knower, knowing and known[49] – grounding our identity in a non-afflicted mode of action. As *puruṣa* is self-luminous, in *kaivalya* '*purusa* stands alone in its true nature as pure light'.[50] *Purusa* no longer needs to know itself reflexively, is peaceful and immutable because it needs/lacks nothing. *Kaivalya* implies a power of 'seeing' in which the dualisms rooted in our egocentric patterns of attachment, aversion, etc., have been transformed into unselfish ways of being with others.[51] 'Seeing' is not only a cognitive term but implies purity of mind, i.e. it has moral content and value. *Kaivalya* does not destroy feeling or encourage neglect or indifference. On the contrary, the process of cessation (*nirodha*) steadies one for a life of compassion and discernment and is informed by a 'seeing' in touch with the needs of others.

Yoga goes beyond the position of classical Sāṃkhya which seems to rest content with a discriminating knowledge (*viveka*) leading to an absolute separation between *puruṣa* and *prakṛti*. At the end of the day, *prakṛti*'s alignment with the purpose of *puruṣa* appears to be all for nought. Yet, if *puruṣa* were completely free to start with, why would it get 'involved' with *prakṛti*? *Puruṣa*'s 'entanglement' does intelligise *prakṛti* which on its own is devoid of consciousness.[52] The end product of puruṣa's 'involvement' with *prakṛti*, the state of liberated omniscience, is enriching and allows for a verifying and enlivening of human nature/consciousness. Classical Sāṃkhya's adherence to an absolute separation, implying a final unworkable duality between spirit and matter, amounts to an impoverishment of ideas. In Yoga, however, knowledge can be utilised in the integrity of action and being. Thus, Vyāsa states that the knower is liberated while still alive (*jīvanmukta*).[53] The *puruṣa* is 'alone' not because it is a windowless monad but because it transcends the faulty mechanics of *saṃyoga*, is unaffected by the *guṇas* and *karma*.

Can *puruṣa*'s existence embrace states of action and knowledge, person and personality? The tradition of Yoga answers in the affirmative. Vyāsa asserts that having attained a state of perfection beyond sorrow, "the omniscient *yogin* whose afflictions and bondage have been destroyed disports himself [herself] as a master".[54] The enstatic consciousness and pure reflection of the *sattva* of the mind 'merge' in *kaivalya*,[55] resulting in a natural attunement of mind and body in relation to *puruṣa*. The karmic power of *prakṛti* ceases to have a hold over the *yogin*, the karmic ego having been exploded.

The *yogin*'s attention is no longer sucked into the vortex of the conflicting opposites (*dvandvas*) in *saṃsāra*, is no longer embroiled in the polarising intentionalities of desire: the vectors of attraction and aversion. Free from the egoic intrusions of worldly existence, the *yogin* is said to be left 'alone'. The *puruṣa* can express itself in the time-space continuum in a particular body and with a particular personality. Yoga does not deny the existence of individuality; it allows for a trans-egoic development which is not the dissolution of the individual person and its personality but, rather, which includes their extension into the recognition, moral integrity and celebration of the interconnectedness of all beings, all life. Enstasy (*kaivalya*) is lived simultaneously with the mind or 'consciousness-of'. The link between the enstatic consciousness and the world is the purified *sattva* of the mind.

We must question assertions to the effect that, having attained liberation, the psychical apparatus of the *yogin* is destroyed,[56] or that the *yogin*'s body lives on in a state of catalepsy until death.[57] What disappears for the *yogin* is the 'failure to see' (*adarśana*),[58] or the world-view born of *avidyā*, not *prakṛti* itself. The purified mind and the evolutes of *prakṛti* (e.g. intellect, ego) can now be used as vehicles for an enlightened life of interaction and service, such as imparting knowledge to others: the purity and cognitive power impersonated in the guru is transformed from an end into an available means. When one accomplished in Yoga opens one's eyes to the world of experience, the knower (*puruṣa*) will be one's true centre of existence. The *guṇas* (i.e. *vṛttis*) will be subordinate to the knower.[59] Once the final stage of emancipation is reached, the lower levels of insight previously gained are incorporated, not destroyed. Only *puruṣa*'s misidentifications with phenomena are ended. When it is said that one has realised *puruṣa* through *nirodha*, it is meant that there is no further level to experience for one's liberation. *Nirodha* does not indicate the denial of formed reality or the negation of relative states of consciousness. Nor is it rooted in a conception of oneself which abstracts from one's identity as a social, historical and embodied being. *Nirodha* refers to the expansion of understanding necessary to perceive every dimension of reality from the direct perspective of pure, untainted consciousness.

If Patañjali had destroyed his perception of forms and differences, how could he have had such insight into Yoga and the intricacies of the unenlightened state? If through *nirodha*, the individual form and the whole world had been cancelled for Patañjali, he would more likely have spent the rest of his days in the inactivity and isolation of transcendent oblivion rather than presenting Yoga philosophy to others! Rather than being handicapped by the exclusion of thinking, perceiving or experiencing, one can say that the liberated *yogin* actualises the potential to live a fully integrated life in the world. The *yogin* simultaneously lives as it were in two worlds: the dimension of unqualified (*nirguṇa*) existence and the relative dimension (*saguṇa*), yet two worlds which work together as one. I conclude here that there is no reason why the liberated *yogin* cannot be portrayed as a vital, creative, thinking, balanced, happy and wise person. Having adopted an integrative orientation to life, the enlightened being can endeavour to transform, enrich and ennoble the world. I am therefore suggesting that there is a rich affective, moral, cognitive and spiritual potential inherent in the realization of *puruṣa*, the 'aloneness' of the 'power of consciousness'.

CONCLUDING REMARKS

Although many valuable contemporary scholarly writings on Yoga have helped to present Patañjali's philosophy to a wider academic audience, it is my contention that Patañjali has far too often been misinterpreted or misrepresented thanks to the use of inappropriate methodology: partial and misleading definitions of Sanskrit yogic terms and reductionistic hermeneutics. Many scholars have repeatedly given ontological definitions and explanations for terms which, I maintain, are more appropriately understood with an epistemological emphasis. Consequently, the specialised sense inherent in Yoga soteriology is diminished. The soteriological intent of Yoga need not preclude the possibility for an integrated, embodied state of liberated selfhood. A bias is invariably created within the language encountered in the translations and interpretations of the *YS*, resulting in an overemphasis on content, due consideration not having been given to form, structure and function. It is crucial to study the process of Yoga contextually, as it is lived and experienced by the *yogin*, and not simply to impute a content-system to the whole process. The bias extends to the ontological priorities of *puruṣa* over *prakṛti* and by consequence the priority of axiology over epistemology. *Puruṣa* is generally explained as the enlightened and ultimately hegemonic principle of pure consciousness, our true identity which alone has intrinsic spiritual value. *Prakṛti*, we are often told, is the non-spiritual cosmogonic principle comprised of the three *guṇas* (*sattva*, *rajas* and *tamas*), has a deluding, binding yet paradoxically subservient nature, and eventually disappears from the *yogin's* purview thus having no real value in the liberated state. It is not clear that the language of the *YS* is explanatory. It could equally be descriptive, in which case the axiological and ontological priorities would collapse, thereby challenging the widely held view that the relationship between *puruṣa* and *prakṛti* is exclusively an asymmetrical one, i.e. *prakṛti* exists for the purpose of *puruṣa*, and its value is seen only in instrumental terms and within the context of a soteriological end state which excludes it.

In Patañjali's central definition of Yoga (*YS* 1.2) *nirodha* has far too often been understood as an ontological cessation, suppression or 'deadening' of the mind and this misunderstanding has led, I submit, to some major interpretive errors. First, one can witness a reductionistic application of positivistic presuppositions to a mystical system: scholars have often concluded that once the stage of liberation has been attained the *yogin* will no longer be capable of experiencing the world since the body-mind has ceased to function. Second, the oral/historical teaching tradition has either been ignored or else this important pedagogical context of Yoga has not been sufficiently taken into consideration. Our hermeneutics must include a way of reading the tradition of Yoga within the culture we are studying. Third, by understanding *nirodha* to mean the ontological cessation or negation of *vṛttis*, many scholars have given a negative, one-sided and spurious definition of Yoga. The result is a volatile concept of *nirodha* that is world-denying and mind-and-body negating, wherein phenomenal reality is dissolved into nothingness or a meaningless existence for the liberated *yogin*. Consequently, Patañjali's philosophy as a whole becomes trivialised and can be viewed as impractical, unapproachable, unintelligible and unattractive.

Puruṣa indeed has precedence over *prakṛti* in Patañjali's system, for *puruṣa* is what is ordinarily 'missing' in human life and is ultimately the consciousness one must awaken to. According to this study, liberation as 'aloneness' (*kaivalya*) need not denote an ontological superiority of *puruṣa*, nor an exclusion of *prakṛti*. *Kaivalya*, I have argued, can be positively construed as an integration of both principles – an integration which, I maintain, is what is most important for Yoga. To break *puruṣa* and *prakṛti* apart, keep one and try to discard the other, is an enterprise which creates psychological and social conflict involving confused notions of 'self' which, I submit, are, clearly inimical to Yoga.

Such notions may have an aversion-orientation (*dveṣa*),[60] e.g. an exaggerated (and impoverished) sense of 'isolation' from the world as in the flight or escape of self with an impulse towards self-negation; or such notions may have an attachment-orientation (*rāga*),[61] e.g. whereby we only succumb to the world and can easily become enmeshed in forms of narcissism and egocentrism by aggressively objectifying and exploiting the world. Both of these extremes – escape from the world and worldly entrapment – must be transcended in Yoga. I have proposed that the *YS* does not uphold a path of liberation which ultimately renders *puruṣa* and *prakṛti* incapable of 'cooperating' together. Rather, the *YS* seeks to 'unite' these two principles, to bring them 'together' in a state of balance, harmony and a fullness of knowledge in the integrity of being and action.

Thus, Patañjali's Yoga need not result in the extinction or the evaporation of our 'personhood' along with the material world; rather, it is more accurate to say that Yoga culminates in the eradication of spiritual ignorance, the root cause of our misidentification with, and attachment to, worldly (or otherworldly!) existence. In this way, Yoga removes our selfishness and suffering (*duḥkha*) rooted in an afflicted and mistaken self-identity (*asmitā*). Liberated from the pain of self-limitation and all destructive personality traits, and having incorporated an expanded and enriched sense of personal identity embodying virtues such as non-violence, compassion and wisdom, the *yogin* can dwell in a state of balance and fulfilment, serving others while feeling truly at home in the world. The *yogin* can function in relation to the world, not being morally or epistemologically enslaved by worldly relationship. Morality and perception are both essential channels through which human consciousness, far from being negated or suppressed, is transformed and illuminated. Yoga combines discerning knowledge with an emotional, affective and moral sensibility. The enhanced perception gained through Yoga must be interwoven with Yoga's rich affective and moral dimensions to form a spirituality that does not become entangled in a web of antinomianism, but which retains the integrity and vitality to transmute our lives effectively. By upholding an integration of the moral and the mystical, Yoga supports a reconciliation of the prevalent tension within Hinduism between spiritual engagement and self-identity within the world (*pravṛtti*), and spiritual disengagement from worldliness and self-identity which transcends the world (*nivṛtti*). Yoga teaches a balance between these two apparently conflicting orientations.

This paper has been an attempt to counter the radically dualistic and ontologically-oriented interpretations of Yoga given by many scholars – where the full potentialities of our human embodiment are constrained within the rigid metaphysical structure of classical Sāṃkhya – and to offer instead an open-ended, morally and epistemologically-oriented hermeneutic which frees classical Yoga of the long standing conception of spiritual isolation, disembodiment, self-denial and world-negation and thus from its pessimistic image. I have elsewhere suggested that Patañjali can be understood as having adopted a provisional, practical, dualistic metaphysics but that there is no proof his system ends in duality.[62]

Patañjali's *YS* has to this day remained one of the most influential spiritual guides in Hinduism. In addition to a large number of people of India, hundreds of thousands of Westerners are actively practising some form of Yoga influenced by Patañjali's thought, clearly demonstrating Yoga's relevance for today as a discipline which can transcend cultural, religious and philosophical barriers. The universal and universalising potential of Yoga makes it one of India's finest contributions to our modern and postmodern struggle for self-definition, moral integrity and spiritual renewal. The purpose of this present study has been to consider a fresh approach with which to re-examine and assess classical Yoga philosophy. There is, I submit, nothing in what I have argued which can be proven to be incompatible with Patañjali's thought. Thus, it is my hope that some of the suggestions made in this paper can function as a catalyst for bringing Patañjali's Yoga into a more fruitful dialogue and encounter with other religious and philosophical traditions, both within and outside of India.

Ian Whicher, Department of Comparative Studies in Literature, Film and Religion, University of Alberta, Edmonton, Alberta, Canada T6G 2B4. Ian Whicher is now Deputy Director of the Dharam Hinduja Institute of Indic Research in the Faculty of Divinity, Cambridge University, England.

NOTES

1 Because of obvious limitations of space, this paper can only present a summary of some of the main arguments given in an earlier, more thorough study which is presently being revised for publication. WHICHER,

Ian R. (1992) 'A study of Patañjali's definitions of Yoga: uniting theory and practice in the Yoga-Sūtras, PhD thesis, Cambridge University. I have not offered a critical analysis of Vyāsa's commentary for the purpose of trying to determine how far Vyāsa correctly explains the *YS*. Rather, the study draws upon the wealth of philosophical and experiential insight which the *VB* brings to aid our understanding of the *YS*. For the Sanskrit text of the *YS* and the *VB* I have used *Pātañjala-Yogasūtrāṇi*, edited by K. S. Āgāśe (1904) (Poona, Anandāśrama Sanskrit Ser., 47). Unless otherwise specified, all translations are my own.

2 *YS* 1.2, p. 4. The modifications or functions (*vṛtti*) of the mind are said to be fivefold, namely, 'valid cognition' (*pramāṇa*), 'error' (*viparyaya*), 'conceptualisation' (*vikalpa*), 'sleep' (*nidrā*) and 'memory' (*smṛti*) (YS 1.6), and are described as being 'afflicted' (*akliṣṭa*) or 'non-afflicted' (*akliṣṭa*) (YS 1.5). *Citta* is an umbrella term which incorporates 'intellect' (*buddhi*), 'sense of self' (*ahaṃkāra*) and 'lower mind' (*manas*), and can be viewed as the aggregate of the cognitive, conative and affective processes and functions (*vṛtti*) of phenomenal consciousness, i.e. it consists of a grasping, intentional and volitional consciousness.

3 Monier-Williams, Sir M. (1899) *A Sanskrit-English Dictionary* (Oxford, Oxford University Press) p. 884.

4 Āranya, Swāmi Hariharānanda (1963) *Yoga Philosophy of Patañjali* (Calcultta, Calcutta University Press) p. 1; and Dvivedi, M. N. (1930) *The Yoga-Sūtras of Patañjali* (Adyar, Madras, Theosophical Publishing House) p. 2.

5 Taimni, I. K. (1961) *The Science of Yoga* (Wheaton, IL, The Theosophical Publishing House) p. 6; and Leggett, Trevor (1990) *The Complete Commentary by Śaṇkara on the Yoga Sūtras* (London, Kegan Paul) p. 60.

6 Woods, J. H. (1914) *The Yoga System of Patañjali* (Cambridge, MA, Harvard University Press) p. 8; Koelman, G. M. (1970) *Pātañjala Yoga: From Related Ego to Absolute Self* (Poona, Papal Athenaeum) p. 237; and Feuerstein, Georg (1979) *The Yoga-Sūtra of Patañjali: A New Translation and Commentary* (Folkstone, UK, Wm. Dawson) p. 26.

7 Larson, G. L. & Bhattacharya, R. S. (Eds) (1987) *Sāmkhya*: A Dualist Tradition in Indian Philosophy, Vol. 4 of *The Encyclopedia of Indian Philosophies* (Princeton, NJ, Princeton University Press) p. 28; and Varenne, Jean (1976) *Yoga and the Hindu Tradition* (Chicago, IL, University of Chicago Press) p. 87.

8 Tola, F. & Dragonetti, C. (1987) *The Yogasūtras of Patañjali, On Concentration of Mind* (Delhi, Motilal Banarsidass) p. 5; and Chapple, Christopher Key & Yogi Ananda Viraj (1990) *The Yoga Sūtras of Patañjali* (Delhi, Sri Satguru Publications) p. 33.

9 *VB* 2.18, p. 84; on *saṃyoga* see *YS* 2.17, p. 79.

10 *VB* 2.6, p. 9646.

11 *YS* 2.3–5, pp. 59–63.

12 *YS* 1.4, p.7.

13 *YS* 2.3–9, pp. 59–65.

14 See, for example, Vivekānanda, Swāmi (1977) *The Complete Works of Swāmi Vivekānanda*, 8 Vols (Calcutta, Advaita Ashrama), e.g. vol. 2, pp. 255–256 and vol. 8, p. 48, which takes a very negative approach to the

mind. In an otherwise excellent book, Varenne, op. cit., note 7, appears to support a mind-negative approach to Yoga and qualifies a statement by adding ". . . the *chitta*, whose activity . . . yoga makes it an aim to destroy . . ." (p. 114).

15 Whicher, op. cit., notes, chapter four.
16 See for example *VB* 1.5, p. 10; *YS* 2.15, p. 74. 4.9, p. 181; and *YS* 4.8, p. 180, 4.24, 199.
17 *VB* 2.24, p. 95.
18 *YS* 1.8, p.12.
19 *YS* 3.9, p. 122.
20 *VB* 1.8, p. 13.
21 Whicher, op. cit., note 1, chapter four.
22 For a deeper analysis of this analogical understanding of consciousness see Whicher, op. cit., note 1, chapter 3.
23 *YS* 2.26, p. 96.
24 *YS* 3.49, p. 167.
25 *YS* 1.51, p. 54.
26 Müller, Max (1899) *The Six Systems of India Philosophy* (London, Longmans, Green and Co.) p. 309.
27 Eliade, Mircea (1969) *Yoga: Immortality and Freedom* (Princeton, NJ, Princetown University Press); Koelman, op. cit., note 6; Feuerstein, op. cit., note 6; and Larson, op. cit., note 7.
28 *YS* 2.29, p. 98.
29 *VB* 2.28, p. 98.
30 *YS* 1.48, p. 51.
31 *YS* 3.54–55, p. 174.
32 *VB* 1.18, pp. 21–22.
33 *YS* 1.3, p. 7.
34 *YS* 4.34, p. 207.
35 *YS* 3.54, p. 174.
36 *YS* 4.7, p. 180.
37 *YS* 4.29, p. 202.
38 *YS* 4.30, p. 202.
39 *VB* 4.7, p. 180.
40 *YS* 1.16, p. 19.
41 *VB* 1.16, pp. 19–20.
42 Zaehner, R. C. (1974) *Our Savage God* (London, Collins) pp. 97–98.
43 Scharfstein, B.-A. (1974) *Mystical Experience* (Baltimore, MD, Penguin) pp. 131–132.
44 Feuerstein, op. cit., note 6, p. 81.
45 *YS* 1.33, p. 38.
46 *YS* 2.35, p. 107.
47 *YS* 2.25, p. 96.
48 Feuerstein, Georg (1980) *The Philosophy of Classical Yoga* (Manchester, Manchester University Press) p. 24.
49 *YS* 1.41, p. 43.
50 *VB* 3.55, p. 175.
51 *YS* 1.33, p. 38.
52 *YS* 4.19, p. 194.

53 *VB* 4.30, p. 203.
54 *VB* 3.49, p. 167.
55 *YS* 3.55, p. 175.
56 Koelman, op. cit., note 6, p. 249.
57 Feuerstein, op. cit., note 6, p. 142.
58 *VB* 2.23, p. 91.
59 *YS* 4.18, p. 193.
60 *YS* 2.8, p. 65.
61 *YS* 2.7, p. 64.
62 Whicher, op. cit., note 1, chapter 6.

8

Morals and Society in the Light of Advaita Vedānta

A Reflection

Michael Zammit

In a diary entry dated 21st August 1914, Wittgenstein launched his philosophical enquiry with an admission of having failed to make sense of our understanding of and concern for other people. This was right at the beginning of the war and the young Wittgenstein aptly described in universal terms a deeply entrenched inability of his to relate to his fellow soldiers.

> We tend to take the speech of a Chinese for inarticulate gurgling. Someone who understands Chinese will recognize 'language' in what he hears. Similarly, I often cannot discern the 'humanity' in a man.
>
> (Wittgenstein, 1980)

On another battlefield, in another culture, equally vicious, Prince Arjuna turns to the Lord Krishna, his charioteer, for advice concerning the nature of this selfsame paralysis that strikes at the heart of civilisation, threatening it seriously with dissolution.

Wittgenstein resorts to 'language' perhaps covertly echoing the western attitudes to rationality solidly grounded on the ancient, traditional word-based religions. The concern with language and the similitude drawn between it and 'humanity' fortunately provide prescriptively a way out of the dangerous labyrinthine situation. War is the contradiction of dialectic. The skills for discerning 'the humanity' in men (like those for language) may be innate and universally provided but (as with language) they also need to be cultivated, nurtured, educated. In the Vedāntic tradition the cultivation of those skills serving the purpose of discerning 'the humanity' in men, takes the shape of a moral programme leading to a dissolution of the feeling of isolation, and to a strengthened awareness of others; but it does not stop there. For Vedānta language is certainly a means for putting the end in sight, though out of reach. Conflict is surely the contradiction of dialectic, yet this in turn is not satisfying and certainly not liberating.

Wittgenstein uses the German '*menschen*' for the translated term, 'humanity'. Unfortunately the English term is generic and hints to some 'thing', some essential general entity. On the other hand

> The German word tends to be used to pick out some particular character, concern or even weakness of an individual.
>
> (Tilghman, 1991)

Therefore

> We must keep in mind, . . . that the remark evidences no interest in getting at the 'essence' of the human, but instead in what it is to understand a particular person, his thoughts, feelings and so on, in some particular situation.
>
> (Tilghman, 1991)

The Vedānta philosophy begins right here at this juncture. It addresses humanity at large by reference to the individual human being. Wittgenstein's frank admission expresses vividly the failure that Western philosophy has suffered ever since it embraced wholeheartedly the tenets of Cartesian dualism. It is an admission which the whole of Western civilisation as we know it, and live it, needs to address. Here indeed lies the value of examining some of the principle notions of *Sanātan Dharma* which with a universal gesture may provide even the *mahātmā* Wittgenstein with some means for discerning 'the humanity' in his fellow men, answering our eager call for someone who understands the 'humanity'.

> The word *Sanatan* is made up of two words: *Sada* and *Tan*. *Tan* means the body, inner body. *Sada* means eternal, the 'Body of Eternal Religion', that is *Sanatan Dharma*. *Sanatan Dharma* is the religion of the *Atman* – the natural laws of the *Atman*.
>
> (Saraswati, 1992)

* * *

In Advaita Vedānta the distinction is made between worldly knowledge, through which one associates with things or events, thence deriving pain and/or pleasure; and true knowledge which does not bind, which lies behind the structure of worldly knowledge supporting and inspiring it.

> This is spiritual knowledge. With this we rise above the results of pain and pleasure and enjoy bliss even in the midst of actions.
>
> (Saraswati, 1992)

Elsewhere His Holiness Sri Shantanand Saraswati elaborates on this theme in an enlighting passage which I will quote fully:

> Knowledge is unlimited and available at all times. It manifests itself according to the needs of the time. It is only available when the need arises. The stream of love and truth is one, but man catches it in two different ways, by heart or by mind. By heart he means his love, by mind he means his knowledge. But in fact the stream of love and truth is always the same. It is always present in the world but people will only take as much as their destiny offers, or as they need.
>
> Knowledge is not bound to any land or place. No place is favoured. Knowledge is everywhere, all over. If certain types of people are prepared at a place, they will receive it. Preparation of mind is the only key to where this knowledge will descend. If people at a particular place take to the ordinary way of life, they will get ordinary knowledge. If at a certain place people are preparing themselves for higher knowledge, certainly it will be available. No place is particular for knowledge.
>
> Anywhere, anytime, anybody who is looking for this knowledge must get it, because the Absolute is not for a single race, colour, creed or nation.
>
> (Saraswati, 1992)

The question is: What is meant by people preparing themselves for higher knowledge? What is meant by preparation of mind? Who teaches it?

Knowledge manifests wherever the attention needs to be applied, in any dialogical situation between any teacher who knows and any student who really wants what is being offered. Such roles are taken up in all relational circumstances and events wherever two or more people meet. We will all be teachers or students, sometimes several times in the same conversation. The teacher *is* the student.

What is the mark of a true teacher? The question arises from a recognition that as with 'language', the awareness and appreciation of 'the humanity' in men and therefore higher knowledge, depends entirely on tuition. A note of caution is justified here since the veneration and adulation of false leaders and teachers has sometimes led to atrocities of great shame for mankind.

> We never do evil so fully and cheerfully as when we do it out of conscience.
>
> (Pascal, 1970)

One needs to be intelligent and turn away from fanaticism and idolatry.

The Sanskrit term for teacher, '*guru*', is cognate with the Latin '*gravis*' and primarily means 'heavy, weighty'; then it also refers to

> . . . any venerable or respectable person (father, mother or any relative older than one's self); as also a spiritual parent or preceptor from whom a youth receives the initiatory mantra or prayer, who instructs him in the shāstras and conducts the necessary ceremonies up to that of investiture which is performed by the Āchārya. The word is derived from '*gur*' to raise, lift up (or to make effort), and this in turn is from the '*dhātu*', the seed form '*gṛī*', to call out, to invoke, to mention with praise.
>
> (Monier-Williams, 1974)

The mark of a teacher is steadfastness, respectability, brightness and the ability to respond to situations intelligently. A truly creative situation becomes one in which the teacher/student roles are not allowed to fossilize so that the positions taken up do not become stiff and rigid. Higher knowledge is creative and responsibility is preferred to blind, mechanical reaction. In the *Bhagavad Gītā* a man of knowledge is called *Mahātmā*, one whose self is great and noble.

> At the end of many births, the man of wisdom comes to me (realizing) that Vasudeva is the all: he is the noble-souled (*Mahatman*), very hard to find. [Disc. VII v. 19.]
>
> (Sastri, 1981)

Such a man is taught by comparison, by analogy, by the likeness to himself, to see the same Self everywhere.

> Whoso, by comparison with himself, sees the same everywhere, O Arjuna, be it pleasure of pain, he is deemed the highest Yogin. [Disc. VI v. 32.]
>
> (Sastri, 1981)

This therefore is the first and fundamental tenet of *Sanātan Dharma*, and it goes a long way towards any upgrading of social norms. Seeing that whatever is pleasurable or painful to himself is similarly pleasurable and painful to all beings, a *Mahātmā* will cause no pain to any being, will do no harm and will devote himself to right knowledge.

For such a one society becomes a celebration in sharing the company of *all* human beings; all those that have been, all those that are and that ever will be. The perspective of the Advaitin penetrates the obvious to cull the innermost recesses of the causes and motives of all human actions. His span of vision is widespread and covers the whole spectrum of human nature – from the wretched to the noble, from the dull to the enlightened. The Self, the *Ātman*, he himself underlies it all, pervades it all . . . eternal, unmoving most ancient, the *Ātman* is known (by the *Mahātmā*) to be the Self of all. Whatever anyone, anywhere, seems to do, starts from it, is supported by it and eventually dissolves back into it. The laws of the *Ātman* are the moral laws making the very existence of human society, humanity at large, possible.

In sharp contrast to this 'the dualist's behaviour must forever be hesitant'. For him the tendency

> . . . has been to rely on some distinction between philosophical theory on the one hand and practical behaviour on the other . . . Philosophy never becomes a question of acting . . . because he has no desire to upset the usual pattern of his daily business and, during the course of his philosophical enquiry, life will go on as it always has.
>
> (Tilghman, 1991)

Mithya-jñāna, illusory, mere theoretical knowledge, the source of affection and aversion, is never replaced by *Viveka-jñāna*, right knowledge, whereby the person becomes mindful of *Shāstra* (the Teaching) and is no longer subject to the sway of pleasure and pain.

* * *

Wittgenstein's investigations trace the rise of the Cartesian picture of human beings to the mistaken theory that in language, words mean what they name – a notion that tends to underestimate or even ignore the complex creative system wherein words are dynamically current and alive. If words mean what they name then a person's mental vocabulary would be a private language. Mental events and states would be private objects, allowing for the possibility of people being merely physical bodies inhabited by non-physical minds or souls, turning human beings into a strange amalgam of something that changes and something inhabiting it – making them predictable and easily conformable.

> It follows from Wittgenstein's attack on the very idea of private language that when the dualist says he doubts, whether he says he has specific doubts about this person being in pain or a general doubt about people having any mental life whatsoever, he is not really saying anything at all. He presumably means, let us say, the word 'pain' in the way we all understand it . . . yet in his expression the word is torn loose from its familiar anchorage in life . . . His words are like wheels idling and his language has gone on holiday.
>
> (Tilghman, 1991)

On the other hand the grammar-philosophy of the Sanskrit language, together with the magnificent *mantra shāstras* displace the very possibility of the notion of a private language by tracing and locating the sources of all articulate expression to the universally accessible creative principle in man. In effect the privacy of 'tongues' (as opposed to 'language') cannot be contradicted in the sense that to a non-Chinese speaker, Chinese *is* the private domain of a limited number of people. But the geography of the emergence of language as traced in the Sanskrit grammar-philosophy, spells out the notion that a 'tongue' is merely a reflection, albeit inert and inanimate, of a natural language that all human beings share. A language the best imitation of which is the Sanskrit tongue.

For the purpose of gaining an appreciation of higher knowledge the seeming private ownership of language, and therefore of mind, needs to be relinquished. Vedānta provides the means for doing this. With this objective in view Vedānta prescribes Advaita, non-duality – a difference-less attitude to society rooted in a special type of activity based on the practice of the discipline of non-attachment to the fruit of action (*vairāgya*).

* * *

The purpose of any action, (i.e. the result), like fruit carries within itself the seeds of further actions. This is attractive because the propagation of events provides a powerful fertility metaphor fired by the desire for immortality. Since everlasting life is so ardently desired by all human beings, attachment to the fruits of one's actions becomes anathema to fulfillment, satisfaction and success.

The legitimate urge for the fullness of happiness, omniscience and everlasting life is echoed by an insane attempt aimed at reducing the universal into the particular. Thus recurrence, repetition and idle habitual behaviour are, by a most subtle twist, given support and motivated by the very true human aspiration for the *Ātman*, the immortal. Such a vicious attempt calls for an equal and opposite virtuous *saṇkalpa* – a resolve firmly adhering to the ideal of dissolving *ahaṇkāra* (the ego) – a *dharma* for a renewed world-order inspired by *sanātan* (eternal) principles.

* * *

Sanātan Dharma provides for the 'preparation of mind' referred to by Sri Shantanand Saraswati. The mind in Vedānta is called '*antaḥkar-aṇa*', an inner instrument. 'Inner' in the sense of it not being available to the immediate scrutiny of the 'outer' senses of sight, hearing, taste, touch and smell.

The *antaḥkaraṇa* is complex and composed of several organs, the sovereign being *buddhi*, the intellect – that which, in man, is capable of reflecting the light of the *Ātman*, that by which anyone may discern the truth in anything and discriminate between eternal, never changing principles and transient, ever changing modes of creation. This awareness needs to be drawn out and cultivated (*gṛī*). *Sanātan Dharma*, the religion of the *Ātman*, thus becomes a means for the education of the *buddhi*, placing before it the natural laws of the *Ātman*.

> An example of a natural law is that if somebody wants to speak lies all the day, he just cannot do it. It is impossible because it is not the nature of the Atman to speak a lie. But if somebody wants to speak the truth all day, he can do it. It is not impossible. This is so because the nature of *Atman* is to be truthful – *Atman* truth.
> (Saraswati, 1992)

Sanātan Dharma addresses all men at all times and assumes the total absence of innate or unavoidable sources of conflict between one human being and another. It is not at all necessary to embrace *Sanātan Dharma* since every religion, if followed truthfully, reveals the same basic concept, the same central principles forged from a keen awareness of the unity and the inherent identity of all men.

Thus even at the heart of the Florentine Renaissance for instance, we find the tenets of Advaita expressed in unambiguous terms by men such as Marsilio Ficino (b. 1433). He addresses his friends, the recipients of his letters, by appellations such as 'Magnanimus', a term that literally means *Mahā Ātman*.

In one such letter entitled 'De Humanitate', Ficino writes to Tommaso Minerbetti saying:

> Individual men, formed by one idea in the same image, are *one* man. It is for this reason, I think that of all the virtues, wise men named only one after Man himself: that is humanity, which loves and cares for all men as though they were brothers, born in a long succession of one father.
>
> Therefore, most humane man, persevere in the service of humanity. Nothing is dearer to God than love. There is no surer sign of madness or of future misery than cruelty.
>
> (Ficino, 1975)

To 'love thy neighbour as thyself' in the Vedānta of non-duality, is an injunction based on the *dharmic* tenet stating that 'the Self, the *Paramātman*, is real'. To the practicing student of Vedānta the world starts to become understood (and experienced) from a substantially different emotional ground (called *bhāwana*). Insofar as the *ahaṅkāra* (the ego) is abandoned, in exactly the same measure is one's neighbour *known* as oneself.

In the *Brihadāraṇyaka Upanishad*, Prajāpati's instruction to mankind is 'to give'. Shaṅkara explains:

> Distribute your wealth to the best of your power, for you are by nature avaricious.
>
> (Madhavananda, 1975)

This is not the easiest of lessons to learn especially since (as is plainly stated) one is actually contradicting one's own nature (albeit 'avaricious'), and yet it is prescribed for liberation (*moksha*). Its reach is wide and subtle:

> '*Rā dāne*'; in the act of giving, giving up, communicating, imparting, teaching, restoring, adding, donation and gift . . . in these acts there arises the seed sound '*rā*'.
>
> '*Rā*' means to grant, bestow, give, impart, yield and surrender, and from it the Sanskrit derives '*rai*', meaning property, possessions, goods, wealth, riches.

> '*Rai*' in turn becomes '*re-*', stem of '*res*', a thing; which stem, with the suffix '*-alis*' in Latin, becomes '*realis*'.
>
> (Monier-Williams, 1974)

This fascinating derivation links the term 'reality' to the act of giving via the Sanskrit etymology, supplementing and enriching our understanding of the notion of the real. It is saying that the real arises in the act of giving, the real is experienced as an effect of renunciation. The real is the supreme *Ātman*, the *Param Ātman*.

> Attachment means to consider as ours what really belongs to God. Our body, our house, our wealth, our son etc. Give up this feeling and you get rid of all your troubles. Do not think that the world around you is insubstantial. Rather it is your feeling of attachment to it that is insubstantial. Whatever is happening around you is right. What is wrong about it is the view you are taking of it. If you could correct your viewpoint, you would be happy!
>
> (Saraswati, 1992)

* * *

In conclusion it may be said that for the Vedāntin, human beings are human beings all the world over, made in the image of the one Self of all, the *Paramātman*; and making allowance for differences in place and circumstance there is nothing especially good or especially bad about any one person.

As a step towards an ideal, the concept of brotherhood may be excellent, but the assumption of duality that is inbuilt into it is laden with the possibility of conflict and violence. To take an archetypal instance of this, the first human child born according to the Bible, was a murderer and its brother was its victim. The notion of brotherhood falls short of truth. It needs to develop into the Vedāntic realisation that 'I am the Self of all'; if it is going to serve humanity at all.

> The social and moral implications of this doctrine are clear. The doctrine of the unity of the spirit is the foundation of all morality, both social and individual. No one tries to harm himself; so how can one who *knows* that each and every living being is his own Self, harm anybody? There is no room here for narrow nationalism or psychological individualism. The greatness of the doctrine of Advaita makes nonsense of all war, social

exploitation and desire to achieve national superiority; it strikes at the roots of social and individual evils and leaves no room for international friction; it permits no inquisition, but gives freedom to each and everyone to live a life of righteousness.

(Shastri, 1985)

Michael Zammit, University of Malta

REFERENCES

FICINO, M. (1975) *The Letters of Marsilio Ficino, Vol. 1.* (London, Shepheard-Walwyn) pp. 100–101.

MADHAVANANDA SWAMI (Trans.) (1975) *The Brihadāraṇyaka Upaniṣad with the commentary of Śaṅkarācārya* (Calcutta, Advaita Ashrama).

MONIER-WILLIAMS, M. (1974) *A Sanskrit-English Dictionary* (Oxford, Oxford University Press).

PASCAL, B. (1970) A. J. KRAILSHEIMER (Trans.) *Pensées* (Harmondsworth, Penguin Bks. Ltd.) pp. 272.

SARASWATI, Sri SHANTANAND (1992) *Good Company* (Shaftesbury, Element Bks. Ltd.) pp. 91, 109, 110, 124, 139.

SASTRI, A. M. (Trans.) (1981) *The Bhagavad Gita* (Madras, Santa Bks.).

SHASTRI, H. P. (1985) *Direct Experience of Reality* (London, Shanti Sadan) pp. 37, 38.

TILGHMAN, B. R. (1991) *Wittgenstein, Ethics and Aesthetics: The View from Eternity* (London, the Macmillan Press Ltd.) pp. 92, 98, 99, 101, 102.

WITTGENSTEIN, L. (1980) G. H. von WRIGHT (Ed.) P. WINCH (Trans.) *Culture and Value* (Chicago, University of Chicago Press).

9

The Function of Theatre in Society

A Reading of the Nāṭyaśāstra

Daniel Meyer-Dinkgräfe

Theatre is frequently regarded as a mirror of the society that produces it in its different forms. The function of theatre, it is then held, is to awaken the spectators to the problems of life in society. In reaching the spectators, theatre can adopt two main channels: the intellect (mainly addressed by Brecht's alienation effect), or the emotions (Aristotle's catharsis). Any combination of the two is possible.

The major Indian treatise on drama and theatre, the *Nāṭyaśāstra*, goes much further in its claims for the position of theatre in society. The origin of the *Nāṭyaśāstra* dates back several thousand years. Originally handed down in an oral tradition, it was written down between the first century B.C. and the eighth century A.D.-scholars disagree about the exact date of the manuscripts (Kale, 1974, p. 1). The authorship is ascribed to Bharata Muni, although this issue is debated also among scholars (Srinivasan, 1981). According to the text, when the Golden Age (*Kṛtayuga*) had given way to the Silver Age (*Tretāyuga*), the gods, with Indra as their head approached the creator, Brahma, asking him to create 'an object of diversion, which must be audible as well as visible' (Ghosh, 1950, I.12). As members of the lowest caste, the *Śūdras*, were not allowed to listen to the Vedas and were thus excluded from their purifying effect, Brahma was asked to 'be pleased to create another Veda which will belong to all the Colour-groups (*varṇa*)' (ibid.). Brahma created the *Nāṭya*, drama, as a fifth Veda, compiling it from the four main vedas *Ṛg-*, *Sāma-*, *Yajur-*, and *Atharvaveda*.

> The recitative (*pāṭhya*) he took from the Rgveda, the song from the Saman, the Histrionic Representation (*abhinaya*) from the Yajus, and Sentiments (*rasa*) from the Atharvaveda, [and] thus

> was created the Nāṭyaveda connected with the Vedas principal and subsidiary (*vedopaveda*), by the holy Brahman who knows [them] all. (ibid., I.17–18)

The reference to '*vedopaveda*' means that the subsidiary Vedas, i.e. *Upavedas*, are also connected with *Nāṭyaveda*: *Ayurveda* (Science of medicine) is related to *Ṛg-Veda*, *Gandharva-Veda* (musical science) to *Sāmaveda*, *Dhanurveda* (Science of archery, social, political life) to *Yajurveda*, and *Sthapatyaveda* (science of architecture) to the *Artharvaveda*.

Thus based on the holy scriptures and created by the creator himself, drama according to the *Nāṭyaśāstra* is a 'mimicry of actions and conducts of people, (. . .) of the exploits of gods, Asuras, kings as well as householders in this world' (ibid., I. 111–112 and I.120). There is 'no wise maxim, no learning, no art or craft, no device, no action that is not found in the drama (*nāṭya*)' (ibid., I.116). The stories to be dramatised are taken from Vedic works and semi-historical texts (ibid., I.119), (*itihāsā*, i.e. *Mahābhārata* and *Rāmāyana*). The benefits of drama for the spectator are many: Drama

> teaches duty to those bent on doing their duty, love to those eager for its fulfillment, and it chastises those who are illbred or unruly, promotes self-restraint in those who are disciplined, gives courage to cowards, energy to heroic persons, enlightens people of poor intellect and gives wisdom to the learned. This gives diversion to kings, and firmness [of mind] to persons afflicted with sorrow, and [hints of acquiring] money to those who are for earning it, and brings composure to persons of agitated mind. (ibid., I.108–109)

Drama furthermore is conducive to 'fame, long life, intellect and general good' and will 'educate people' (ibid., I.114–115).

How does theatre that follows the detailed instructions of the *Nāṭyaśāstra* hope to achieve all these beneficial effects it claims to have? In specific situations laid down in the play (determinant, *vibhāva*), the actor has to use specific means of histrionic representation (consequents, *anubhāva*) to create the dominant emotional states (*sthāyibhāva*). There are eight dominant states, love, mirth, sorrow, anger, energy, terror, disgust and astonishment (ibid., VI.17). Those dominant states combine with transitory states (*vyabhicāribhāva*) and temperamental states (*sāttvikabhāva*). There are thirtythree transitory states, such as discouragement, weakness, apprehension, envy, intoxication; and eight temperamental states: paralysis, perspiration, horripilation, change of voice, trembling, change of colour, weeping and fainting (ibid., VI. 18–21). The temperamental states refer to expressions of emotion usually considered to be in the domain of the autonomous nervous system and beyond the influence of the will (Ambardekar, 1979, p.26.). The combination of dominant states, transitory states and temperamental states leads to the major underlying sentiment of the play, *rasa*. *Rasa* has been translated as aesthetic experience, sentiment, taste, or flavour. The eight sentiments are the erotic, comic, pathetic, furious, heroic, terrible, odious, and marvellous. The eight dominant states correspond directly to the eight *rasas*.

Having described this interaction of dominant states, transitory states, and temperamental states in creating a specific sentiment (*rasa*) in the context of specific dramatic situations (determinants), the *Nāṭyaśāstra* goes on in substantial detail to describe the consequents, i.e. the means of histrionic representation. Individual chapters deal with gestures of minor limbs, hands, other limbs, combinations of movements, different gaits; different parts of the stage have different specific functions in the play; rules of prosody and metrical patterns are established, as well as rules on the diction of the play, on modes of address and intonation. Whereas the chapters mentioned so far may easily claim universality beyond the limits of the time and place of origin, this is more problematic with chapters on the rules of the usage of local (Sanskrit) dialects, kinds of Sanskrit drama and structural elements of those plays. All elements, however, whether universal or restricted to the plays known in the time of the writing or compilation of the *Nāṭyaśāstra*, have one aim in common: they are all descriptions of how to achieve the major sentiment or sentiments (*rasa*) in the performance.

It is rewarding to assess the *Nāṭyaśāstra* in the light of the psychology of its own sphere, psychology as it developed in India. I will limit my analysis to the concepts of Vedic psychology as recently reformulated by Maharishi Mahesh Yogi. He is the disciple of the late Swami Brahmananda Saraswati (1869–1953), who held the position of Śaṅkarācārya of Jyotir Math for the last 13 years of his life. This is one of four monasteries in India founded by the sage and philosopher Śaṅkara to safeguard the tradition of his Advaita Vedanta philosophy. Brahmananda Saraswati has been called 'Vedanta incarnate' by India's first President, Radhakrishnan (Campbell, 1975). As Brahmananda Saraswati's disciple, Maharishi Mahesh Yogi is in the direct line of Śaṅkara's Advaita Vedanta philosophy. In recent years, Maharishi Mahesh Yogi has, together with faculty at Maharishi

International University in the USA, reformulated Indian psychology as Vedic psychology (Orme-Johnson, 1988).

Vedic psychology proposes '(. . .) an architecture of increasingly abstract, functionally integrated faculties or levels of mind' (Alexander, 1990, p.290). This hierarchy ranges from gross to subtle, from highly active to settled, from concrete to abstract, and from diversified to unified (ibid.). The senses constitute the grossest, most highly active, most concrete and most diversified level of the mind, followed by desire, the thinking mind, the discriminating intellect, feeling and intuition, and the individual ego. Vedic psychology uses the term 'mind' in two ways: 'It refers to the overall multilevel functioning of consciousness as well as to the specific level of thinking (apprehending and comparing) within that overall structure' (ibid.). Underlying the subtlest level, that of the individual ego, and transcendental to it, is the Self, 'an abstract, silent, completely unified field of consciousness' (ibid.). Each subtler level is able to 'observe and monitor the more expressed levels' (Alexander, 1986). Thus, the emotions, apparently the main target of performance according to the *Nāṭyaśāstra*, are subtler than the intellect or mind. Consequently, taking *rasa* to refer to the level of the emotions, a performance can affect spectators more deeply if the performance is directed at the spectators' emotions. Moreover, the emotions are 'closer' to the transcendental level of the mind, the Self, thus allowing easier access to this field. Empirical evidence suggests that transcendental consciousness is a field that links all individuals (Travis, 1989), parallel to Jung's concept of the collective unconscious, only that pure, transcendental consciousness is proposed to be directly, consciously experienceable, e.g. through meditation techniques such as Transcendental Meditation

Rather than assuming *rasa*, translated as 'sentiment' to refer solely to the level of the emotions, its range can be extended to the level of transcendental consciousness. The performer, initially, creates *rasa* in himself, arising from the transcendental Self as the basis of the mind, and encompassing, by definition, not only the emotions, but all levels of the expressed mind, i.e. ego, emotions, intellect, mind, desire and senses. This state of *rasa* is communicated to the spectators on all those levels of the mind, the most important of which is the basis, transcendental Self.

Thus, the functioning of performance is dependent on the level of consciousness of both the performer and the individual spectators. This applies to all levels of the mind, including its basis, transcendental consciousness. Vedic psychology not only describes distinct levels of the mind, but also proposes higher stages of the development of consciousness, stages that go beyond the ordinary states of waking, dreaming, and sleeping. The development is characterised initially by glimpses of a simultaneity of experience of transcendental consciousness together with either waking, or dreaming, or sleeping. When transcendental consciousness is permanently experienced together with any of the other three, this state is called cosmic consciousness, or *Turyateet Chetna*.

The further developed the consciousness of the performer, understood according to the concepts of Vedic psychology described above, the better will the performer be able to produce *rasa* within himself, and the more impact will he have on the spectators on all levels of the mind. The more advanced the consciousness of the spectators, the more will they be able to receive the stimuli from the performer, again on all levels of the mind. Theatre, then, can be perceived as an instrument of developing consciousness, both for the performer and the spectator, because of the mutual feedback on the basis of the proposed unified field of transcendental consciousness.

Viewed from the perspective of Vedic psychology, then, theatre in line with the *Nāṭyaśāstra* is able to significantly influence the consciousness of both actor and spectator. The effect of that influence is not limited to the performance: changes in consciousness are permanent, and accumulative; theatre in line with the *Nāṭyaśāstra* has the dimension of 'transformation', as opposed to 'transportation', in Schechner's terminology (Schechner, 1985, p.125). Repeated exposure to performance will cause development of consciousness in both actor and spectator. As both are more and more active on the level of a unified field of consciousness, linking all individuals, no matter whether present at a particular performance or not, an enlivening of that field will have beneficial effects also on those members of a society who do not participate in the performance. The field nature of pure or transcendental consciousness, the Self as described by Vedic psychology, is corroborated by EEG studies:

> In ten trials, EEG was concurrently measured from pairs of subjects, one practicing Transcendental Meditation and the TM-Sidhi-technique of 'Yogic Flying' (Yfg) – said to enliven the proposed field of consciousness – and the other performing a computer task. . . . [A]nalysis indicated that coherence changes in the . . . band sensitive to TM and Yfg, consistently led coherence changes in the other subject's . . . band. A clear relationship was

seen among subjective reports, coherence patterns, and strength of intervention effects (Travis, 1989, p. 203).

Given that theatre can affect the consciousness of actor and spectator, and also the consciousness of individuals not involved in the performance at all, several issues need further discussion: how to safeguard that this very powerful tool is not misused for manipulation; what effect will the theory have on the 'canon' of plays currently performed in theatres around the world; and what will be the implications for new writing?

Daniel Meyer-Dinkgräfe, Department of Theatre, Film and Television Studies, University of Wales Aberystwyth, 1 Laura Place, Dyfed, Wales, SY23 2AH

REFERENCES

ALEXANDER, CHARLES N., ROBERT W. CRANSON, ROBERT W. BOYER, DAVID ORME-JOHNSON (1986) Transcendental Consciousness: A Fourth State of Consciousness beyond Sleep, Dream, and Waking, in JAYNE GACKENBACH (Ed) *Sleep and Dream. A Sourcebook* (New York, London, Garland Publishing).

ALEXANDER, CHARLES N. *et al.* (1990) Growth of Higher Stages of Consciousness: Maharishi's Vedic Psychology of Human Development, in: CHARLES N. ALEXANDER & ELLEN J. LANGER (Eds.) *Higher Stages of Human Development. Perspectives on Human Growth* (New York, Oxford, Oxford University Press).

AMBARDEKAR, R.R. (1979) *Rasa Structure of the Meghaduta* (Bombay, Andreesh Prakashan).

CAMPBELL, ANTHONY (1975) *The Mechanics of Enlightenment. An Examination of the Teaching of Maharishi Mahesh Yogi* (London, Gollancz).

GHOSH, MANOMOHAN (1950) *The Nāṭyaśāstra. A Treatise on Hindu Dramaturgy and Histrionics,* Ascribed to Bharata Muni (The Royal Asiatic Society of Bengal: Calcutta).

KALE, PRAMOD (1974) *The Theatrical Universe, A Study of the Nāṭyaśāstra* (Bombay, Popular Prakashan).

ORME-JOHNSON, DAVID (1988) The Cosmic Psyche, *Modern Science and Vedic Science* 2:2, pp. 113–163.

SCHECHNER, RICHARD (1985), *Between Theatre and Anthropology* (Philadelphia: University of Pennsylvania Press).

SRINIVASAN, SRINIVAS AYYA (1980) *On the Composition of the Nāṭyaśāstra* (Reinbek, Dr. Inge Wezler Verlag Für Orientališche Fachpublikationen).

TRAVIS, FREDERICK T. and DAVID ORME-JOHNSON (1989) Field Model of Consciousness: EEG Coherence Changes as Indicators of Field Effects, *International Journal of Neuroscience* 49:3, 4, pp. 203–211.

10

Paths to Perfection

Yoga and Confucian*

Frank R. Podgorski

At first sight, to juxtapose the 'vision' etched by Confucius, Mencius and their followers side-by-side with the inner paths recommended by Patañjali, Īśvarakṛṣṇa and the Yoga tradition seems foolish. The thrust of these Chinese and Indian paths to perfection seems sharply contradictory; they point to two very different experiences. The Sāṃkhya-Yoga tradition attests to a concentrated 'inner journey', to a radical probing of 'inwardness'. From the time of the Indus Valley civilisation (c.2,500 BCE), Yogis have focused on probing 'inner-space'. Indian explorations of the psyche, the human spirit, and the body-mind-spirit continuum have become renowned. Ultimately, Yoga identifies the hidden meaning of everyone as '*puruṣa*'. '*Puruṣa*' is our deepest 'consciousness', 'spirit', 'illumination', or simply our authentic and genuine hidden identity as a human being. This 'self-discovery', claim the Yogis, is verified by journeying within oneself. Quite naturally then, this search for '*puruṣa*' became a preoccupation and an all-consuming goal for the Yogis – even at the cost of an almost total disregard for the social order. Traditional values such as family, society, social growth and development became insignificant. Is it any wonder then that the great scholar of Yoga, Mircea Eliade, criticised Yoga as ultimately 'selfish' and self-centered?

Nothing would seem to contrast more sharply with this experience than the catalyst for human growth emerging from the Confucian tradition. The Chinese thrust is markedly external, proposing both societal and individual paths of progress and perfectibility. Long before Five-Year Plans, Confucius advocated social development

*Previously published in *Asian Philosophy*, Vol. 4, No. 2, 1994.

produced through an awakening of 'human consciousness'. Focusing on the 'four seeds'[1] of human potential, Mencius tested the Confucian intuition of innate human goodness of the 'heart-mind' (*xin*) by specific acts and actions of verification. Confucian *li*, prescribed modes of human conduct, challenge the potential of every human being. The emerging Confucian ideal then focused on each individual located within a specific societal context; precise acts and actions challenge each person to a fuller and more complete understanding and appreciation of the meaning of humanity, society, and their underlying foundations. If a particular act or rite or mode of conduct (*li*) catalyses the human foundation of *ren*, it is valuable; if not, it ought to be discarded. With such a practical approach to 'social engineering', is it any wonder that some thinkers have described Confucianism as almost three millennia of probing the mystery of all that it means to be a human being situated within the milieu of a particular society? In dramatic contrast to the inward search of the Yogis, Confucianism attested to what Joseph Needham later described as a "naturalistic universe"[2] containing an almost "gestalt-like cosmogonic Unity"[3] of humanity (*ren*), earth or nature (*di*), and Heaven (*tian*) linked within a mammoth "organismic cosmology".[4] Thus the germs of Confucius and Mencius developed into explicit attempts to discover the meaning of humanity and human conduct within the realities of family, home and society. Such external 'self-cultivation' and verification is far from the solipsistic inner journey of the Yogis.

Yet are there meeting-points? Are there ideals common to these two very different plans for human self-discovery? In the spirit of an exploratory conversation, the models of human development emerging from these two traditions will be studied.

THE YOGA TRADITION

What does a Yogi seek? Exactly what do Yogis mean by '*puruṣa* in *kaivalya*' (consciousness in total isolation); what is this '*samādhi*' proclaimed by so many generations of Yogis?

Within India, the Yoga tradition is commonly known as the Sāṃkhya-Yoga *darśana* (perspective). Implicit in this name is the assumption that the techniques and practices of Yoga can be understood fully *only* in the light of the cosmology, metaphysics and psychology of this related Sāṃkhyan tradition. Although the roots of Yoga spirituality may be traced to several Indus Valley archaeological finds as well as to a variety of Vedic, Upaniṣadic and Epic texts, including especially the celebrated *Bhagavad-Gītā*, two somewhat later texts, the *Yoga Sūtra* and the *Sāṃkhya-kārikā*, refined the spiritual journey proposed by Yoga. These two texts succinctly link Yoga techniques with Sāṃkhyan theory. Significantly from the close of this classical era (c. fourth century AD) until our age, very few changes in Yoga have taken place. If we wish to discover *puruṣa*, we must begin by studying the perspective emerging from these classical texts.

Yoga invites to a profound inward journey which radically challenges each Yogi to disengage, decondition, and overcome completely what is commonly referred to as phenomenal life or the realities of daily living. Thus the basic Yoga orientation contrasts sharply with the traditional Confucian concern for the realities of human society. So radical a change is proposed by Yoga that Mircea Eliade wonders whether the Yogi who attains '*puruṣa*-realisation' ought still be considered human.[5] Yet the liberated Yogi does proclaim a permanent identification as a 'consciousness' completely separated from all forms of matter (*prakṛti*). In order to appreciate this liberated consciousness, we must turn to the Yoga texts to observe how this Sāṃkhya-Yoga "psycho-spiritual journey of transvaluation"[6] is understood. As that inner journey during which a Yogi shifts from an identity tied to ego to a far more profound sense of self-understanding as 'consciousness' totally removed from all vestiges of materiality emerges, four moments of increasingly rarefied consciousness become distinguishable. Let us now follow this yogic journey of inner quest.

OUR MOMENT OF HUMAN AWARENESS

Ahaṃkāra which translates both as 'self-awareness' and 'ego-assertion' is the Yogic description of the first moment of human awakening, our initial awakening to human consciousness. As each person awakens, the realisation soon dawns that we are really a paradox. On the one hand, it is most natural to posit identity in the very forms of matter which envelop and apparently define us; emerging human consciousness awakens but is limited by a particular body, ego, and mind which interpret, modify and colour our awareness. Yet immediately these very surrounding material forms are observed to be always changing and ever in flux. Analysing this, the *Sāṃkhya-kārikā* begins by describing every human being as 'suffering' (*duḥkha*) precisely because of a foundational dysfunction. To entrust total identity to any form of frustrating, ever-changing matter is precisely the human dilemma, protest the Yogis. Common human consciousness routinely settles for an identity which is too humble, for far less than what a human person truly is.

Yoga cosmology maintains that 23 hidden elements of noumenal matter (*prakṛti*) – forms of materiality so fine that they are unobservable to sense experience – underlie all phenomenal experience. Thirteen of these elements unfold into the subtle material unit that becomes the human psyche whereas ten other more clustered forms of 'matter' evolve into all that becomes objective reality. Yoga theory maintains that these twenty-three noumenal elements support and evolve into all phenomena of common experience. Within this perspective, *ahaṃkāra* (self-awareness or ego assertion) is critical and decisive; it formulates the fundamental human distinction between 'a subject which knows' and an object which is 'known', thus enabling human knowledge and acts to unfold. Some Yoga commentaries even proclaim *ahaṃkāra* to be the real creator of each person and the entire phenomenal world.

Yet the Yoga tradition actually sees the formulation of the human psyche and the formation of each individual as a descent or fall from a previously unmanifest idealised state to our current human dilemma of misplaced identification. Potential matter (*prakṛti*), stimulated by the proximity of consciousness (*puruṣa*), evolves into *ahaṃkāra*, that 'self-awareness' or 'ego-assertion' which allows human beings and our observable world to become manifest. Although the texts depict our human situation as a moment of suffering, this is not entirely an 'unhappy moment'. Indeed, *ahaṃkāra* introduces the unique value of human consciousness; it is the first human step in the search for *puruṣa*.

Although it is most natural that everyone, awakening to consciousness, almost automatically identifies the self with our surrounding body, mind, psyche and ego, the Yogis charge that this is a radical underestimation and denigration of the nature and value of the human condition. Life is so much more than mere ego. As long as one remains content with only an empirical identity, a frustrating life of 'suffering' (*duḥkha*) continues. From this radical human underestimation, Yoga proposes a 'psycho-spiritual' journey to authentic identity. Significantly, at the very beginning of this journey, the Yoga Sūtras detail explicit efforts to still all movements of body, mind, psyche and ego. Equally significant, the investment of an identity in *ahaṃkāra* is openly challenged. *Ahaṃkāra* is even called a 'conceit' or 'pride' (SK XXIV: *abhimāna*); such pride is precisely the overexaltation of observable material identity. There is 'something more', Yoga proclaims.

On account of all this, Yoga recommends a deliberate sustained effort to break away from all forms of ego-identity; it points to the deliberate pursuit of a more enduring sense of existence. This intense concentrated discipline is the key to Yoga. The very light of limited, frustrated human consciousness suggests and gives promise of a more illuminating 'consciousness' awaiting within ourselves.

THE MOMENT OF THE PSYCHE

Once the limitations of a misplaced sense of identity have been acknowledged, a specific Yogic healing cure is prescribed. The texts describe an ever-deepening process of interiorisation, an ever-opening process of mental discrimination, a search for even more 'light'. Deliberately stilling body, mind and the senses, Yoga concentrates more directly on consciousness. Contemplating such 'light' results in a gradual defocusing on 'matter'; slowly the identities of the Yogi changes. Our basic instrument of knowledge, the psyche, becomes recognised as an independent unity called the 'subtle body'. This 13-dimensional subjective psyche, together with its supporting sheath[7] is discovered to be a unit capable of retaining a basic sense of individuality. Although no longer tied to the gross matter of our observable world, this meta-empirical unit retains an attachment to subtle matter. Yet, insofar as interior spiritual 'light' dominates consciousness more, so proportionately does the Yogi's meta-empirical ego become less linked to matter; the ego now defines itself in subtle and no longer in gross matter.[8] This shift in identity is the second major step in the Yogic journey. This realisation parallels our common human aspiration to immortality, our projection of a presumed identity thought to be capable of lasting forever.

Yet even though considerably more 'light' has been realised, matter (*prakṛti*) still lingers in a recognisable form; an ego-identity defined in subtle matter still perdures. As long as egoness remains, so also does the pain of misidentity. "Suffering is of the nature of things until the deliverance of the subtle body." (SK LV). An ego-identity articulated in subtle matter is again but a temporary identity in quest of a more perduring and authentic identification. Yogis call this the moment of the 'subtle body'.

THE MOMENT OF WISDOM

Yoga now speaks of a moment of transition, a 'final yet liberating self-recognition', a wisdom of 'cosmic consciousness' which the Sāṃkhyan has labelled '*buddhi*', a moment of profound spiritual learning which immediately precedes total liberation from matter. *Buddhi* is that pregnant moment when the 'light' of *puruṣa* becomes so attractive that all desire for ego-assertion fades and dissolves. An ever-widening appreciation of the unlimited range of consciousness overcomes attraction towards any form of phenomenal experience. Authentic identification can only be *puruṣa*, never any lingering strand of *prakṛti*. Egoness opens to a more profound I; the Yogi is now on the brink of total self-discovery.

Traditionally, *buddhi* is considered a moment of profound wisdom. What has been learned? The Yogi has mastered the laws of nature. He now knows that matter both unfolds and refolds in a cycle designed to awaken total consciousness. Consequently, he is able to diagnose and overcome his foundational misidentity with the various costumes of matter. Matter is but a tool whose sole purpose is the liberation of *consciousness*.[9] *Consciousness* is now appreciated as radically different from all forms of materiality. The brilliance of *puruṣa* becomes clearer and more dominating; even our basic human distinction between a subject which knows and object which is known fades as human knowledge opens to transphenomenal wisdom.

The Yogi is now on the verge of learning a unique lesson: authentic identity must be found in that which is other than matter. Initially, human awareness introduced reflection, the beginning of an ever-deepening process of interiorisation. Reflection first separated the body, the mind, the will, the emotions, and finally even the ego, from this hidden and deeper consciousness. Now all that remains is the experience of authentic identification as that consciousness which is totally other than all forms of matter.

THE MOMENT OF LIBERATION

It is but one short yet radical leap from *buddhi* to the radiance of consciousness in total isolation (*samādhi; puruṣa* in *kaivalya*). Contemplative realisation is now an apt descriptive. The ego having been abandoned, the Yogi focuses directly on the 'light' of consciousness (*puruṣa*). Herein is uncovered the deepest meaning of I, the answer to that primordial question of identity first raised by *ahaṃkāra*. 'I' realises genuine and lasting meaning, I admits that I am neither ego nor mind nor emotion; I proclaims I am unentangled consciousness, pure knowing, perfect seeing. Transphenomenal identification is awakened and freed from all entanglement in matter; a previously concealed sense of self emerges. This yogic liberation resembles what several other religious traditions term salvation. In a strikingly similar passage, the Western monk Thomas Merton writes:

> Contemplation is not and cannot be a function of an external self. There is an incredible opposition between the deep, transcendent Self that awakens in contemplation, and the superficial, external self which we commonly identify with the first person singular . . . This superficial I is not our real self. It is our 'individuality' and our 'empirical self' but it is not the hidden and mysterious person in whom we subsist before the eyes of God. This I that works in the world, thinks about itself, observes its own reactions, and talks about itself, *is not the true I* . . . This self is doomed to disappear as completely as smoke from a chimney. *Contemplation is precisely the awareness that this I is really 'not I' but an awakening of the unknown I that is beyond observation.*[10]

Samādhi or *puruṣa* in *kaivalya*, the goal of the Yogis, testifies to a release into the absolute realms of consciousness following an austere, disciplined journey or inner search. The Yogi opens a whole new sense of identification; an entirely new mode of existence emerges. For the realised Yogi, liberation means the uncovering of a formerly hidden but authentic self. Although this transition in understanding, this transvaluation, takes place within, it is thought capable of completely freeing the Yogi from the phenomenal world. Perfect consciousness overcomes the fundamental human dilemma of misplaced identification. We are far more than mere individual egos.

Yet how has the Yoga tradition understood this consciousness? *Puruṣa* resembles a lamp which illuminates. Ordinarily human knowledge is filtered and coloured through the shrouded medium of *ahaṃkāra*; it is thus but a partial vision, an imperfect way of knowing. In contrast, the brilliant illumination of the liberated Yogi is a pure seeing, a perfect knowing, an isolated consciousness, a perfect contemplation. This Yoga experience claims to infinitely surpass and transcend limited human seeing and knowing. Yogic speculation suggests 'isolated consciousness', radiant seers and brilliantly enlightened knowers as the ultimate Yogic goal.

What effect does the uncovering of authenticity have on the Yogi? What reorientation is demanded? The answer has to be total: the realised Yogi is challenged to radically reorient fundamental attitudes and values. No longer can the Yogi judge himself to be simply a human being; rather transphenomenal *puruṣa* reorients all basic values and judgments. An entirely new perspective emerges. Even the Yogi's former assumption of entanglement within matter must be re-evaluated and discarded as a mere empirical perspective. The liberated Yogi ponders the mystery and paradox of *puruṣa*'s eternal freedom. "No one is bound, no one is released . . . Only matter in its various forms is bound and released." (SK LXII)

Who am I? *Puruṣa* is the clear and unequivocal answer of the Yogis. The liberated Yogi proclaims: 'I am unentangled consciousness, pure seeing, an authentic self which always was free but yet never fully appreciated and realised'. This radical epistemic change, this total reassessment, this recognition of a formerly hidden mode of being and existence is Yogic liberation; here everyone discovers a permanent and authentic identification. The testimony of the Yogis then is that we are not matter but rather consciousness or spirit to which all forms and shapes and unfolding of matter eternally testify.

Fig. 1 summarises and maps the Sāṃkhya-Yoga psycho-spiritual path to human perfection.

THE CONFUCIAN PERSPECTIVE[11]

Shifting focus from our Yoga model, we now turn to the Confucian perspective.

In dramatic contrast to Yoga's inward search for the transphenomenal, China's focus has never been confronted with the charge of 'world-fleeing selfishness' that critics sometimes bring against the ascetical practices of the Yogis. Confucianism has always concentrated on stimulating and developing the maximal potential of 'the human', humanity and society. From the time of Confucius (c. 551–479 BCE) right up to and including our own day, the Chinese mind has always been intrigued with questions of human development. Within this humanistic laboratory, China has discovered a profound understanding and respectful appreciation for the integral and intertwined depths of each human being. So special is this insight that some Westerners speak of this experience as a Chinese description of 'immanence' or 'sacredness'.[12]

When Ancient China began to probe 'humanness', an initial

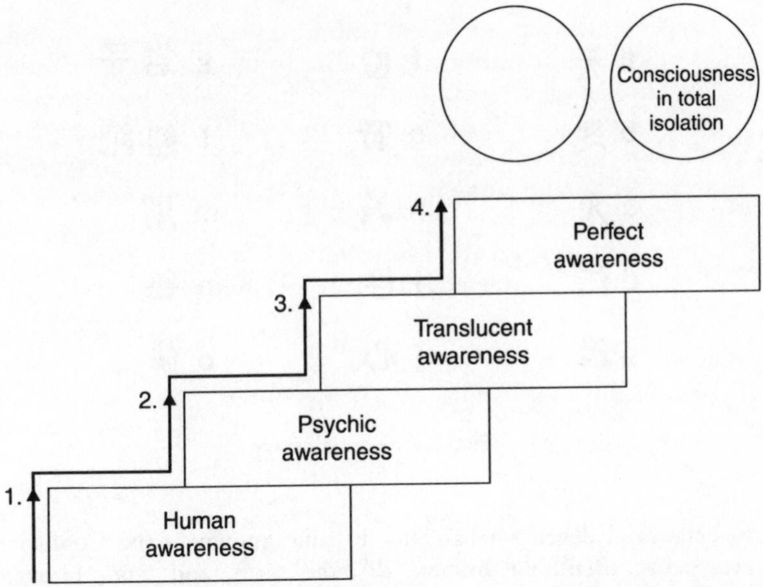

FIG. 1. A Sāṃkhya map of inner journey

problem confronted the Chinese mind at the outset. What word or concept could possibly symbolise the richness of the basic experience of being a human being, of simply being 'human'? What ideogram could express all that it means to be human? *Ren*[d] the symbol chosen, is really a combination of two ideograms, one indicating human experience, the other emphasising 'two' and perhaps even suggesting 'community'. An immediate implication of this basic ideogram is that a single solipsistic person in total isolation is an anomaly and perhaps even a contradiction in nature. A single totally isolated person, such as the Yogis idealised, seems less than fully human to the mind of China. Rather, *ren*[d] implies that 'humanness' must always be understood in terms of relationships. This foundational ideogram hints at the Community and the 'humanness' and humaneness that China would come to explore with such thoroughness in the centuries ahead.

Like a visionary architect, Confucius etched a blueprint for a worldview that concentrated on stimulating human growth and development. All depends on human perfectibility. Yet as the very foundational ideogram *ren*[d] emphasises, a human being is by nature either isolated nor alone; rather three pivotal pillars gradually emerge

a 天	f 禮	k 君子
b 地	g 智	l 禮記
c 人	h 誠	m 周
d 仁	i 性	n 德
e 我	j 心	o 儒

FIG. 2. Chinese glossary

to detail and develop what later became known as the Confucian perspective. *Ren*[c], the human, *di*[b], the earth, and *tian*[a], Heaven, interrelate and intertwine within a wondrously harmonious whole. The rhythms of all three must be heard if one is ever to cope with the mystery of existence; similarly any viable plan for growth and development must respond to the exact challenges of each pillar. Accordingly, the Confucian Classics[13] developed precise plans for integrated, enlightened growth. Significantly, this Chinese focus on growth and development is described in terms of 'self-cultivation'.

The Confucians sounded a note of optimism, a hope grounded in a unique understanding of the nature (*xin*[i]) of the human. According to the Han thinkers, 'whatever is' has its own proper nature and identity: yet every nature seeks its own fulfillment. All existence in every particular shape and form resembles a huge interlinked gestalt-like living organism.[14] Harmony and growth will characterise this organism, the macrocosm, this oneness, only when each human personally identifies with each of the realms of existence. The Classics identify the Sage as the exemplar of this attitude. Yet this organism depends on the harmonious growth of each cell or microcosm. When this occurs, the whole organism will expand to full potential; simultaneously each individual cell will awaken to a sense of mutual interdependence and greater worth. For the human being then, 'self-cultivation' became a Sage-like personal identification with each of these foundational pillars.

As Confucius studied the chaos of his age, he searched for the cause of such disorder. If society be in crisis, he concluded, it is because human beings, inhibited from authentic growth and development, have settled for less satisfying and more self-serving goals. Yet 'whatever is', nature, contains within itself a foundational orientation towards perfection; when that development is impeded, frustration, chaos and disorder enter society. All that is needed, then, is for each human to become sensitised and awakened to this spontaneous, natural thrust towards expressing what is genuinely good for self and society. Confucians sought to awaken, sensitise, and stimulate these spontaneous inner promptings; indeed, development of just such a sensitivity became the primary goal of self-cultivation. Thus, in spite of the chaos of their day, Confucius and the Confucians articulated an extraordinary faith in humanity and human potential.

If Confucius pointed to human potential, Mencius (c. 371–289 BCE) refined the paths for cultivating this human goodness or virtue. Mencius specified and detailed our innate human instincts as four; these roots or seeds or beginnings are dormant within all. All are naturally endowed with these at birth; yet nourishment and care is demanded for the cultivation and development of these seeds.

> The feeling of compassion or commiseration is the beginning of humaneness or benevolence [*ren*[d]]; the feeling of shame and dislike is the beginning of righteousness [*yi*[e]]; the feeling of deference and humility is the beginning of propriety [*li*[f]]; the feeling of right and wrong is the beginning of wisdom [*chi*[g]]. Men have these Four Beginnings just as they have four limbs. Having these Four Beginnings, but saying that they cannot develop them is to destroy themselves . . . If anyone with these Four Beginnings in him knows how to give them the fullest expansion and development, the result will be like fire beginning to burn or a spring beginning to shoot forth.[15]

The human race is similar to a child with limitless potential. Although children naturally love their parents by instinct, these same beginnings must be carefully nourished and cultivated lest they wither. Such cultivation implies the extension and expansion of this goodness outward to others, to family and community, to society, and even towards specific identity with earth and earth-processes as well as Heaven. Self-cultivation is orderly discipline and training which begins within and yet expands ever outward. Just as correction may often be necessary lest a child wander and stray, so also disciplined self-cultivation is demanded lest our natural spontaneities be challenged by competing self-aggrandising desires of self-interest and selfishness. Harmony depends on inspiring or educating natural human spontaneity to appropriate acts and actions; this is the naturalness, the *ren*[d], which though now cloaked within each human, is capable of uniting *ren*[c], *di*[b], *tian*[a].

How then is this spontaneity to be inspired? Curiously, the Confucian answer is through appropriate *li*[f] (etiquette, ceremonies, rites). The Confucian teachers may have been descendants of the *ru*[o], those ceremonialists who served as the official upholders and preservers of tradition for the Court. Foremost among the responsibilities of the *ru* was the creation of *li*[f]. With the possible exception of *ren*[d] no other term is more fundamental to the Confucian perspective. Prior to Confucius, the meaning of *li*[f] had been restricted to specific rituals and ceremonies usually associated with the 'superhuman' or 'divine'. Confucius expanded and extended *li*[f] to include every possible type of human conduct, action and etiquette. Does this adaptation of the ideogram for ancient 'ceremonial' suggest that the awe associated with rituals can be extended to include every conceivable form of human act and action?[16] Are all human actions able to become 'sacred'?[17]

'Sacredness' or even 'holiness', according to some contemporary commentators gradually came to mean the blossoming of the 'seeds' of potential latent within each human being. As music introduces new levels of awareness and consciousness, so also does *li*[f] invite to more profound rhythms and fuller cadences of human experience and existence. Paradoxically, cultivating *li*[f] liberates and frees each person from naively clinging to narrow individualism and lingering selfishness. New levels of awakened 'consciousness' beckon.

Contemporary scholarship has recently begun searching for this fuller understanding of *li*[f].[18] The *Li Ji*[1] is not only an elaborate catalogue of conduct and a detailed social-ethical code; it is so much more. According to Professor Herbert Fingarette, an awakened Confucian life may be considered "one, vast, spontaneous and holy rite".[19] That radical distinction between the sacred and the secular that has muddied so much of Western religious thought is inapplicable to China. Rather from a Confucian perspective, the human community as such is itself a sacred meeting place, a crossroads, the intersection for a truly sacred and awesome rite. Within this human community, the growth, development and the awakening of all may even be considered sacramental moments.[20] *Li*[f] can stimulate, challenge and expand this process of growing awareness.

As *li*[f] inspire expansive growth, they challenge our moral sensitivity and consciousness; they point to a more complete understanding of who we are as well as to a deeper awareness of our specific responsibilities to society and even to the cosmic whole; in a word, *li*[f] fosters the genuine growth of *ren*[d]. Yet so powerful and so effective are *li*[f] that they are sometimes described as having an almost 'magical'[21] quality about them. A *junzi*[k] is described as radiating a certain naturally transformative power; he has so fused *li*[f] with his own personality that the almost alchemical result of contact with him is invariably 'virtue' (*de*[n]). So powerful and so effective and, indeed, so 'magical' is a *junzi*[k] that:

> He is able to give full development to his nature. Able to give full development to his own nature, he can do the same to the nature of others. Able to give full development to the nature of creatures and things, he can assist the transforming and nourishing powers of Heaven and Earth. Able to assist the transforming and nourishing powers of Heaven and Earth, *he may with Heaven and Earth form a Trinity.*[22]

Is such an ideal really possible? With what attitude ought one to respond to the catalyst of *li*[f]? The answer is total sincerity (*cheng*[h]), an all encompassing meta-virtue capable of transforming and leading all to authenticity.

> Sincerity is the way of Heaven, and to discover how to be sincere is the way of Man. There has never been a person who was completely sincere who did not move others. Nor has there ever been a person who was not sincere and yet could move others.[23]

Total sincerity, if fully unleashed, promises to awaken the profound interrelationships which intertwine *ren*[d], *di*[b], and *tian*[a] within a unique mutually dependent, cross-fertilising oneness. This oneness suggests what Western religious thinkers sometimes describe as 'transcendence' and yet others as immanence'. Within the human centre of the 'heart-mind' (*xīn*[j]) of everyone, an elevating bond and identification with all existence awaits discovery; here is the Confucian promise of *ren*[d]. We are far more than mere solitary individuals; we experience solidarity and identity with every other form and level of existence, be it human, cosmic or even divine. To this expansive self-understanding, the Confucian invites.

Within the vast Confucian literature, the models and lists of schemata for growth and development are multiple and often overlapping. Perhaps the dialect of this awakening of levels of 'consciousness' may be understood in terms of a journey, a journey both inward and outward. Mencius drew his lessons from nature; just as seeds must first establish and root themselves in the rich nutrients of soil and only then push outward and upward to give forth fruit, so also ought each human being first probe *ren*[d], which then leads most naturally outward and upward to yield ever-richer fruits. The human journey proceeds along this path of gradual self-discovery. Initially, all wonder at existence and marvel at the discovery and experience of life itself. Disciplined self-cultivation, probing self-reflection, and necessary self-correction all challenge 'consciousness' during this inward dimension of life's journey; en route, *li*[f] challenge, motivate, expand and draw the searcher outward to an awareness of the fuller dimensions of 'humanness'. By journeying within, we become aware of the potential of *ren*[d], our natural inclination to goodness which lies dormant within the rich soil of our 'heart-mind' (*xin*[j]). Here the real test of *ren*[d] begins. Maturity and growth demand outward movement to others and to society to share the richness uncovered within. This is the real test of virtue.

As an awakened *ren* begins to move outward, a variety of communities are encountered. Finally, society the earth or nature, and even Heaven all invite fuller reflection on all that it means to be human. Each community challenges to an expansion of consciousness. As a sense of personal identity broadens, absolute sincerity (*cheng*[h]) is again the critical virtue. An emerging sense of identification with the oneness of *ren*[d], *di*[b], and *tian*[a] demands that each new level of consciousness be verified, tested and probed by a variety of appropriate actions. Eventually this became the classic Neo-Confucian principle of 'unity of knowledge and action', the norm of verification for human conduct.

Confucian self-cultivation parallels what the West often vaguely terms 'immanence' in its literature. In the West, immanence is usually explained as the exact opposite of transcendence; such a perspective all too often fails to probe the 'sacred indwelling presence' which it so boldly proclaims. One great value of the Confucian perspective is that it does just this; it has persistently probed, explored and experimented with the meaning of 'the human' while searching for a fuller understanding of 'humanness'. While deeply aware of the richness embedded within *ren*[d], Confucian *li*[f] challenges us to ever fuller understandings of the linkages and relationships which both flow from and bind together each human with all of *ren*[d], *di*[b], and *tian*[a].

This awakening demands that all latent human potential be stimulated, challenged and expanded to fullest perfection. Harmony or the interrelationship of all existence is thus a central Confucian teaching. A solitary, isolated individual, such as a Yogi, is, for a Confucian, truly an anomaly and certainly less than a human being. Yet by means of a journey both inward and even more importantly outward, a fuller and more profound understanding of *ren*[d] – *ren*[d] in solidarity with all that is – can be awakened. For the Confucian, all this is central to being human.

A CONVERSATION

If by some magical trick of the Yogis, we were able to bring to Zhou and Han visionaries of ancient China into conversation with the creators of the classical Yoga tradition of India, the possibilities of a most interesting conversation would certainly be present. Both would speak of the value of the human, both would attest to a potential hidden within the depths of each human. Although both would speak of the predicament of false self-aggrandisement caused by a mere ego-identity, each would recommend the deeper values of different modes and levels of consciousness. Both would agree that there is much more to the human condition than ordinarily meets the human eye. Yet how different the Indian and Chinese maps and guides to this more profound understanding of self-identity would be!

Patañjali, Īśvarakṛṣna, Kapila, Śaṅkara, and the Yogis would wish to speak, above all else, of *puruṣa*, that hidden infinite which they name 'consciousness'. '*Puruṣa*-experience' is medicinal and healing in itself, they would argue; awakening to the depths of 'consciousness' cures the human dilemma of facile misidentification with various masks of 'matter' and material formations. Yoga invites us to function in an entirely new way, they would argue.

The principal challenge of life, claim these Yogis, is to crack or break open the human ego, to plumb the limitless depth and range of pure 'consciousness'. Liberated Yogis propose an "epistemic transvaluation",[24] an experiential awakening to a transphenomenal understanding of ourselves as ultimately infinite 'consciousness', a 'consciousness' totally freed and utterly independent of our temporary imprisonment within specific physical bodies or particular formations of matter. All bodies and all material forms have but one goal, to bring about this more complete or fuller appreciation and experience of isolated consciousness, '*puruṣa* in *kaivalya*'. By means of a dramatic and radical epistemic transvaluation, the Yogis propose the freeing and liberation of each individual from all bondage within our common world of daily experience; simultaneously Yoga proclaims the unique, lasting and infinite value hidden within every human being.

While acknowledging and championing the value of the human and while agreeing with the Yogis that the principal human predicament is certainly our self-aggrandising ego, the praxis recommended by the Confucians is very different. Confucian virtues promote an ever expanding awakening to levels of 'consciousness' catalysed by a series of practical tests within the cauldron of everyday life. Not reflective introspection but practical effectiveness and verification within lived reality is the Confucian ideal. Whereas Yogis probed and explored the depths of 'consciousness' located within, Confucians tested their intuition of 'cosmic unity'[25] and a 'harmonious whole' by recommending a movement which is both inward and outward. If the Yogis mapped a vertical inward descent, the Confucians pointed to a catalyst which inspires a movement from an initial inner perception consciously outward in an explicit plan designed to awaken personal identification with every aspect and dimension of existence. The development of human nobility (*junzi*) in personal character, as well as the cultivation of a milieu of a humane and awakened human society, serve as a challenge to inspire each person to maximal potential. This ideal became the Confucian goal. It is this more external vision which the Confucian wishes to describe.

Critical to the Confucian perspective is the catalysing role of self-awakening that a number of natural communities play in the education or self-cultivation of each person. To stimulate this process, precise *li*[f] are created with a clear purpose, to challenge each of these 'seeds' to their fullest potential and development.

Yet the key to Confucian growth and development is really the explicit challenge which a variety of hierarchically structured natural communities present to these foundational 'germs' hidden within each human being. If the family be the cradle or primordial educator of the human person, several other challenges explicitly stimulate each individual to an expansion of self-understanding. Such natural communities become the school or university leading each person to a more complete discovery of all that it means to be human, to a clear sense of identification with all dimensions and forms of existence. "The family is the prototype of all human communities. The forms of human fellowship represented in the family furnish the model by which to understand all forms of communal interaction, whether they be social, religious, or political. Indeed, some even think that this 'family-ism' results in a perspective in which, unlike in the West, the individual has no identity separable from that of the group."[26] Confucian self-cultivation fosters the opening of just such an expansive consciousness. The 'seeds' of humanity having been located within, the Confucian genius is to explicitly challenge each human to maximal development by specific acts and actions. *Li*[f] draws, expands, and leads *ren*[d] ever outward to a clear realisation and to the linkages shared between *ren*[c], *di*[b], and *tian*[a].

Curiously, not unlike the Yogic analysis of the human dilemma, self-seeking, self-aggrandisement, and self-centredness are identified by Confucius as the principal human problem; however, for the Confucians, selfishness is understood as that which inhibits expansive consciousness and thus prevents the fullest development of all the potential noted within the 'heart-mind' (*xin*[j]) of each human being. Whereas the Yogis wish to probe the human Ego so as to *still* egoistic affirmations, the Confucians challenge this internal consciousness to expand beyond our current limited, empirically-observable horizons to a greater sense of explicit identity which all dimensions of existence. Confucian *li*[f] challenge *ren*[d] to a fuller understanding of all that it means to be human. To be fully human, in the Confucian view, is to be awakened to the totality and the harmonious interrelatedness of all that is, of all existence in all its multiple shapes and forms. This expansive plan for maximal human growth and development is the initial contribution that the Confucians would wish to introduce into any conversation exploring the nature of the human.

Were our imaginary conversation between Patañjali and Confucius to deepen, several threads of common agreement would most certainly arise. Both spiritual masters believe in the 'infinity' hidden within every human being, a richness attributable to a veiled 'personal identity' which transcends ordinary human perception. Both also proclaim the perfectibility or the potential of each human being, although both identify the principal human dilemma as selfishness or egocentric over-assertiveness. Thus both Patañjali and Confucious have faith or a core belief in human potential, although their proposed paths or means for liberating this fullest meaning *differ* radically. Contemplatively oriented Yoga searches within so as to liberate the infinite and limitless value (*puruṣa*) of each human being. Yoga proposes a radical reassessment of all knowledge by means of what later commentators have termed an 'epistemic transvaluation'; *puruṣa* is thereby unveiled as utterly free infinite consciousness. Thus through Yoga contemplation, all humans discovers that they are far more than the egocentric entity they once judged themselves to be. On the other hand, the Confucians probe the potential perceived within human experience; they deliberately challenge human consciousness and human society to awaken and expand to its fullest potential through identification and awareness of the linked organic unity which binds together *ren*[c], *di*[b], *tian*[a]. Through specific acts and actions, each human is challenged and inspired to awaken to the fullness of human identity and potential.

Were our conversation to expand to a genuine dialogue, a major topic of discussion would be epistemology. How does one know? How does one know the 'knower'? Yogic *puruṣa*-realisation is empirically unobserved and, therefore, ultimately unverifiable except by Yogic experience. Not only would this Yogic insight seem at best a poetic vision or perhaps a mystical intuition, the Confucians would also argue that such a 'self-centred' vision could undermine the very foundations of society. Yogic contemplative exercises and experiences could easily lead to escapism, thereby, in the view of Confucius, 'proving' their unhumanness. Were Patañjali to reply by distinguishing between various levels of perception, knowledge, understanding, wisdom, and the richness of this Yoga experience as an aid to total human understanding, Confucius might respond by saying that if Patañjali is correct, then ultimately every human being is infinite, again a conclusion which Confucius himself would challenge for lack of explicit proof. Perhaps Mencius might empathise, but even this somewhat later Confucian orientation would still concentrate on practical growth and development achieved through the test of specific human acts and actions. Human acts performed within society are the infallible means of awakening to an explicit experience of the organic unity of intertwined *ren*[c], *di*[b], and *tian*[a]. Thus for Confucians, the focus is on each human being and human potential: this human person is always located and situated within the natural environment of a particular society. Humanity and society will achieve full potential and perfectibility when stimulated by challenging appropriate human acts and action. The norm of verification is the growth and development of each individual and society.

As our introductory conversation approaches this more demanding realm of dialogue, a hint arises that perhaps Yoga and Confucianism, rather than being viewed as contradictory and antithetical, may even be viewed as complementary and mutually enriching. Both affirm and strongly develop the unique richness detected within human experience: whereas Yoga probes inwardly, proclaiming mystical and contemplative insights, Confucianism searches to inspire and draw out *ren*[d] to a fuller experience and awakening to all that it means to be human. Perhaps, then *puruṣa* and *ren*[d] may be two sides of the same coin, two dimensions of experience, one stressing internal depth and the other external possibilities. If so, a dialogue between Patañjali and Confucius would have much to say to our age.

Frank R. Podgorski, Department of Asian Studies, Seton Hall University, South Orange, New Jersey 07079, USA.

NOTES

1 Mencius, 2A.
2 Needham, Joseph (1956) *Science and Civilization in China*. Vol. 2: *History of Scientific Thought* (Cambridge: Cambridge University Press).
3 More, Frederick W. (1971) *Intellectual Foundations of China* (New York: Knopf) pp. 3–28. Cf. also Thompson, Laurence (1969) *Chinese Religion: An Introduction* (Belmont, CA: Dickenson).
4 Yearley, Lee H. (1983) A comparison between classical Chinese thought and thomistic thought, *Journal of the American Academy of Religion*, Vol. LI, (3), 1983, pp. 427–458.
5 Eliade, Mircea (1969) *Yoga: Immortality and Freedom*, Bollingen Series No. 56 (Princeton, NJ: Princeton University Press) p. 94 ff.
6 Podgorski, Frank R. (1984) *EGO: Revealer-Concealer – A Key to Yoga* (Landham, MD: University Press of America) pp. 203–242; and Podgorski (1977) Psycho-spiritual transvaluation, *Journal of DHARMA*, 11(2), pp. 152–163. Both sources contain a much more detailed description of the Yogic understanding of spiritual journey.
7 This subjective psychic instrument consists of *buddhi*, *ahaṃkāra*, *manas*, five *buddhīndriyas*, five *karmendriyas*, all governed by the expressions of *ahaṃkara*; its supporting sheath would be the five subtle elements of sound (*śabda*), touch (*sparsa*), form (*rūpa*), taste (*rasa*), and smell (*gandha*).
8 Subtle differs from gross matter only in being finer or lesser accumulations of *prakṛti*.
9 *Sāṃkhya-Kārīkā*, LVII: *puruṣavimokṣanimittam*.
10 Merton, Thomas (1962) *New Seeds of Contemplation* (London: Burns & Oates) pp. 5–6.
11 Podgorski, Frank R. (1981) Self-cultivation: a Chinese view of religious experience, in: Thomas, Mampra (Ed.) *Religious Experience: Its Unity and Diversity* (Bangalore: Dharmaram Publications) pp. 40–62.
12 Finagrette, Herbert (1972) *Confucius, The Secular as Sacred* (New York: Harper Torchbooks) p. 17. Please note the recent discussion of Finagrette's work in *Philosophy: East-West* (1978–1980).

13 The traditional *Five Classics* and *Four Books*.
14 Northrop, F. S. C. (1946) *The Meeting of East and West: An Inquiry Concerning World Understanding* (New York: The MacMillan Company). Note also More, Needham and Thompson, op. cit., notes 3, 2 and 3.
15 Mencius 2A, Cf. also Yearley, Lee H. (1975) Mencius on human nature: the forms of his religious thought, *Journal of the American Academy of Religion*, 43, pp. 185–98.
16 Munro, Donald (1969) *The Concept of Man in Early China* (Stanford, CA: Stanford University Press); Munro (1977) *The Concept of Contemporary China* (Ann Arbor, MI; The University of Michigan Press) Cf. also Tu Wei-ming (1968) The creative tension between *Jen* and *Li*, *Philosophy East-West*, 18(1).
17 Fingarette, op. cit., note 12, p. 17.
18 Cf. Tu Wei-Ming, op. cit, note 16 and Ching, Julia (1977) *Confucianism and Christianity* (New York: Kodansha International). Cf. also Podgorski, Frank (1976) An ancient Chinese model of celebration, *Jeevadhara* (Kerala, India), VI (35) pp. 429–432.
19 Fingarette, op. cit., note 12, p. 17 and *passim*.
20 Yearley, op. cit., note 4.
21 Fingarette, op. cit., note 12, *passim*.
22 *Chung Yung* XXIII.
23 Mencius 4A, p.12.
24 Lad, Ashok (1967) *The Concept of Liberation in Indian Philosophy* (Gwalior: Shri Krishna Press) p. 104. "The transition from the state of bondage to liberation is epistemic; change is required in our outlook . . . What is required is not the transformation of atman, but only the transvaluation of it."
25 Needham, op. cit., note 2.
26 Yearley, op. cit., note 4, p. 428.

11
The Characteristics of Confucian Ethics

Xiao Wei

Originating from the Pre-Qin period, Confucian ethics has a history of over two thousand years. It has not only been the essential basis of Chinese culture, but has also influenced the world greatly. It has become the spiritual wealth commonly shared by countries in East Asia and South-Asia such as Japan, Singapore, Thailand, Indonesia and Malaysia. Confucian thought is now still to a large extent influencing people in their thinking and behaviour in many ways.

However, what is Confucian ethics? This is indeed a very complicated question. I will only focus attention on the major characteristics of Confucian ethics through which I hope to present a very general picture.

From my point of view, Confucian ethics possesses the following five characteristics: heaven combines human beings into one; introversion; experience; entirety; and normativity. Let us start from a brief explanation of the Confucian school, then move on to a description of these characteristics one by one.

Confucius (551–479 B.C.) was the creator of the Confucian school. Someone has depicted Socrates as Confucius in Western culture, which is a very interesting metaphor. But in my opinion, Confucius has exercised much more influence over Chinese culture than Socrates has over Western culture.

Confucius and his disciples were born at the end of the Spring and Autumn Period which was a time of great social disorder. All kinds of moral rules and rituals (*li*) had been overturned and society was in a state of anarchy. The situation reflected the collapse of the old patriarchal clan system. Confucius wanted to put society back into order, so he established a set of rules which were intended to maintain the relationships between rulers and ministers, fathers and sons, husbands and wives, between brothers, and between friends.

Confucian ethics stemmed from *Ru* which originally denoted a particular profession, namely, those who gave expert advice on rituals and regularly gave instruction on them. But Confucius built an academic school based on *Ru*, so Confucian ethics is more than just *Ru*.

Confucius' main work is the *Analects* which he did not write himself. It was written by his disciples who collected dialogues and exchanges that they remembered having with Confucius.

We can divide the development of Confucian ethics into three important historical stages. The first stage is the Pre-Qin period in which Confucius and Mencius and Xun Zi were the main representatives. The second stage is the Han Dynasty. Dong Zhongshu was the main representative of Confucian ethics in this time. Up to the Shong and Ming Dynasties, Confucian followers built Neo-Confucianism whose main representatives were Zhang Zai, Wang Yangming, and Zhu Xi.

I. HEAVEN COMBINES HUMAN BEING INTO ONE (*TIAN REN HE YI*)

To my understanding, the subject-object relation takes the shape of dualism in traditional western philosophy. That means a human being is independent of the world which seems to be attached to the human being by chance. In brief, there is an external relationship between the human being and the world. Nevertheless, it is quite different in Chinese traditional ethics. When we talk about the relationship between heaven and a human being, the very important point is that heaven combines human beings into one.

The implications behind this viewpoint are, firstly, that heaven communicates with the human being, and secondly, that heaven is similar to the human being. For the first theory, Mencius was the first person who claimed that heaven communicates with human beings and the virtue of heaven is embodied in the mind-nature of a human being. The way of heaven connects with the way of the human being. The universal noumenon is the source of morality of a human being and that morality is an expression of the universal noumenon. In this case, the universal noumenon contains the sense of morality; on the other hand, morality also contains the sense of the universe. The reason that a human being is distinguished from animals is that the mind-nature of a human being combines with heaven.

Mencius said: 'Those who exercise their minds to the full come to understand their congenital nature; and if they understand their nature, they understand heaven. They keep their minds alive and nourish their nature and so serve heaven.'[1]

The Neo-Confucians of the Shong-Ming Dynasty developed Mencius' thought; they thought of heaven and the human being as a whole. Zhang Zai said: 'Heaven is called Father, the Earth is called Mother. I am so insignificant that in a muddled kind of way I dwell between them. Therefore with regard to what directs the movements of heaven and earth, I am a part of its nature. All men are my brothers from the same womb, all things my companions.'[2] That means, we live in a big family, father is heaven, mother is earth, brothers are other persons, my companions are all things.

Neo-Confucians also built a mind-nature school and a principle school which thought 'Mind is heaven', 'Mind is principle.'

Another theory is that heaven is similar to the human being. The proposer of this was Dong Zhongshu in the Han Dynasty. According to him, heaven is the master of the human being. Heaven could share thoughts and feelings with a human being. Heaven also has the air of pleasure and anger, the heart of joys and sorrows. These are very similar to that of the human being. So heaven and human beings are actually one and the same thing. The rulers must obey the commands of heaven, for if they don't, punishment will ensue. When a country is flourishing, there are bound to be omens of happy augury; when it is about to fall into ruin, there are bound to be omens of calamity.

The significance of '*Tian ren he yi*' in ethics can be expressed in several ways. Firstly, as moral duty is close to you, you can treat others as kindly as you do your parents, brothers and sisters at home. So you do not have a burden of moral duty. It is natural for you to act morally. Secondly, the moral nature of a human being externalises the nature of heaven which in turn externalises the moral rules of the human being. So, morality has a high authority in this world. Thirdly, the theory stresses the position of a human being in the universe. The human being is a pivot which channels heaven and all things.

II. INTROVERSION

Though heaven will communicate with a human being in Confucian ethics, the virtue of heaven always embodies the mind-nature of the human being. Then the mind of the human being, of course, is a link-point to channel the relationship between heaven and human beings.

It follows that if one wants to pursue morality and become a sage, instead of pursuing it from outside himself, he needs to seek it from his own inner mind. Master Confucius said: 'Heaven is far away from us, but a human being is close to us. Is *Ren* (humanity) far away too? If I do want to possess *Ren*, it comes to me itself.'[3] Heaven in Confucian ethics is different from God in Western ethics. In Western ethics, people are eager to justify the existence of God, but in Confucian ethics, heaven is simply regarded as the source of value. To know its existence is more than enough, and nobody seeks to justify it.

Zhuang Zi who is the main representative of Daoism also said that a sage does not consider and justify things which are beyond the six dimensions (top/bottom, front/back, left/right).

Therefore, morality should be pursued by making efforts towards one's inner mind. The essence of Confucius' thought is *Ren*. He used *Ren* to channel the relationship between the rules of heaven and the rules of human beings. *Ren* is an innate merit inherited from one's own mind. *Ren* is the fundamental element that distinguishes a human being from animals and other living things. *Ren* is based on the intimate relationship of the family. Even if Confucius did not concern himself about the goodness of human nature directly, his use of *Ren* had already contained the idea indirectly.

Mencius developed this point of Confucius and proposed the goodness of human nature directly. He pointed out that the human being has four senses which are the tender shoots of morality.

Mencius said: 'All men have a sense of compassion for others.' 'What I mean by all men having a sense of compassion is that if, for instance, a child is suddenly seen to be on the point of falling into a well, everybody without exception will have a sense of distress. It is not due to the reason of any close intimacy with the parents of the child, nor the reason of a desire for the praise of neighbours and friends or the reason of disliking to be known as that kind of man. From this point of view, we observe that it is inhuman to have no sense of compassion, inhuman to have no sense of shame over wickedness, inhuman to have no sense of modesty and the need to yield place to a better man, inhuman not to distinguish right and wrong. The sense of compassion represents the tender shoot of individual morality, the sense of shame that of public morality, modesty that of ritual propriety, the sense of truth and error that of wisdom. Men have these four tender shoots just as they have their four limbs . . .'[4]

Though everybody has the four senses, it is only possible for them to become a sage and a virtuous person. The reason why there are some differences between the noble-minded man and the low-minded man is that the noble-minded man retains his own senses but the low-minded man loses them. Mencius suggested that moral training aims at maintaining and nurturing the heart and bringing the lost heart back.

Neo-Confucianism developed Mencius' point. Wang Yangming said: 'My mind is exactly the universe. The universe is exactly my mind.' The mind goes up to the noumenal position of the universe.

Confucian ethics was therefore developing according to an introspective line. We pursue morality from the self and the inner mind. In Western philosophy, the self emphasises self-harmony which is regarded as a precondition for achieving a relationship with others and society. However, Confucianism sees the essence of the self as introspection and self-criticism. Confucius' disciples engage in self-examination on three aspects everyday: Is my personality insidious? Do I treat my friends untruthfully? Haven't I reviewed the knowledge which I learnt today? Mencius said, when you respect others, but they do not respond to your, you should discover by introspection whether you really respect others. *Ren* is just like a bow, if you want to hit the target successfully, you must take your own exact position first. So Confucian ethics believes that self-criticism is a precondition for achieving a harmony with others and society. The concept of the self in Confucian ethics is quite different from that in Western philosophy.

III. EXPERIENCE

Western ethics inherits Greek psychology and explains all human mental processes via belief and desire. The concept of morality involves reference to the human faculty of reason. The main tradition in Western ethics is rationalist. In Western ethics, morality mainly depends on reasoning and analysing. Thus, it has established metaethics and moral epistemology which are abstruse and sophisticated.

However, Confucian ethics sees morality in a different way, which emphasises human emotions and feelings. Morality is experienced through the mind of people in their ordinary life. Confucian ethics does not focus on formal justification in detail. It also does not have a tight theoretical system. Truth means the combination of experience and practice. It is quite enough to explain life-experience. It also does not weigh words in detail. Confucian ethics does not lay stress on logical justification. How then to get morality? The answer is to learn it through one's personal experience. The more you experience, the more the chance of sudden 'disillusion.' Chan Zhong was the creator of Chinese Buddhism. Although he was illiterate, he was still a good example of disillusioning morality which was achieved in his relaxed daily life. There are many flowers in Spring and the moon in Autumn. There is a nice cool breeze in Summer and snow in Winter. If you do not have things to worry about, today is a good chance for you to understand morality. Sometimes Confucian ethics calls experience intuition. By contrast to Western ethics, Confucian ethics considers intuition as an experiential faculty rather than a rational faculty. In Confucian ethics, the mind is not abstract, but vivacious and concrete. The mind contains emotions and feelings which are based on the blood-bond relationship. For example, Confucian suggested the 'Three Years' Funeral' when one's parents died. How can we explain this rule? Confucius said, one could not leave one's parents' arms during the first three years after one was born. Similarly, when one's mother or father died, one should have a three years' funeral in order to repay one's parents' loving kindness. This is a way to introspect on one's moral duty through the role of experience. The dead person reminds us to take care of living persons.

Confucian ethics addresses experience and practice. In the history of Confucian ethics, there were some debate on problems such as 'Does knowledge exist before practice or is the opposite true?' However, the purpose of such debate is not to form a moral epistemology, but to put knowledge into practice. Knowledge and practice should be combined together. Zhu Xi said, a sage does not want to say how the pear smells, you should taste it by yourself. What is morality? Nobody can tell you. You could not know morality until you practised it for yourself. Why has Confucian ethics been handed down for so long a time? The reason is that it essentially stresses daily experience, emotions and feelings which are based on the blood-bond relationship. In fact, Confucian ethics uses experience not only to discover desirable conventions derived from traditional culture, but to let them become accumulated psychologically in the individuals' mind.

IV. ENTIRETY

Compared with Western philosophy, Confucian ethics has another characteristic – 'entirety', which means that the world, the universe, human society, animals and plants are integrated into a whole. In addition, each of them is also an organic whole. Take traditional

Chinese medical science as an example. If you have a headache, a Chinese doctor will give medicine not only for your head but also for your whole body. This situation reflects the different ways of thinking in the Eastern and the Western world. Chinese doctors consider the whole body when trying to cure diseases in the parts. That is, through regulating the energy and blood of the whole body, they reach the goal of curing diseases in individual parts.

'Entirety' has two meanings. Firstly, it considers the universe and human society as an organic whole, as in '*Tian ren he yi*' mentioned before. Secondly, the organic whole fixes the human being in his subjective position, because the human being knows objective laws of nature through their morality which is learned from experience. Thus, entirety is in reality the moral subject. That is why we see that the universe has the feature of morality. On the other hand, the human being has a feature of the universe.

Entirety makes Confucian ethics into a social ethics. We think of human society as an organic whole, which is based on the blood-bond relationship. Confucianism divides all human relationships into five kinds: rulers and ministers; fathers and sons; elder brothers and younger brothers; husbands and wives; friends and friends. We call this classification 'The Five *Lun*'. Each *lun* has its own rules associated with morality. The important task of Confucian ethics is to justify the rules which can be applied to everyone. Three of the five *lun* indicate family relationships, and the rest can be understood as based on family relationships. The relationship between rulers and ministers can be regarded as being equal to that between fathers and sons. The relationship between friends can be seen as being similar to that between brothers. Thus, the whole of society is actually a web which is based on the blood-bond relationship. Each person is a link-point in this web. They must obey their own moral duty. In Confucian ethics, the Western idea of the individual does not appear: we have only different social roles. Confucian ethics fixes instead an individual in a social role and pays more attention to the whole value of the society. It suggests a collectivism which asks an individual to sacrifice his own interest for the social interest. Thus, we have a set of moralities for a loyalty to rulers and dedication of one's life to the cause of the country. According to Confucian ethics, every person, every role and every class has its own morality, therefore the next characteristic of Confucian ethics is normativity.

V. NORMATIVITY

The essence of Confucian ethics is normative ethics. *Ren* is the fundamental principle of morality. Under the guide of *Ren*, there was a complete normative system which was built by Confucius and developed by Mencius, Xun Zi and others.

Ren of Confucianism came from *Li* (ritual) of the Zhou Dynasty. *Li* is actually a kind of primitive ritual of which the basis and core are to respect and offer sacrifices to ancestors. These primitive rituals applied to all men equally rather than only to some noble-men. They represented the worship of totem, taboo and respect to old persons. These primitive rituals were not laws, but they had the sense of law. We can call them the common-law which had not been formalised. They organised primitive society as a powerful realm of super-structure and ideology which kept society in order.

Confucius replaced ritual with *Ren*. He transferred *Li* from outward mind to inward mind. He addressed moral emotions and feelings which were based on the blood-bond relationship and included in *Li*. He combined *Ren* with *Li*, and so established Confucian ethics. Though *Ren* is virtually a set of moralities, it contains more humanity than *Li*. *Ren* is a normative frame which is composed of many structures.

FILIAL PIETY AND FRATERNAL DUTY (*XIAO* AND *TI*)

This is the basis of *Ren*. It unfolds *Ren* on the basis of the blood-bond in length and breadth. Filial piety means respecting one's parents in length. Fraternal duty means to be friendly with one's brothers and sisters in breadth.

ZHONG SU

This is the principle of *Ren*. To do one's very best for the sake of others is *Zhong*, to extend this beyond oneself is *Su*. *Zhong* like *Su* involves extending oneself to include others. *Zhong* is the positive aspect of extending oneself to include one's fellow men, *Su* is the negative aspect. Confucianism emphasizes that a *Ren* man is sure to be very good at considering others. Because of what he desires for himself, he can consider other men and know what they desire. Because of what he does not desire, he can consider others and know what they do not desire. Thus through knowing other men's desires by his own desire, in wanting to become a solid man in society, he makes other men solid: in wanting success for himself, he makes other men successful. Mencius said: 'I treat the aged in my family properly and extend this to the aged in other men's families, and treat the young in my family properly and extend this to the young in other men's families.'[5] *Zhong Su* is actually the extension of *Xiao Ti* as applied to the whole society.

TO LOVE EACH OTHER

This is the spirit of *Ren*. It derives from *Xio Ti* and *Zhong Su*. Love, firstly, means 'loving relatives'. The love based on the blood-bond relationship is the deepest basis of *Ren*. 'Loving relatives' is very important because it adopts the old system of the patriarchal clan and agricultural family. Love also means loving others. This involves the relationship between individual and society. Its purpose is to retain peace and unity within the society.

TO REHABILITATE *LI* (RITUAL)

This is the aim of *Ren*. Confucius said: 'To restrain the self in order to rehabilitate *Li*, we call this *Ren*.' How are we to follow *Ren*? 'Do not look at anything which is counter to the rituals, do not hear anything which is counter to them, do not speak anything which is counter to them, do not move in any way which goes counter to them.'[6] *Li*, of course is not the *Li* of the Zhou Dynasty, rather feudal moralities which are used to assure a harmonious society. The fundamental feature of old China is the combination between the blood-bond relationship and the patriarchal system. The principle of *Ren* is determined by the nature of society and serves it. It is worth while mentioning feudal moralities relevant to women in Confucian ethics. For example, 'Man superior to woman', 'Three obediences and four virtues' and so on. Dong Zhongshu suggested 'the three bonds or cardinal guides and five constant virtues' which means that rulers are the cardinal guide of ministers, fathers are the cardinal guides of their sons, husbands are the cardinal guides of their wives. Women obey their fathers before they are married, and obey their husbands after they are married, and obey their sons after their husbands die. Thus, women were reduced to the lowest level of feudal society.

BRIEF EVALUATION

I want to give a brief evaluation of Confucian ethics as follows:

1. Confucian ethics is a harmony ethics. It brings a harmony between heaven and the human being, society and the individual, the self and his own mind. *Tian ren he yi* is actually a harmony between a human being and nature. Introspection and experience are the causes of self-harmony. Entirety and normativity result in harmony of society. This spirit of Confucianism is expressed by such sentences as: 'Training self, harmonising family, managing country and keeping peace in the whole world.'
2. As compared with Western ethics, Confucian ethics pays more attention to daily experience, emotions and feelings, and the blood-bond relationship. It touches the nature of the human being and attempts to put society in order. To some extent, Confucian ethics have been threading a different path from that of Western ethics; but they can be complementary to each other and have been making a great contribution to human civilization together.
3. Confucian ethics is a practical ethics. It seems that philosophers always want to put their ideas into practice. Because of this, Confucian ethics could not have been perplexed by other religions and superstitions.

However, we should contemplate Confucian ethics from another side in order to find some problems.

1. The tendency of entirety and normativity submerges the individual in Confucian ethics. Instead of the individual in Western ethics, in Confucian ethics he has only a social role. It stresses society rather than the individual and ignores the active function of the individual in society. Therefore, Confucian ethics lays the ground for a feudal autocratic system.
2. Confucian ethics to some extent places restrictions on the development of the human being. Why I draw this conclusion is that Confucian ethics is really a moral ontology which sees human value only from the moral aspect. If one is a sage, he need not acquire other abilities than morality. To concentrate on morality means virtually to limit the development of other abilities.
3. The mind-nature theory of Confucian ethics is a closed system which couldn't explain why human nature is good rather than evil. It also couldn't illustrate why one person should act on his own mind. The

essence of mind is actually Confucian moral principles which are made by Confucius and his followers. On a superficial view, Confucian ethics addresses one's conscious dynamic function in a moral choice, but in fact, this choice couldn't break away from the fixed frame which was laid down by Confucian ethics. At the end of the day, Confucian ethics served the feudal domination in old China.

Confucian ethics is currently facing a serious challenge in China. Economic reform has brought many new ideas concerning values. A pluralism of values has already become a tendency. Chinese people wonder whether it is possible that there will appear a new stage of the development of Confucian ethics to be adapted to today's radical changes.

Most Chinese agree to remain with our traditional culture and apply it to economic reform. How should we use it? This is a very important problem that every Chinese should consider.

Economic reform brings many contradictions between society and the individual. The essence of the reform is to focus benefits on the concrete individual, thus it is not enough to stress social interest as Confucian ethics did. We need a new ethics to serve this economic reform. How should we establish it? This is also a problem which Chinese people need to deal with.

Xiao Wei, School of Humanities and Social Sciences, Tsinghua University, Beijing 100084, People's Republic of China

NOTES

1 Mencius: *The Book of Mencius.*
2 Zhang Zai: *Works.*
3 Confucius: *Analects.*
4 Mencius: *The Book of Mencius*
5 Ibid.
6 Confucius: *Analects*

REFERENCES

Fung Yu-Lan: *The Spirit of Chinese Philosophy,* London: Kegan Paul, Trench, Trubner, 1947.
Rhys, E. (ed.): *Chinese Philosophy in Classical Times*, London: J. M. Dent, 1937.
Singer, P. (ed.): *A Companion to Ethics*, Basil Blackwell, 1991.
Zhu Yiting: *The History of Chinese Traditional Ethics*, Huadong Normal University Press, 1989.

12

Moral Values and the Daoist Sage in the *Dao De Jing**

Robert E. Allinson

In the corpus of the *Dao De Jing* it is possible to find statements which appear to imply that nothing at all can be said about the Dao; statements which can be construed to state or imply that all value judgements are relative; statements which appear to attribute moral behaviour to the actions of the Daoist sage; statements which appear to attribute immoral or amoral behaviour to the sage. The question then is, how to make sense of these seemingly contradictory statements?

The interpretation taken in this paper is that the Daoist standpoint exists (a standpoint being defined as a self-consciously held view) only from a standpoint which is outside the Daoist standpoint. The Daoist standpoint is not, strictly speaking, a standpoint at all. The very first line of the *Dao De Jing* can be taken to mean that the Dao can never be made into a standpoint. Therefore, anything said about the Dao must arise from a standpoint outside the Daoist standpoint. All statements about the Dao or the Daoist sage will only possess a limited and qualified truth value. Among these statements which possess a limited and qualified truth value, the criterion of a coherence theory of truth will be employed to sort out which statements are more likely to be more 'correct' descriptions of the values and behaviour of the sage than others. Textual evidence from within the *Dao De Jing* reveals that there appears to be an ethical hierarchy of values. For example, kindness is considered a higher value to follow than ritualistic action (chapter 38). Statements which can be taken to state or imply that all value judgements are relative will be examined to determine if another interpretation of their meaning is possible.

* Previously published in *Asian Philosophy*, Vol. 4, No. 2, 1994.

What of statements which appear to attribute immoral or amoral behaviour to the Daoist sage? First, such statements must also be made from outside the Daoist standpoint. Second, assuming from above that there is a hierarchy of values such that kindness is closer to the Dao than cruelty, then statements which appear to attribute cruelty or indifference to the behaviour of the sage must be examined carefully in order to determine if another interpretation of their intention is possible. Since the text of the *Dao De Jing* is replete with statements attributing good behaviour to the sage, and only very few statements can be found which are possible to interpret as attributing amoral or immoral behaviour to the sage, it makes more sense to seek an alternative interpretation of these statements than to attempt to seek alternative interpretations of a contrastingly greater number of statements which seemingly attribute good behaviour to the sage. Another way of putting this is that the principle of interpretation relied upon is based upon the criterion of finding the greatest coherence among the greatest number of statements to be found within the text.

The conclusion from the above investigation is that from the standpoint outside the Dao, the Daoist sage can best be understood to be acting from a 'standpoint' of goodness in itself. This, however, cannot be goodness for itself because it would not be aware of itself as goodness.[1] From the side of the Daoist sage such a characteristic cannot meaningfully be said to exist. The attempt to describe the standpoint of the Dao is in some ways like the transcendental misapplication of the categories in Kant. All that Kant could say of the thing-in-itself was that it existed (even this is moot). The attempt to describe the standpoint of the Dao is unlike the transcendental misapplication of the categories in Kant in that certain descriptions of the sage, it is argued below, are less false than others. In this sense, there are lesser and greater degrees of truth contained in varying attempts to render a description of the Daoist sage, though no description can, by definition, be absolutely true.

It would now be of interest to illustrate how the interpretation offered above can be employed to understand certain statements in the *Dao De Jing* so as to render some seemingly paradoxical statements less paradoxical. It is doubtful that any interpretation, including this one, can remove all paradoxicality. The impossibility of removing all paradoxicality is a result of the inherent limitations of language which is the substance of the very first statement found in the *Dao De Jing*, "The Dao that can be spoken about is not the constant Dao". In other words, any description of the Dao is not of the Dao. In Kantian language, any description of the thing-in-itself makes it into an appearance such that it is no longer the thing-in-itself that is being described. It does not mean, for Lao Zi, that we can say nothing about the Dao – otherwise there would have been no point in writing the *Dao De Jing* – it only means that whatever we say about the Dao will be only partially true. However, it is the contents of the partial truths about the Dao which are of the greatest interest.

If the first two statements in the *Dao De Jing* are analysed closely, much can be learned. The first statement, "The Dao that can be spoken about is not the constant Dao" would appear to suggest that the Dao is not capable of being linguistically described. As soon as some linguistic description is given of the Dao, the Dao that has thus been described is not the Dao to which one had been referring. There is a difference between the Dao and its description. The described Dao is not the real Dao. Thus, any description of the Dao will fail to yield the true nature of the Dao. Does this mean that all description is pointless? If all description were to be considered pointless, then there would be no point in proceeding. If Lao Zi proceeds, then he must consider that description has some merit or the entire *Dao De Jing* is a self-contradiction and meaningless. On the basis of this being a meaningful work, it follows that the attempt to describe the Dao has some value rather than no value at all. It might prove useful to consider the value of attempted Dao description as the attempt to render a partial and limited understanding of the Dao which will never be completely accurate.

The second statement of the *Dao De Jing* provides a further clue to the nature of the problem of Dao description. The second statement is: "The name that can be named is not the constant name". This statement makes it evident that the problem can be seen to lie in the nature of the relationship of language and the Dao. Whatever linguistic description is given of the Dao, it misses its target. It does not follow that all linguistic description is of no use. What does follow is that one must always bear in mind that any linguistic description of the Dao cannot be strictly speaking true. Every linguistic description of the Dao must miss its target. It remains an open question as to whether some linguistic descriptions must be misdescriptions; it remains open whether certain misdescriptions can be less false than others. But one implication remains true throughout the text to follow: whenever one is speaking about the Dao, one must be outside the Daoist perspective. From inside the Daoist perspective no linguistic description is possible. It remains an open question whether certain linguistic descriptions which take place outside the Daoist perspective can be less false than others.

After having said all this, what can we say about the moral evaluations that are found within the *Dao De Jing*? From the above analysis, from the Daoist standpoint, no moral evaluations can be made since any moral evaluation is linguistic. All language usage occurs, by definition, when one is outside the Daoist standpoint. Hence, according to the above analysis, when one is outside the Daoist standpoint, moral evaluations can be made and there is no problem with statements that claim that good can be favoured over bad. One can only make value statements when one is outside the Daoist standpoint, but it does not follow that all values are of equal worth.

If it is the case that all values are not of equal worth, then why is it certain statements in the *Dao De Jing* appear to imply that all values are relative to each other? For example, what of the classic statement that appears at the beginning of chapter two that "It is because the whole world knows that the beautiful is the beautiful that there is the ugly, and knows that the good is the good that there is the bad"?[2] In Professor D. C. Lau's analysis, and mine, the emphasis here is on the conceptual knowing that there is good and not the ontological existence of good. When one becomes aware of goodness as goodness, that is the origin of the *concept* of badness. Lao Zi is not saying that goodness cannot have ontological existence without badness in a kind of Pelagian sense. Daoism is not the same as Zoroastrianism. Nor does it follow from this that there is a relativity of value with respect to goodness and badness.[3] It only follows that if one comes up with a conceptualisation of goodness it must be that there is a conceptualisation of badness as well. The category (not the existence) of goodness (or beauty) could not arise without the co-temporary arising of the category of badness (or ugliness).

One of the reasons that some scholars have thought that Lao Zi was a relativist was that they took this discussion of opposites in chapter 2 as a kind of metaphysical Yin Yang discussion of opposites, such as is to be found in the *Yijing*. But if the distinction between goodness and badness is an epistemological and not an ontological one, then the discussion of opposites which follows in chapter 2 most likely is a further illustration of the opening point rather than an argument that all opposites are ontologically linked together. The statements in chapter 2 are, once again, statements that imply that all values are epistemologically correlative to each other, not that all values are ontologically of equal worth.

That not all values are ontologically of equal worth can be shown by an abundance of statements in the *Dao De Jing* which show a preference for good actions over evil actions. Of special interest are statements which show that within good actions, there is a hierarchy of values. That a hierarchy of values can be alluded to would seem to further support the notion that values are not of equal worth. In chapter 18 it is stated that:

> When the great way falls into disuse
> There are benevolence and rectitude;
> When cleverness emerges
> There is great hypocrisy;
> When the six relations are at variance
> There are filial children;
> When the state is benighted
> There are loyal ministers.[4]

This would seem to imply that the great way is above benevolence and rectitude, both of which in turn are higher values than hypocrisy. Filial piety is a virtue, but of conditional importance as it comes into being only when family relations are awry. Likewise the loyalty of officials arises only when the state is in disarray.

An even more detailed and specified hierarchy of positive values appears in chapter 38:

> A man of the highest virtue does not keep to virtue and that is why he has virtue. A man of the lowest virtue never strays from virtue and that is why he is without virtue . . . Hence when the way was lost there was virtue; when virtue was lost there was benevolence; when benevolence was lost there was rectitude; when rectitude was lost there were the rites. The rites are the wearing thin of loyalty and good faith and the beginning of disorder.[5]

Here, the man of highest virtue is above morality. This being above morality means that his actions are identical with morality and thus he has no need of external principles of morality to follow. One step beneath the Daoist standpoint is the step of self-conscious following of moral principles. Following moral virtue is a step above benevolence. Benevolence in turn is a higher value than rectitude; rectitude in turn is a higher value than following pure ritualistic behaviour. In fact not only is this a highly specified hierarchy of moral value but it is difficult to find such a structured hierarchy of moral values in any other philosopher, Eastern or Western.

Such detailed examinations of the layers of positive values lend support to the interpretation of the *Dao De Jing* as a text which embraces the thesis that not only are all values not of equal worth but their relative worths can be classified in a vertical hierarchy. The notion that moral values can be ranked in a hierarchy also suggests that it is not without precedent that within Daoism there is the suggestion of degrees of truth. In other words, if values can come closer and closer to the reality of the sage, then it is also possible that in the description of the sage it is possible to arrive at a description which is closer in its approximate truth value than other descriptions. This lends support to the previous thesis that, while the Dao cannot be described in absolute terms, certain descriptions may be less false than others.

It is also important in this connection to consider that the highest moral value is the action of the sage which is goodness without being aware of itself as being goodness. In fact, it is in the very awareness of or labelling of itself as goodness that the action falls outside the Daoist standpoint. This would seem to imply not only that the sage is perceived as good but that the kind of goodness of the sage is that sort which is not aware of itself as being good. The goodness of the sage is defined as a goodness that is good in itself but not for itself.

There are further statements in the *Dao De Jing* which lend support to the notion that the proper understanding of the sage is that the sage is perceived as morally good, but that the goodness of the sage is such that the sage is not himself aware of his goodness.

In chapter 79 of the *Dao De Jing* the statement can be found:

> It is the way of heaven to show no favouritism.
> It is for ever on the side of the good man.[6]

This seems to be an intriguing attempt on the part of Lao Zi, to attribute goodness to the sage (here referred to as 'the good man') while earlier asserting that the sage is not aware of the goodness from which he acts as being goodness – or as flowing from a value judgement. This would appear to be perfectly congruent with the argument in chapter 38. Virtue is ascribed to the sage but it exists precisely because the sage has no concept of it as being virtue.

Chapters 77 and 81 also reflect that the action of heaven is for the good and hence not morally neutral or morally evil. In chapter 77 it is stated that "It is the way of heaven to take from what has in excess in order to make good what is deficient".[7] In chapter 81, it is clearly stated that, "The way of heaven benefits and does not harm".[8] In chapter 27, it is stated that, "Therefore the sage always excels in saving people, and so abandons no one".[9] In chapter 49, it is stated that, "Those who are good I treat as good. Those who are not good I also treat as good. In so doing I gain in goodness."[10]

The only way of making sense of these statements is to say that from the standpoint of the sage, there is no concept of goodness but that good action is the unerring result of the action of the sage. The description then, of the sage, from the standpoint outside Daoism (even his self-description must be perceived from a standpoint outside Daoism proper)[11] is that the action of the sage is good. The only way of understanding the action of the sage from the standpoint outside Daoism is that from this standpoint it must be presupposed that the sage is operating from an unerring ontological goodness which is goodness in itself, that is, a goodness which intends towards goodness but which is not goodness for itself, that is, a goodness which is aware of itself as being goodness.

There is, however, at least one puzzling statement which would appear, from the standpoint outside the Daoist standpoint, to attribute immoral or amoral attitudes or behaviour to the Daoist sage. This is the notorious 'Straw Dogs' passage from chapter five. In H. G. Creel's translation, it is rendered as follows:

> Heaven and Earth are not benevolent;
> they treat the ten thousand creatures ruthlessly.
> The sage is not benevolent; he treats the people ruthlessly.[12]

H. G. Creel took these statements to mean that:

> The enlightened Daoist is beyond good and evil; for him these are merely words used by the ignorant and foolish. If it suits his whim, he may destroy a city and massacre its inhabitants with the concentrated fury of a typhoon, and feel no more qualms of conscience than the majestic sun that shines upon the scene of desolation after the storm. After all, both life and death, begetting and destruction, are parts of the harmonious order of the universe, which is good because it exists and because it is itself. In this conception of the Daoist sage, Daoism released upon humanity what may truly be called a monster. By any human standards, he is unreachable and immovable; he cannot be influenced by love or hate, fear or hope of gain, pity or admiration.[13]

This interpretation is based upon identifying the notion of the Dao as being above value concepts, with the Dao being indifferent to values. As discussed above, other passages indicate that, while the sage is not aware of goodness, his action is good in the eyes of others. So Creel's interpretation is based upon a confusion between ontological and evaluative realms of description. In addition, Creel's interpretation would be contradicted by the passages quoted above which attribute good or moral behaviour to the sage.

Through an examination of various English language translations, one can ascertain how the interpretation of the Daoist sage as a moral monster or at least as amoral still prevails today. In a recent translation by Victor H. Mair, one finds:

> Heaven and Earth are inhumane;
> they view the myriad creatures as straw dogs.
> The sage is inhumane;
> he views the common people as straw dogs.[14]

In a recent translation by Thomas Cleary, one finds:

> Heaven and earth are not humane;
> they regard all beings as straw dogs.
> Sages are not humane;
> they see all people as straw dogs.[15]

Rhett Y. W. Young and Roger Ames directly translate their interpretation of the sage as being amoral in their version:

> Heaven and Earth are amoral;
> They consider the myriad things to be straw dogs.
> The sage is amoral;
> He considers the common people to be straw dogs.[16]

But the sage cannot be amoral, as demonstrated by chapters 8, 27, 49, 79 and 81. Thus the concept of amorality is inappropriate and inaccurate to the concept of the sage. Neither can the action of Heaven be described as amoral if one considers chapters 77, 79 and 81. It would therefore appear to be significantly and systematically misleading to the serious reader of Daoism in general and the moral philosophy of Lao Zi in particular to attribute amorality either to the sage or to Heaven.

A translation which is closer in spirit to the meaning of the text is to be found in John C. H. Wu's version:

Heaven-and-earth is not sentimental;
It treats all things as straw-dogs.
The Sage is not sentimental;
He treats all his people as straw-dogs.[17]

According to a slightly amended version of Holmes Welch's translation, a literal translation (for pedagogical purposes only!) resolves the issue of meaning:

Heaven Earth not benevolent
Regard Ten Thousand Things as straw dogs
Sage man not benevolent
Regards Hundred Families as straw dogs
Heaven Earth's between [space] it resembles bellows
Empty but not depleted
Move it and more issues
Much talk quickly exhausted
Better keep Middle[18]

In this version, there is a similarity between chapter 5 and chapter 38 in the respect that the sage does not act from the concept of benevolence. It does not follow that the sage acts from ruthlessness or amorality. How does one explain the action of the sage as "Regarding Hundred Families as straw dogs"? (The straw dogs were employed in ritual purposes and treated with the greatest deference before they were used as an offering and then discarded and trampled upon as soon as they had served their purpose).[19]

While this statement would seem to defy any ingenuous explanation, perhaps this passage is attempting to explain that the Daoist sage, while always acting so as to promote the good, does not show favouritism. In this sense, though he is deferential to all human beings, he does not show special favouritism to any.

It may also be that this is a sort of practical directive. In dealing with human beings, one is bound to run up against very obstinate and obstreperous people. In a sense, then, if a person one is trying to help does not respond to the decorousness that is accorded to all, then that person is simply discarded. The sage cannot suffer fools. He acts in accordance with his goodness that is not aware of itself as goodness. But if a person who is being offered assistance does not respond to this, the sage does not get involved in protracted attempts and arguments; his time is too precious for this. He must get on with more important matters. This explanation certainly does account for the phrase, "Much talk quickly exhausted". The idea of a bellows also seems to suggest an action that is both moderate and moderated, and completed within one action.

If the above explanation of the notorious 'Straw Dogs' passage is acceptable, then the action of the sage is still one which is consistent with goodness that is unaware of itself as goodness but has the added property of being a goodness that knows how and when to expend itself in order to get on with the proper work of being a sage.

Further puzzling passages appear in chapter 3:

> Not to honour men of worth will keep the people from contention; not to value goods that are hard to come by will keep them from theft; not to display what is desirable will keep them from being unsettled of mind.
>
> Therefore, in governing the people, the sage empties their minds but fills their bellies, weakens their wills but strengthens their bones. He always keeps them innocent of knowledge and free from desire, and ensures that the clever never dare to act.
>
> Do that which consists in taking no action, and order will prevail.[20]

While one may wish to disagree with Lao Zi's advice to the ruler which seems to be a counsel of bread without circuses, one must bear in mind that Lao Zi's definition of what amounted to good ruling might differ greatly from the definition of good ruling according to Western concepts of democracy. The relevant feature here is that Lao Zi is committed to what he considers to be a good kind of governance. This is very different from making Lao Zi out to be either advocating immoral or amoral behaviour for the Daoist sage-king.

To sum up: all descriptions of the sage are from outside the Daoist standpoint, and hence are not descriptions of the Dao which is above all descriptions, including value judgements.[21] Even the description of the sage as being good without being aware of himself as good is a description which is from the side of the observer outside the Daoist circle. It is, however, perhaps the least false description that can be made of the Daoist sage according to Lao Zi. It is clear from the majority of statements to be found in the *Dao De Jing* that the sage is perceived as acting from goodness rather than perceived as being immoral or amoral. The Daoist sage is perceived from the outside as acting from goodness which is a goodness in itself but not for itself. The notorious Straw Dogs passage is not really contradictory to this and is a species of practical advice on how to act from goodness in itself.

From the standpoint outside of Daoism, there is a scale of values and all values are not relative although they are conceptually relative to each other. In fact, moral values are ranked in a hierarchy with the lowest moral values being the furthest from the Dao and the highest moral values most closely approximating the actions of the Daoist sage. Such a classification of moral values suggests that moral values embody greater and higher degrees of value as they approach the Dao. It may not be inadmissible then to consider that the description of the sage as moral, while from the absolute standpoint is false – or to speak more precisely – not applicable, comes closer to describing the reality of the sage than the description of the sage as amoral or immoral, and hence is the least false description of the Daoist sage.

Robert E. Allinson, Department of Philosophy, The Chinese University of Hong Kong, Shatin, NT, Hong Kong

NOTES

1 One may think here of the concept of 'innocent' when applied to the child. From the point of view of the adult, the child is 'innocent'. But from the child's point of view, the child is simply being himself or herself. The category of 'innocence' only makes sense when contrasted with a level of experience that the child has not yet encountered. The concept of 'play' when applied to the child is another example of this phenomenon. For the adult, the categories of 'work' and 'play' have a meaning. The child simply acts; he or she is not aware of the meaning of 'play'. It is interesting in this connection to consider that Lao Zi compares the Daoist sage to a new born child: "One who possesses virtue in abundance is comparable to a new born babe" (translation by D. C. Lau), cf. also chapter 10. Such a comparison both supports Lao Zi's description of the sage as operating from a perspective of goodness which is not aware of itself as goodness and implies that human nature is originally good. Further evidence for this viewpoint may be found in chapters 20 and 48, which make the argument that the way of learning the Dao is to unlearn, thus implying that imperfections are acquired and must be unlearned so as to return to one's original nature. This nature must be conceived of as good since the sage, who by definition acts from it, acts for the good (cf. chapters 8, 27, 49, 77, 79 and 81). That this nature is universally distributed – at least in potential form – is indicated by the fact that the sage's influence will be such that people will naturally transform themselves (without the need of ethical imperatives); cf. chapter 57.

2 This translation is found in LAU, D. C. (1958) The treatment of opposites in Lao Tze, *Bulletin, School of Oriental and African Studies*, xxi(2), p. 347.

3 Ch'en Ku-ying's argument appears to confuse the claim that all values are conceptual correlatives; e.g. it makes no sense to have a concept of good without a concept of evil with the claim that all values are relative: "Lao Tzu's intention is . . . to explain the relativity of value judgments . . . the second sentence, 'everyone understands that which makes "goodness" good, and thus the concept of badness arises' explains the relative nature of standards and their interdependence with their antithesis'. CH'EN KU-YING (1977) *Lao Tzu, Text, Notes, and Comments*, trans. Rhett Y. W. Young & Roger Ames (San Francisco, CA: Chinese Materials Center) p. 59.

4 *Dao Te Ching*, trans. D. C. Lau (1989) (Hong Kong: Chinese University Press).

5 Ibid.

6 Ibid.

7 Ibid. This is different from the circle of changes described in the *Yijing* which is a circular cycle from fullness to emptiness and from emptiness to fullness, whereas this movement is obviously only one way, from the excess to the deficient. The confusion of the cyclical changes of the *Yijing* with the Yin-Yang of Daoism also may have historically influenced the reading of the Daoist sage as being amoral. For a lucid discussion of the differences between the cyclical changes of the *Yijing* and the one way changes of the Yin-Yang of Daoism, see D. C. Lau op. cit., note 2. It is also clear from Lau's discussion why the correlative epistemological disjunctions introduced in chapter 2 of the *Dao De Jing* (the classic source of the frequently cited good-evil, beautiful-ugly contrasts) are neither cyclical changes nor one-way changes but are conceptual contrasts and not strictly speaking ontological Yin-Yang properties at all. One could, if one liked, think of them as conceptual Yin-Yang correlatives so long as one did not inflate these correlative properties into ontological existences.

8 Ibid.

9 Ibid. Water is likened to the Dao in that it benefits in chapter 8: highest good is like water. Because water excels in benefiting the myriad creatures without contending with them and settles where none would like to be, it comes close to the way. (Ibid.)

10 Ibid.

11 It must also be understood that any self-description of the sage as good or description of Lao Zi's of the sage as good are descriptions which exist for pedagogical purposes. The sage cannot believe that he is really good (*ex hypothesi* such a belief would rule him outside sagedom, cf. chapter 38). In any event, the sage can mispeak; he is not and need not be, after all, a philosopher. One may well then ask on what basis does the non-Daoist (or the non-sage) arrive at moral evaluations of the Daoist and on what grounds should the Daoist consider such moral evaluations justified or justifiable. The answer to such a question can only be that the levels of value indicated in chapter thirty-eight are ontological as well as normative levels. As one progresses in one's moral development, one embodies values which come more and more close to approximating the moral development of the

sage. It is this ontological incorporation of moral worth that makes evaluative judgements possible. However, it is the same progress of moral development that eventually transcends all such value judgements. Such judgements arise only, as with the metaphor of the boat in Buddhist literature, when one needs to reach the other shore. When one reaches land, one does not continue to carry one's boat upon one's back. To enlarge upon the Buddhist story, whenever one wishes to return to help ferry others across, one reboards the language boat (no mention of a return boat trip is made in this story but such a return is consonant with the notion of the Boddhisattva). To enlarge and perhaps alter Wittgenstein's ladder metaphor, when one wishes to speak, one descends one's ladder again. The ladder of language, according to the view presented herein, is necessary both for ascending and descending. For Wittgenstein, when one reaches the top, one discards the ladder of language: one remains silent. In Daoism, or at least in this account of Daoism, the philosopher becomes the spokesman for the sage. Insofar as the sage appears to be making value judgements, he speaks *qua* philosopher, not *qua* Daoist sage.

12 Creel, H. G. (1953) *Chinese Thought from Confucius to Mao-Tse-tung* (Chicago, IL: The University of Chicago Press) p. 111.

13 Ibid., pp. 112–113.

14 Mair, Victor H., trans. (1990) *Dao Te Ching, The Classic Book of Integrity and the Way* (New York: Bantam Books) p. 63.

15 Cleary, Thomas trans. (1991) *The Essential Dao* (New York: Harper Collins) p. 11.

16 Ch'en Ku-ying (1977) *Lao Tzu, Text Notes, and Comments*, trans. Rhett Y. W. Young & Roger Ames (San Francisco, CA: Chinese Materials Center) pp. 20, 69.

17 Wu, John C. H., trans. (1989) *Dao The Ching* (Boston, MA: Shambhala) p. 11.

18 Welch, Holmes (1965) *Daoism, The Parting of the Way* (Boston, MA: Beacon Press) p. 42.

19 *Tao Te Ching* op. cit., note 4, p. 9.

20 Ibid.

21 For further reading in the issues of valuation and transvaluation, and the permissible pedagogical usage of evaluative language from a transevaluative standpoint, one may be referred to Allinson, Robert E. (1986) Having your cake and eating it, too: evaluation and trans-evaluation in Chuang-Tzu and Neitzsche, *Journal of Chinese Philosophy*, 13(4), pp. 429–443. For a more complete and detailed analysis with respect to Zhuang Zi, one may be referred to Allinson, Robert E. (1989) *CHUANG-TZU For Spiritual Transformation: An analysis of the Inner Chapters* (Albany, NY: State University of New York Press) especially chapter 8. Additional discussion of the issues of evaluation and transevaluation may be found in Allinson, Robert E. (1988) The concept of harmony in Chuang-Tzu, in: Robert E. Allinson & Shu-hsien Liu (eds) *Harmony and Strife: Contemporary Perspectives, East and West* (Hong Kong: The Chinese University Press); and Allinson (1988) Zen and Lao-Tzu: an essay in intercultural hermeneutics, (Kyoto: The Institute for Zen Studies) *Zen Studies Today* 6.

Glossary of Asian Terms

This Glossary contains only those terms which are not immediately defined in the body of the text.

Key:
Ar = Arabic. Ch = Chinese, Jap = Japanese, Pa = Pali, Skt = Sanskrit.

abhimāna (Skt) conceit, pride
abhinaya (Skt) histrionic representation
'adab (Ar) literature of courtesy and urbanity
ahaṃkāra (Skt) self-awareness
aidagara (Jap) human relations
anatta (Pa) no-self, no-soul (from *anātman* (Skt)
anubhāva (Skt) consequent
avidyā (Skt) spiritual ignorance

bodhisattva (Skt) seeker or attainer of enlightenment
buddhi (Skt) cosmic consciousness

cheng (Ch) sincerity
chi (Ch) wisdom
citta (Skt) mind, intelligence, reason

darsána (Skt) approach to spiritual goal
dharma (Skt) social and religious duty
duḥkha (Skt) suffering

guru (Skt) spiritual teacher

ḥadīth (Ar) saying and doings of the Prophet and companions
ḥilm (Ar) mildness, gentleness

insāniyya (Ar) humanity
jāhiliyya (Ar) barbarism of pre-Islamic age
jen (Cha) benovolence, humaneness, humanity
jihād (Ar) holy war
junzi (Ch) nobility

kaivalya (Skt) isolation from matter
kalām (Ar) dialectical tradition of Islam
karma (Skt) action, ritual action, merit or demerit acquired
ku (Jap) the Absolute

li (Ch) propriety, rules of behaviour
loka (Skt) place

nāṭya (Skt) drama
ningen (Jap) human being
nirodha (Skt) cessation, process leading to spiritual liberation
nirvāṇa (Skt) cessation of rebirth
nisyān (Ar) forgetfulness
nyorai (Jap) God

pāṭhya (Skt) recitative
prakṛti (Skt) matter
puruṣa (Skt) individual soul, knower

rasa (Skt) aesthetic experience, sentiment, taste, flavour

samādhi (Skt) trance, perfect spiritual state, concentration
saṃsāra (Skt) cycle of birth-death-rebirth
sāttvikabhāva (Skt) temperamental state
senru (Jap) absolute totality
sthāyibhāva (Skt) emotional state
sunna (Ar) example of the Prophet

ta'dīb (Ar) disciplining, education, refinement
tai'yo-ron (Jap) substance and function
tathāgata (Skt) 'thus-gone', the Buddha
tian (Ch) heaven

vibhāva (Skt) determinant
vṛitti (Skt) modification, mental processes
vyabhicaribhava (Skt) trasitory state

xin (Ch) heart-mind

yoga (Skt) union, path or discipline to spiritual liberation

Name Index

Note: This is a selective index, only containing names which appear in the body of the articles. Further references appear at the end of each article.